AMERICA'S
NATIONAL GALLERY OF ART
A Gift to the Nation

AMERICA'S
NATIONAL GA

LLERY OF ART

A Gift to the Nation

Philip Kopper

Harry N. Abrams, Inc., Publishers, New York

*This book is dedicated with love to my wife,
Mary Carll Kopper, who loves art also.*

**This publication has been made possible by
generous support from the Charles E. Smith
Companies and the Artery Organization, Inc.**

Edited by Edith M. Pavese

Designed by Tom Suzuki

Art assistance by Kathleen Sims, Ed Zielinski, Constance
Dillman, Katherine Allen, Timothy Cook and Virginia
Suzuki

Typeset in Adobe Garamond by Wordscape

Color Separations by the Lanman Companies

Printed and bound in Italy by Amilcare Pizzi

Library of Congress Cataloging-in-Publication Data
Kopper, Philip.
     America's National Gallery of Art: A gift to the nation
     Philip Kopper.
        p.   cm.
     Includes bibliographical references and index.
     ISBN 0-89468-159-1
     1. National Gallery of Art (U. S.)   I. Title.
N856.K66 1991
708.153—dc2O   90-28788
                                          CIP
ISBN 0-8109-3658-5 (Abrams)

Contents

Foreword

The National Gallery of Art evolved through a unique partnership between the Federal Government of the United States and the American people. In what may well be the largest single gift ever given to a government by a private citizen, Andrew Mellon (who served as Secretary of the Treasury under three Presidents) donated his private collection to the nation, built a splendid gallery to house it, and provided a generous endowment to support certain key activities. In addition to these tangible contributions, Mellon gave our country another great and lasting gift by the very form of his donation: the National Gallery of Art was structured not as a memorial to the generosity of its founder but as a catalyst for the generosity of others. Never intended to bear its founder's name, the National Gallery was conceived as a home for future gifts, whether single works of art or entire collections.

Each work in the National Gallery's permanent collection represents a private donation—either of artwork itself or of funds for its acquisition. Although no federally appropriated funds have ever been used to secure a work of art for the National Gallery, the 75th Congress did pledge, however, the faith of the Government of the United States in its enabling legislation. In so doing, it guaranteed a secure home for the nation's art collection, as well as a staff to care

for it. Today, the Federal Government, along with private benefactors, continues to make it possible for the Gallery to conduct many of its programs without charging admission fees to the public.

Supported by this combination of public and private funding, the National Gallery of Art has made extraordinary advances during its first fifty years—achievements that are described in this anniversary volume. This book not only recounts the early history of the Gallery but also reflects the devotion of the many men and women who have worked during the past five decades to ensure its success.

Andrew Mellon's grand gift to the United States is a world-renowned institution dedicated to the preservation, exhibition, and interpretation of great works of art. All of us can take great pride and satisfaction in knowing that it will enrich the lives of generations to come.

George Bush

THE WHITE HOUSE
WASHINGTON

Acknowledgments

TO HAVE BEEN INVITED to write a history of the National Gallery of Art on the occasion of its fiftieth anniversary was a high honor and a challenge. The book, published by Harry N. Abrams, Inc., became a more complex collaboration between writer, museum and publisher than many of its kind. In the process it came to focus on the people who had made the Gallery what it is: its extraordinary founder, his major successors—a remarkable group of patriot/philanthropists—and on the Gallery's professional staff. Thus I am privileged to acknowledge many debts to Gallery People, past, present and tangential.

My thanks first go to Frances Smyth, the Gallery's gifted editor-in-chief, who initiated this rewarding project and championed it through thick and thin. Her staff made crucial contributions as well, especially Abigail Walker, Meg Alexander and Chris Vogel. Edith Pavese, my colleague on a previous Abrams museum book, came on as editor when the manuscript was nearing completion and the final text benefitted from her manifold skills. I am proud to see my words adorned by Dennis Brack's spectacular new photographs—as well as by historical pictures that our able researcher, Carol Mickey, unearthed. And I am grateful to Tom Suzuki for his deft design and production management.

My special gratitude goes to Paul Mellon, formerly trustee, president and chairman, now honorary trustee and ever the Gallery's devoted champion. He could boast of an association with the museum longer and closer than any other person's—except he never boasts. When asked, he gave generously of his time and unconditionally provided recollections, counsel and even some documentation from family papers.

Next, two old Gallery hands deserve my particular thanks and recognition. William J. Williams, a senior member of the Education Department, has been an art historian here for a quarter of a century and commands much of the Gallery's institutional memory. His careful, critical reading of the text and captions, as well as his own store of stories, have been invaluable. A. C. Viebranz, a driving force in the Gallery's oral history project, also read the text with great care and offered helpful comments. Long before that, moreover, Al Viebranz introduced me to Gallery lore and shared the fruits of his research into Andrew Mellon's efforts to found the museum. His colleagues in the Gallery Archives worked tirelessly on my behalf, kept their doors open at odd hours, and gave me house room. Thus my thanks as well especially to Gallery Archives Chief Maygene F. Daniels, architectural archivist Richard E.

Saito and archives technician Martha J. Shears. I also thank Kurt Helfrick, Robin Van Fleet and oral historians John Harter and Anne Ritchie.

Many members of the Gallery's professional ranks made themselves and their good offices available to me. Thus I thank a veritable legion: from director J. Carter Brown, for both his views and sustained interest in the project, to senior curator Charles S. Moffett who offered stores of learning, to a guard in the garage Gregory Stevenson, for his unfailing efficiency and hospitable sense. Variously for providing information, sharing knowledge, educating me in general, or just going an extra mile, in particular I thank Gordon Anson, Caroline H. Backlund, Kathryn K. Bartfield, Robert Bowen, David Brown, David Bull, Deborah Chotner, Nicolai Cikovsky, Jr., Elizabeth A. Croog, Tam Curry, Susan Davis, Eric Denker, Ariadne Y. DuBasky, Lamia Doumato, Carol Eron, Anne B. Evans, Suzannah J. Fabing, Ruth E. Fine, Sarah Fisher, James Grupe, Valerie Guffey, John Oliver Hand, Anne Hawkins, Daniel Herrick, Genevra O. Higginson, Philip C. Jessup, Jr., Willow Johnson, Ruth Kaplan, Carol Kelley, Franklin Kelly, Joseph J. Krakora, Mark Leithauser, C. Douglas Lewis, Angela LoRé, Alison Luchs, Thomas F. J. McGill, Jr., Maria Mallus, Henry A. Millon, Franklin Murphy, Thomas O'Callaghan, Jr., Gaillard Ravenel, Andrew Robison, Nan Rosenthal, J. Russell Sale, Mary Suzor, Jane Sweeney, Christopher A. Thomas, D. Dodge Thompson, Elizabeth A. C. Weil, Arthur K. Wheelock, Jr. and Katie Ziglar.

Outside the Gallery, for various courtesies and insights I am grateful to Richard Bales, Thomas Beddall, Steven Bedford, John E. Benson, the late Margaret Bouton, Evangeline Bruce, Carroll Cavanagh, the late Howard Devree, William Dunlap, Betty Foy, Pat Good, Ellsworth Kelly, Linda Kikuchi, Eric Lindquist, Bunny Mellon, Theodore A. Miles, Joanne B. Moore, Oliver Murray, Lynn Nicholas, Edwin B. Olsen, Charles Parkhurst, Meryle Secrest, Janet Stewart, Mrs. Newman A. Townsend, Jr. and John Wilmerding. As to particular items of information, many are specified in the Notes and Sources section of the book.

Finally, please know that this work would not have been finished but for the patience and encouragement of my wife, Mary, and for the diverting (sometimes distracting) inspiration of our son, Tim.

PHILIP KOPPER

The Shrine and the Metropolis

I t might be called a village, if this community of

a thousand souls were set in some mountain fastness, a single wisp of smoke from all its chimneys

barely smudging the infinite sky of a Frederic Church landscape. It could be called a shrine, if these

were nuns and priests serving a church with an altar adorned *in nomine patri* by Fra Angelico—or

Rouen Cathedral where Monet proved the mysteries of light. It is not quite either and partially

both—at once a society dedicated to art and a pilgrims' destination. Yet to let it go at that is to cut its

identity short, for its pilgrims are not only reverent seekers of Truth in the Visual who come here in

droves or singletons, checking backpacks and briefcases alike at the door, thank you. These buildings'

pilgrims—some 17,163 on an *average* day—include all manner of people:

A scholar in tweeds come to study a single

group of Flemish drawings of special rarity; T-shirted children who wonder at Calder's mobile, then

discover they can prance each pose of George Segal's four *Dancers*—but for just a minute, while his

white statues fix their motion forever;

❦ Body-builders whose muscles flex as they pause before a Bellows boxing scene;

❦ The halt riding wheelchairs provided gratis at the insistence of the first chief curator, who was lamed by polio himself;

❦ Clatches of Washington's chic set sporting the latest in attire to see a special exhibition within a week of its debut;

❦ American Legionnaires killing time (as GIs did here fifty years ago) but now looking for the Dalí—"That's what I call real painting";

❦ Sikhs in pairs, their wives following in a rainbow of saris, their voices soft as wind through lotus leaves;

❦ A renowned actor (timid without greasepaint) who pays homage to Manet's Hamlet but takes delight in Picasso's *Family of Saltimbanques*;

❦ Two elderly babushkas with their mother whispering dismay, startled by the moving sidewalk in the Concourse;

❦ Queen Elizabeth II, among other heads of state who ask to visit this renowned museum;

❦ A Tyrolean couple discussing Fragonard in solemn tones and learned terms. (One day in the cafeteria, I counted the foreign tongues within earshot: five, plus something in the noonday din that proved to be Pig Latin prattled by two New Jersey girls. My count was short: a recent survey polled visitors from every state and fifty-five foreign nations.)

❦ Here they come, young

The Shrine and the Metropolis

and old, smart and naive, smug and curious, you and I, for at least as many reasons as there are works of art—70,576 at the last inventory.

❦ It is a shrine as surely as Raphael answered his patrons' sacred ambitions when he adorned one small square panel with the Dragonslayer and a large round one with that most serene Madonna. A shrine to Art for all mankind.

❦ It is a university in its community of scholars, both tenured and temporary: curators, librarians, educators and

lecturers; the eminent Center for Advanced Study in the Visual Arts with its passing parade of scholars; what amounts to a small university press; and a phalanx of young researchers compiling the definitive systematic catalogue of diverse collections.

🦌 It is an institution that will outlive us all, because the aegis of its charter makes its trustees self-perpetuating and its buildings the charge of the United States.

🦌 It is a family initiative, once overseen by Mellon's son-in-law, then governed by his son and benefitted by his daughter who funded such gifts as the only Leonardo portrait in the western hemisphere.

🦌 It is a village, of course, this hamlet of a thousand souls—999 fulltimers at last count—who welcome so many times their own number.

🦌 It is a monument no less than architect John Russell Pope's waterside rotunda honoring Jefferson barely a mile away as the gull flies.

🦌 It is a gift to the nation first by one man, Andrew W. Mellon, then endlessly enriched with the donations of many others.

🦌 It is a city that by day bustles with woodworkers and gardeners, archi-

tects and accountants, data processors and archivists. It is also city enough to employ three full-time musicians and enough freelance instrumentalists for a small orchestra that performs in the Garden Courts.

🍎 It is a city that never sleeps, a bastion where armed guards from a company of hundreds keep watch by day and by night, with the aid of an arsenal of space-age tools.

🍎 It is a corporation with a chairman of the board, a trustee-president, and a director to whom report a deputy director, administrator, treasurer, secretary-general counsel, external affairs officer and the dean of the study center.

🐦 It is a gallery that displays for brief periods an endlessly changing card of exhibitions, many of which bring together works of art that never hung in the same room before—nor will again. The exhibition per se, one learns here, is a work of art itself, a brief composition of elements that make each other resonate.

🐦 It is a museum dedicated to the study, preservation and exhibition of its priceless art, thus an institution with more than fifty curators and their associates, four registrars, ten art handlers, six scientists, twenty-three conservators, and a like number engaged in designing and installing exhibitions. In addition, there are well-staffed offices for corporate relations, public information, special events, visitor services, and all the facilities management and security such a city/fortress requires.

🐦 It is private: Not a single acquisition has been purchased with government money; all are given by private donors or bought with privately donated funds. It is private, too, because the original gift accompanied an endowment fund that pays the salaries of the half-dozen executive officers, who are thus exempted from the Pecksniffian rules and standards of Civil Service.

🐦 It is public, because the United States Congress in accepting the original gift pledged to sustain the building and pay personnel from curators and such to handymen and charpeople.

🐦 It is national, not in championing pictures painted only by Americans but in possessing an array of masterpieces worthy of belonging to this entire nation, a collection that private generosity over fifty years has made too precious for private ownership today.

🐦 It is international, because it contains examples of the greatest art produced by all the Western traditions that contributed to America and because it draws people from the world over.

🐦 It is a sect with its own icons, witness the soup can (Campbell's of course) on a designer's desk used to hold pencils. Witness the typewriter eraser—the real two-inch

McCoy—glued upright on a bit of cardboard in mini-honor of sculptor Claes Oldenburg's eraser huge enough for an Amazon stenographer at a twenty-foot Underwood. My favorite symbolic joke is a warning painted on a back stairway: on the edge of a low overhang stands a painted bird in profile winsome as a Matisse. It's a sign without words that says "Duck!"

❦ It is fallible (like any human construct)—and admits it, since in its responsible dedication to scholarship, curators continually reassess the authorship of its possessions.

❦ It is perfect, so it would seem, a steward of rare fidelity, a museum that has never made headlines for having had a painting stolen or damaged while on display.

❦ It is younger than many people think, having opened its doors on March 17, 1941, and already become in mere decades an august feature in the cityscape and a landmark in the nation's cultural ken.

❦ It is old enough to have had scholars grow up in its thrall—senior curators remember first coming here as children.

❦ It is formal—regularly holding black-tie events and occasionally banquets in the Rotunda attended by the President when the handlettered invitations stipulate: "white tie and decorations."

❦ Village and shrine,

metropolis and habitat; public, private and

bureaucratic; monument and university; institu-

tion and gift; national and catholic—it is the

National Gallery of Art. ❦

A Grand Opening

Opening night: Taxicabs and limousines jam Constitution Avenue on March 17, 1941, an evening when America remains uneasily at peace, when Franklin and Eleanor Roosevelt celebrate their wedding anniversary and when tout *Washington comes out to attend the opening of the nation's art gallery.*

A s spring approached fifty years ago, America hoped for peace but girded for the world war already raging in Europe and Asia. In New York, Walt Disney's *Fantasia* lit up the Technicolor screen and Lillian Hellman's *Watch on the Rhine* played ominously to packed houses. Charles Dana Gibson judged a soap sculpture contest, while the Kansas City Art Institute added industrial camouflage—the art of concealing factories from the air— to its curriculum. The tonier nightclubs exacted cover charges of six bits from café society swells, and the value of a gift to the nation by Andrew W. Mellon represented $1 million more than the State Department's budget or the price of one battleship. Such choices were on the nation's mind.

March 17, 1941: The *Washington Post* clarioned "50,000 Lost in Duce's Drive; England Past Help, Hitler Says." In Pennsylvania, the morning papers reported on page one, a train wreck was blamed on sabotage. In Georgia, Secretary of State Hull began a short vacation. In Rome, Mussolini's

15

daughter was listed among the last to abandon a hospital ship reportedly torpedoed by the R.A.F. In London, morale was boosted by the recent promise of Lend-Lease, but the submarine *Snapper* was posted missing. In Greece, patriots repulsed a superior force of Italian invaders. In Washington, where crocuses had bloomed two days before, spring fled in the face of fifteen-degree arctic cold. It was the First Family's wedding anniversary and President Roosevelt, sporting a green carnation to honor St. Patrick's Day, took Eleanor downtown to a black-tie event to dedicate the building given to the nation by a second generation Irish-American who made good.

Tout Washington came out that night, despite the bitter cold, for the opening of the National Gallery of Art was the hottest ticket in town. It wasn't a party; food and drink were not served, and the music was marches by the Marine Band. The *New York Times* called it "one of the most distinguished groups of men and women ever assembled in Washington. By train and air, outstanding artists and sculptors, directors of art museums, presidents of universities, connoisseurs and collectors arrived.... All ranks of official, diplomatic and resident society were represented, and a cross-section of the 'Who's Who' and social register of every large city in the United States and several foreign countries were included in the company." Some 6,000 guests were invited; 7,962 showed up.

The doors opened at 8 P.M., and guests began to gather. Then the assemblages of dozens of sanctioned dinner parties swelled the crowd, and the Roosevelts arrived just before the start of the 10 P.M. ceremonies that were programmed down to the half-minute as the proceedings were broadcast on radio coast-to-coast. The Chaplain of the Senate invoked Almighty beneficence; the Chief Justice invited mortal generosity from private art collectors. This was the dedication of the largest marble building in the world, and the richest single gift from any individual to any nation ever. Honored guests and party crashers alike saw the opening of a $15 mil-

lion edifice and the unveiling of art collections valued at more than $80 million—this at a time when cigarettes cost a dime a pack, hotel rooms in Washington went for $4 a night, Brooks Brothers suits for $42 and Cadillacs for $1,354.

The visitors, *Time* magazine observed, "found much to marvel at, much to admire. The four and a half acres of oak-floored galleries were fitted with comfortable, upholstered sofas. In all the 90 galleries on the main floor, light fell with scientifically controlled evenness through laminated glass skylights, which let in diffused sunlight by day, artificial sunlight by night. In the basement, a Dalí dream of convoluted pipes and fans air-conditioned the whole building, from the soaring space of the rotunda to the tiled cafeteria...." Connoisseurs, said *Time*, found strong points in "1) the [Samuel] Kress collection of Italian art, one of the largest and most comprehensive in the U.S.; 2) a gallery of nine over-average Rembrandts; 3) a bevy of British mantelpiece portraits, including Sir Joshua Reynolds' famed $500,000 portrait of Lady Elizabeth Compton; 4) top-flight pictures by Dutchmen Vermeer and Frans Hals, Flemings van Eyck, Memling, Rubens and van Dyck...."

Newsweek cheered: "On the site of the old Baltimore and Potomac Railroad station in Washington where President Garfield was assassinated in 1881, [FDR] formally opened the American Louvre: a National Gallery of Art which ranks with the world's top collections." It gasped at "Raphael's 1510 'Madonna of the House of Alba,' which originally hung in a village church near Naples, passed into the hands of the Spanish Duke of Alba, and from him by way of London in 1836 to Czar Nicholas I...." The magazine touted a painting Lord Duveen had sold to Kress, bragging that Giorgione was "one of the rarest of Venetian masters." (The picture had won the hearts of Christmas shoppers when it hung in the window of the New York City flagship emporium of Kress' chain of 240 five-and-dime stores.) "In addition, there are Titian's 'Venus with a Mirror' which ... Swinburne called a 'proud hosanna of the flesh';

Sir Joshua Reynolds' Lady Elizabeth Delmé and Her Children *oversees part of the crowd which became so pressed that a few people fainted. Of these elegant guests, one in four crashed the party.*

A Grand Opening

19

Gainsborough's portrait of Mrs. Richard Brinsley Sheridan, a popular singer considered by Horace Walpole the foremost beauty of her day, and a ... 'Venus and Bacchus' carted by Napoleon from Florence to Paris as plunder of the Austrian campaign."

Like the press at large, *Newsweek's* ample coverage demonstrated a point that Roosevelt made in his oration, namely that Americans were becoming at least curious about art, perhaps even interested. Further, the nation was fascinated by the monetary values involved—and at a time when the dollar itself was worth at least nine times as much as it is today, so that Mellon's gifts alone would tot up to something close to a billion dollars now, a figure that takes no account of the soaring prices in art since then. The million-dollar *Alba Madonna* alone, according to an educated guesser, could easily fetch $100 million today, were the Gallery trustees ever to offer it for sale, an eventuality about as likely as Raphael's return from the grave.

In presenting the gift to the nation, Paul Mellon, the donor's son, related that the Gallery

is the realization of a plan formed by my father many years ago, soon after he came to Washington as Secretary of the Treasury. He felt the need of a national gallery in Washington, with a collection of art which might serve as the nucleus of a great national collection. He saw in his imagination a building adequate to contain that future, great collection. He hoped that the gallery would become a joint enterprise on the part of the Government on the one hand and of magnanimous citizens on the other. [It was planned to contain a library of books and photographs] that it may serve more fully the cause of education in art, and become a center of scholarship

in this country. For it was my father's hope, and it is ours [his and his sister Ailsa's] that the National Gallery would become not a static but a living institution, growing in usefulness and importance to artists, scholars and the general public.

Thanking everyone involved, from the President for enabling government support to craftsmen for providing their skills and toil, the scion concluded:

This building is the product of many minds, intent on giving America their best; and we are happy to turn it over to you, Mr. President, with my father's collection, to be dedicated forever to the use and enjoyment of the people of the United States....

If the opening was one of the Gallery's finest nights, the President's acceptance speech was vintage Roosevelt. It managed to be conciliatory to the donor and challenging to others; it was both down-to-earth and aristocratic, even witty for a moment. It was a clarion to awaken the nation, a paean to America, a call to greatness for both the people and the museum. He spoke of home, of history, of art and of the troubled world. The gift was a deed of generous patriotism, its acceptance a national act of faith. FDR declared:

It is with a very real sense of satisfaction that I accept for the people of the United States and on their behalf this National Gallery and the collections it contains. The giver of this building has matched the richness of his gift with the modesty of his spirit, stipulating that the Gallery shall be known not by his name but by the Nation's. And those other collectors of paintings and of sculpture who have already joined, or who propose to join…have felt the same desire to establish, not a memorial to themselves, but a monument to the art that they love and the country to which they belong.

There have been, in the past, many gifts of great paintings and of famous works of art to the American people. Most of the wealthy men of the last cen-

Hans Memling's Madonna and Child with Angels, *another of Mellon's original gifts to the Gallery, reflects Flemish ideals—of landscape, architecture and human beauty. Painted after 1479, some thirty years before the Raphael (opposite), it reveals Memling's fondness for his forested, northern homeland as surely as the* Alba Madonna *shows a love of the pastoral, Roman countryside.*

Hans Memling,
Madonna and Child with Angels, after 1479
Andrew W. Mellon Collection

tury who bought, for their own satisfaction, the masterpieces of European collections, ended by presenting their purchases to their cities or to their towns. And so great works of art have a way of breaking out of private ownership into public use. They belong so obviously to all who love them—they are

so clearly the property not of their single owners but of all men everywhere—that the private rooms and houses where they have lovingly hung in the past become in time too narrow for their presence. The true collectors are the collectors who understand this—the collectors of great paintings who feel that

they can never truly own, but only gather and preserve for all who love them, the treasures that they have found.

But though there have been many public gifts of art in the past, the gift of this National Gallery, dedicated to the entire Nation, containing a considerable part of the most important work brought to this country from the continent of Europe, has necessarily a new significance … a new relation here made visible in paint and in stone—between the whole people of this country, and the old inherited tradition of the arts ....

There was a time when the people of this country would not have thought that the inheritance of

art belonged to them or that they had responsibilities to guard it. A few generations ago, the people of this country were often taught by their writers and by their critics and by their teachers to believe that art was something foreign to America and to themselves—something imported from another continent, something from an age which was not theirs—something they had no part in, save to go see it in some guarded room on holidays or Sundays.

But recently, within the last few years—yes, in our lifetime—they have discovered that they have a part…they know also that art is not a treasure in the past or an importation from another land, but part of the present life of all the living and creating peo-

With President Roosevelt at the microphones, dignitaries line the dais to dedicate the National Gallery of Art to the people of the United States. Newsreel cameras record the event and live radio carries it coast-to-coast. Standing at the President's right are: bearded Chief Justice Charles Evans Hughes; next to him, Paul Mellon, who presented the gift in his late father's stead; and, to Mellon's right, Samuel H. Kress, the Gallery's second major benefactor. Eleanor Roosevelt stands at her husband's left beside Vice President Henry A. Wallace.

ples—all who make and build; and, most of all, the young and vigorous peoples who have made and built our present wide country.

It is for this reason that the people of America accept the inheritance of these ancient arts. Whatever these paintings may have been to men who looked at them generations back—today they are not only works of art. Today they are the symbols of the human spirit, symbols of the world the freedom of the human spirit has made....

He said more, but not a word about the Roosevelt administration's effort to discredit Andrew Mellon and hale him into court as a tax dodger. Nothing was said about "economic royalists," nor the plight of thousands still homeless and unemployed in the waning months of the Depression. Nor could a word be said about the measurable popularity this Gallery would achieve. Since that opening night fifty years ago, more than 130 million people have visited this place—roughly the population of the nation when the Gallery was founded.

Fifty years ago, the world was different. The National Gallery of Art emerged as the product of diverse forces—some as frail as the donor in his declining years, some as enduring as his ambitions, some as hopeful as young Paul Mellon, some as pragmatic as the President who was, among other things, the most cultured to occupy the White House since Thomas Jefferson. The museum itself was the confluence of many streams joined in that historic instant, just as it instantly became the font of diverse legacies that now seem major currents in our culture as time sweeps along toward the third millennium.

What follows, then, is the story of its founding, and of its founder, and of his collaborators—variously intimates, strangers, and distant successors of later years. It is the story of "a living institution...dedicated forever...to the use and enjoyment of the people of the United States," a young giant among the august museums of the world. ৯

Before the Creation

Civilization abhors a vacuum no less than nature does, and as sure as people profess love of art and country, so a nation's capital will boast a national gallery. It was inevitable that one would arise in Washington. Yet before a national art gallery worthy of the name was founded and grew to genuine national prominence, a series of them—at least in name or variation thereof—littered the city's chronology for more than a century.

There was Washington's first museum and art gallery of any sort, the establishment which "an humble citizen named [John] Varden" founded circa 1829. As reported a century later, this "Washington Museum" boasted "a number of works of art, the catalogue enumerating 32 of the latter," which in due time were consigned to the nobly named and loftily conceived National Institute for the Promotion of Science and the Useful Arts.

There was that Institute itself, brainchild of Joel R. Poinsett, botanist, South Carolina congressman, Secretary of War under Van Buren, roving diplomat, booster of revolutionary causes in Latin America, and All-American Renaissance Man. Among his special distinctions: He lent his name to the poinsettia, and to the Spanish word *poinsettismo* which was coined to describe "officious and intrusive behavior" of the sort that got him declared persona non grata in Mexico. In short he was a doer and a bounder, and similarly his Institute, founded in 1842, lacked staying power. It got house room in the Patent Office building, until in time its charter simply expired. It never became much more than a caretaker for sundry collections of natural history specimens and various miscellany—including John Varden's surviving pictures. By 1855 all these went to the young Smithsonian Institution, which had its own checkered development.

The notion of a national gallery may have been one of the things John Adams had in mind when he penned his famous mandamus about having to study politics and war so that his sons could practice farming and commerce so that their sons could bask in the high arts and culture. In fact it was his son John Quincy Adams who engineered the birth of the Smithsonian through acceptance of a foreigner's princely bequest "to found at Washington… an Establishment for the increase & diffusion of knowledge among men." James Smithson, wealthy Englishman, amateur scientist, bastard aristocrat and childless bachelor, died in 1829 leaving his estate ultimately to the United States, a country he had never seen. Then seventeen post-mortem years were given over to probate, negotiation, moralizing and Congressional debate. Senator John C. Calhoun, among others, deemed it improper for the republic to accept gifts from foreigners. Another member of Congress feared that if they let one upstart buy respectability with such a bequest, "every whippersnapper vagabond" would follow suit and the Capitol would swarm with vulgar benefactors seeking easy fame. In the end the younger Adams, a former president retired as elder statesman in the House of Representatives, marshalled a majority to put lofty ideals (or simple opportunism) ahead of hubris.

Finally chartering the Smithsonian Institution in 1846, Congress decided, among

other things, that it would be the repository of "all objects of art and of foreign and curious research... belonging or hereafter to belong to the United States, which may be in the city of Washington." Further, its governing body, the seventeen-member Board of Regents, was authorized to construct on the ceremonial expanse west of the Capitol a "suitable building, of plain and durable materials and structure, without unnecessary ornament." The commission went to architect James Renwick, barely thirty and destined for great things during the Gothic revival. He designed a many-towered edifice, a gingerbread fantasy in red sandstone that nonetheless contained "suitable rooms, or halls, for the reception and arrangement, upon a liberal scale, of objects of natural history.... a chemical laboratory, a library, *a gallery of art...*" [emphasis added, of course].

A number of interested parties thought Smithson's "diffusion of knowledge" mandate obviously meant a museum per se to display interesting or esoteric objects for public enlightenment. But Joseph Henry, the eminent scientist from Princeton who became the Smithsonian's first secretary, meant the new institution to concentrate on "increase" through scientific study. Publication of scientific reports would bring "diffusion" enough. At one point, Henry even proposed ceding Renwick's "Castle" to an outfit that wanted to mount exhibitions, like Poinsett's. Apparently Henry disliked museums, and only let the Smithsonian get into the exhibition business when Congress appropriated money to cart the moribund National Institute's collections out of the Patent Office across town and put them on display.

By the time Renwick's Castle was occupied in 1855, the Smithsonian was willy-nilly acquiring art from diverse sources. John Varden's old cache was transferred here. Works by John Mix Stanley, a peripatetic artist and recorder of Indian life, had either been bought-and-paid-for or deposited in the Castle as collateral for loans that bankrolled his expeditions in the field. Then in 1865 a fire destroyed the upper story and

towers of the building along with their contents, including Smithson's remaining personal effects and much of the art collection, particularly Indian paintings by Stanley and William Bird King. Whatever art survived was sent for safer keeping elsewhere pro tem—paintings and sculpture to the Corcoran Gallery, engravings to the Library of Congress. All the *objects* were eventually returned as the Smithsonian came to bear the mark and burden of an athenaeum for exhibitions in addition to its scientific work. The loss of the pictures in the fire was substantial and the first national gallery on the Mall languished. But it did not vanish, especially on paper.

Yet the most ambitious and literally fabulous National Gallery of History and Art ever conceived had nothing to do with the Smithsonian. This was the 1890 brainchild of one Franklin W. Smith, an ambitious builder and promoter from upstate New York who would publicize his plans in a hundred-page bulletin published by the "Offices of the Propaganda for the National Gallery." Smith already had a concrete attraction, a sort of early theme park called the

Pompeia, which replicated the ancient and distant city of Pompeii in Saratoga Springs, the better to edify gentle folk sojourning nearby to take the waters. For Washington, Smith had in mind something grander, less provincial, and substantially bigger. The National Gallery of History and Art, as he proposed it, would comprise a

Columbian Temple [with] the American Galleries surrounding, and the Historical Galleries for the various Periods and Nationalities. They descend by terraces to the Grand Entrance Colonnade. Across the Artificial Lake passes the Forum through the Lincoln and Washington Arches.... The Roman and Greek Courts have areas of about six acres each for reproduction of architectural and historic constructions and remains.... The Gothic and Renaissance Courts have about three acres each.... Sculptures on the pediment of the Parthenon, the frieze &c., are to be left to the interest and generosity of the future....

This grandiose garden, with some full-scale copies of the world's great buildings, would cover more than two hundred acres, namely the entire stretch of ground between the Potomac River and the White House, which itself might be replaced by something grander if Mr. Smith got his way. Mind you, the buildings were not to be just pretty facades; they would *contain* exhibition spaces for art shows and workshops for the creation of copies of antique art, buildings, etc.

If this all sounds more loony than pretentious, it bears mention that Smith's collaborator was none other than James Renwick, by then a distinguished septuagenarian. After the Smithsonian's romanesque castle, he raised the unexcellably neo-Gothic St. Patrick's Cathedral in New York and, near the White House, the original Corcoran Gallery of Art, which now bears the name Renwick Gallery. He died in 1895, but Smith pursued his grandiose and eclectic dream (with generous Congressional support) for several years before going bankrupt.

Freelance efforts aside, back at the Smithsonian its presumed and piecemeal national art gallery gained special legitimacy soon after the turn of the century. This occurred as the result of a legal contest over the estate of Harriet Lane

Most of the Smithsonian's nascent art collection is lost when the upper floors of the new building burn in 1865.

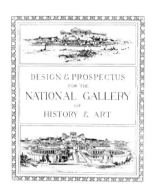

The Smithsonian Institution first occupies James Renwick's many-towered "Castle" in 1855. For decades thereafter it is the chief attraction on the Mall and repository of national art collections, such as they are. For much of the century the Mall boasts a canal, a railway station and acres of bog before it is conceived as the "people's park."

Johnston, a Baltimore philanthropist remembered around Washington as having been President James Buchanan's niece and his White House hostess. In 1906 she died, leaving a substantial collection of old master paintings to the Smithsonian as the nation's art repository until something better came along. A rival beneficiary, an orphans' home in Baltimore, contested the bequest and filed suit, arguing that the Smithsonian *qua* national art gallery was imaginary. The Supreme Court of the District of Columbia found in favor of the Smithsonian, whose art collection was thus judicially confirmed as a national museum per se, however motley its holdings until Harriet Johnston's bequest. By virtue of the court's decision, this national

gallery gained in legal status what it lacked in independence and architectural actuality.

Harriet Johnston's paintings were valuable to the Smithsonian, but as an official foresaw in 1909, the best result of her bequest was intangible. It lay "in the stimulus given to art as a feature of the national collections, [and] in the example set that the government might be trusted as a custodian of art for the people." Charles Freer had already donated his collection of American paintings, his remarkable collection of oriental art, and money for a building on the Mall to house them all. (When this was offered, in 1906, President Theodore Roosevelt practically ordered its immediate acceptance, and Congress avoided the sort of shilly-shallying that had

delayed Smithson's gift, but the Freer didn't open its doors until 1923.) Then one William T. Evans of New York gave a collection of contemporary American paintings to the Smithsonian, and when its new National Museum opened across the Mall from Renwick's Castle in 1910, its central hall was festooned with art.

At about this time, Washington gentry founded the National Society of the Fine Arts, and voiced ambitions of making the capital city "the foremost art center in the western world." Within a decade, Duncan Phillips opened two rooms of his father's Dupont Circle house to the public as an art gallery. This manifested the democratic idea that Phillips expounded: "The sense of well-being and enriched capacity for liv-

ing which art can give" should be "a privilege of the many as well as the technically trained and sensitive few." In other words, art was too important to be left to the esthetes. Soon even the Smithsonian's secretary, now Charles D. Wolcott, would champion art.

"We are the only civilized nation that has not risen to a realization of the real value of art and of important functions of a National Gallery," Wolcott would write. "No important art work has, for art's sake pure and simple, ever been purchased with the approval of the United States Government. The Nation has received as gifts and bequests, art works amounting to more than ten millions in money value, and has expended on their acquirement and care possibly one two-

hundredth part of that amount." In short order, Washington businesses and Smithsonian regents began campaigning for a bigger endowment, and fifteen citizens arranged a loan exhibition to promote interest in the gallery. (By 1929, the secretary would report considerable progress in drumming up official and private support for an art museum. For one, "Mr. John Gellatly, of New York, has made the gift of his extensive collection comprising classic American and European paintings, outstanding specimens of jewelers' art, tapestries, furniture, and oriental art, valued altogether at several million dollars... for eventual exhibition in the National Gallery.")

The mishmash amassed under the Smithsonian aegis all went to the National Museum

of Natural History, across the Mall across from Renwick's Castle. Here exhibition space was now actually dedicated to art. The collections were placed under the stewardship of the Department of Anthropology, a venue then best known for collecting human skeletons and artifacts of various aboriginal peoples. But a move to establish a self-standing national art gallery was afoot within the Smithsonian and among its friends on Capitol Hill. In 1920, this National Gallery became the Smithsonian's seventh bureau by an act of Congress that provided "for the administration of the National Gallery of Art by the Smithsonian Institution, including compensation of necessary employees and necessary incidental expenses."

The following year, a National Gallery Commission was organized for the purpose of getting an actual museum authorized, planned, designed and built, a museum to be filled through the beneficence of America's grand citizens. William H. Holmes, himself a reputable artist who had drawn natural wonders in the West for scientific survey expeditions, was named director of the Smithsonian's yet-to-be-built national gallery. He opined in an interim report: "It can hardly be doubted that, when a building is provided in which contributions can be cared for and presented to the public in the manner they deserve, many collectors seeking a permanent home for their treasures will welcome the opportunity of placing them in the custody of the national institution. The provision of a suitable building for the gallery is all that is necessary to make Washington in the years to come an art center fully worthy of the nation."

With this momentum growing, in 1923 Congress authorized the use of a site on the Mall for an art gallery, namely the space fronting Constitution Avenue between the Museum of Natural History and Seventh Street NW. In its wisdom Congress appropriated no funds, at first, but required the Smithsonian to find the money itself. The regents raised $10,000 from private subscriptions and handed the job to Charles A. Platt, architect of the new Freer Galley on the

south side of the Mall. He was commissioned to conceive a design to "harmonize in general effect" with the Natural History building. Platt chose granite for a three-story gallery "in the Renaissance style" that would cover four acres of ground. Senator Henry Cabot Lodge introduced a bill appropriating $2.5 million to get things started on the building that would comprise both a national gallery of art and, with an eye to London examples, a national portrait gallery. (Both these would eventually open—on other sites and under very different circumstances—while ironically this site would be ceded later for a future sculpture garden of the National Gallery.)

In relatively short order, the Smithsonian's gallery-on-paper had a very palpable collection of art objects. There were two canvases that managed to survive from John Varden's erstwhile Washington Museum, a portrait of Cardinal Mazarin and a *Massacre of the Innocents*, though Director Holmes confided that the pictures were "of no present value due to their advanced state of obliteration." There also were reputed works by Winslow Homer, George Inness, Childe Hassam, Mary Cassatt, William Merritt Chase, Frederick Remington, Frederic Church, Delacroix, Turner, Constable, Stuart, Reynolds, Romney, Gainsborough, Hogarth, even some hopefully attributed to Raphael, Rembrandt, Titian, and a plaster cast of the head of Michelangelo's *David* taken directly from the original marble in Florence. None of these ever found their way into today's National Gallery of Art. Instead these collections became the nucleus of the Smithsonian's National Museum of American Art. That museum, together with Andrew Mellon's dream of a National Portrait Gallery, saved from the wrecker's ball the old Patent Office where Joel Poinsett once housed his ill-fated National Institute.

That's where things stood early in the second quarter of this century when a certain very senior public servant and aging private entrepreneur thought about the eventual disposition of his worldly goods. ❧

Capital and Character

The National Gallery of Art had myriad beginnings. Remembered, they resemble threads in a still unfinished tapestry. In fact, each beginning involved a mortal being who through some toil cheated the grave by becoming involved in something immortal—whether by creating a work of art or by joining an institution, especially this one whose perpetual life has been guaranteed by an act of Congress.

Where have these beginnings occurred? In the upstairs library of the White House, and in Leningrad no less than in Florence, Arles, Tahiti, London. Certainly one beginning occurred when the building opened on the greensward of Washington's Mall. But before the building could rise, the museum had to be conceived and offered to the nation through the President, who accepted it over tea beside a blazing hearth one December afternoon. Before the gift of an edifice could be offered, there had to be a tradition of preserving and honoring art, as in the czars' Winter Palace which the

Andrew W. Mellon, financier, statesman, philanthropist and vision-incarnate of the American aristocrat, poses at the height of his eminence. Painted in 1933 by the leading British society artist, Sir Oswald Birley, the portrait hangs in the place of honor over the mantel in the Gallery's Founders Room.

Bolsheviks had the sense to save. There had to be agents to hear discreetly of art for sale and to ask quiet questions of those who might be interested in buying. Before that there had to be the art itself: the masterpieces and their creators, perhaps famous names in their lifetimes, perhaps unknowns destined to be discovered through the survival of a work that transcended the artist's mortality.

There were many beginnings: in Naples where James Smithson wrote his will, in Delft where the mysterious Vermeer lived, in Peking (as Bejing was then written) where some of Joseph Widener's precious porcelains originated, in Paris where John Russell Pope learned his Beaux-Arts lessons, in Pittsburgh, whence Andrew Mellon came....

For as surely as Zeus birthed Athena from his brow, and Michelangelo carved a *Pietà* sad enough to make men weep, Mellon created the National Gallery of Art. He made it from scratch. This was his child, his ideal, his mistress. The crowning achievement of his life, it reflected that life and its triumphs, failures, prejudices and dreams. In order to see how the museum found its shape and took on a life of its own—as in any living being or human institution—observe the creator to see what was created.

Andrew W. Mellon, who lived more than fourscore years, was a man of his manifold times which were in one extreme rigidly disciplined and in the other explosively boisterous. His life spanned the reign of Czar Nicholas I and Hitler's burning of the Reichstag, the flowering of the Hudson River School and the disappearance of Amelia Earhart, the abolition of slavery and the invention of television, Walt Whitman's *Leaves of Grass* and the making of Walt Disney's *Snow White and the Seven Dwarfs*, the Dred Scott Decision and the New Deal. The world changed during Mellon's lifetime, which began the year the Paris Exposition beatified Delacroix and ended the year Picasso painted *Guernica*.

For most of that life he was one of America's richest men, yet until his seventh decade his name was barely known outside his hometown.

Booming Pittsburgh—young Andrew Mellon's oyster. By 1874 two bridges span the busy Monongahela, linking the old city with the newly annexed South Side, its burgeoning riverside "flats" given to mills, factories, and railways. This bustling, smoking hub of a growing industrial heartland is Elysium for a disciplined youth entering his twenties and becoming a hardheaded banker.

He personally conceived and endowed a national museum, then saw it chartered as an independent and unique instrumentality of the federal government; he lived to see that "the faith of the United States is pledged" to sustain the building his gifts would create and adorn with its first art collection. What he made was not a part of government, but it is nonetheless guaranteed by the government in perpetuity to serve art in the service of all the people of America.

Inevitably or ironically, just as every organization of any ilk reflects the personality of its chief executive, so too a long-lived institution may display the character of its founder. Some facets of this phenomenon seem a plain matter of inheritance, while others are more nebulous. So be it with this National Gallery, Mellon's brainchild and bequest. As an institution it is aristocratic, extravagant, beneficent, insistent upon excellence in almost every particular, influential, willing to use its power for chosen ends. Like its founder it is capable of greatness—and for this it has become justly famous—even if it remains capable of occasional pettiness and human error.

Andrew Mellon has not lacked for biographies. Variously fawning, balanced and muckraking, they focus mostly on his genius career in business and eminent public service. Only one was devoted to Mellon's finest achievement, and it was written by his long-time aide, the Gallery's founding director David Finley. *A Standard of Excellence* contains good data and glimpses of gracious deeds, but both Mellon and his museum deserve better. They are far more interesting and important than perfect, pleasurable consensus allows.

Books about a man like Mellon—financier, then federal officer—focus on professional deeds. No doubt the founding of Alcoa and Gulf are landmark events, but if A.W. Mellon hadn't fueled their development with dollars, others with the Midas touch would have. And any man named to run the Treasury by three Republican presidents in the roaring twenties would probably have pursued the same laissez-faire policies

and been dubbed "the greatest Secretary of the Treasury since Alexander Hamilton." Besides those feats, nay greater than them, Andrew W. Mellon was a man of unique and distinguishing achievement: He founded the National Gallery of Art by giving reputedly the largest single gift by any individual to any nation ever. Few philanthropic acts of such titanic generosity and gentle influence have been performed with his combination of vision, patriotism and modesty. Fewer philanthropists still have made their greatest gesture in a monumental building and then restrained themselves from slapping their name all over it. Plainly named National Gallery of Art at Mellon's insistence, his gift recalls Christopher Wren's cenotaph, which might well be carved on the walls of this museum to remember the donor:

LECTOR, SI MONUMENTUM REQUIRIS, CIRCUMSPICE.
(Reader, if you require a monument, look around you.)

Pittsburgh was a perfectly good place to be born in the nineteenth century, to judge by many who were: Martha Graham, George S. Kaufman, Gertrude Stein, Robertson Jeffers, Mary Cassatt (who touches this history later). By the twentieth it was a popular place to leave too, judging by those who did: all of the above, as well as Rachel Carson, Errol Garner, Gene Kelly, Nellie Bly and Pvt. Thomas F. Enright, the first doughboy to die in World War I. For inventors and investors, industrious Pittsburgh could be a rewarding venue during every upward ride on the Ferris wheel of national business cycles, while even the rushing descents provided opportunities for the cunning as well. All of which has little to do with art and had everything to do with the National Gallery of Art.

From early in the nineteenth century, new waves of immigrant farmers and miners came to Pennsylvania, changing the landscape as they came and being changed in turn. As cities grew, a new class of urban laborers, for example, came

Sir Oswald Hornby
Joseph Birley,
Andrew W. Mellon, 1933
Andrew W. Mellon Collection

to depend on canned goods such as the foods processed by young H. J. Heinz. The Civil War, bloodiest in American history, primed the pumps of Pittsburgh's soon-famous heavy industry, which produced much of the Union cannon. As the century aged, inventions and technological advances combined in spectacular new abilities, markets and opportunities—to dig coal, then not content with coal, to bake it into coke in order to turn iron into steel; to wring oil from the ground; to haul raw freight to factories and finished goods back again. The region provided raw materials and challenges which industrious men mined and refined and smelted and hauled into fortunes—in the process turning land and city coal-black, the air so thick that lamps in the mansion parlors and streetlights often burned at noon. This was the boom town where two rivers met, the Allegheny and the Monongahela to form the Ohio—unless it was the Styx. Pittsburgh was positively (and negatively) Dickensian during what was the Gilded Age elsewhere and what might be called here the Mellonian Era.

Andrew William Mellon, a native son of this teeming region, used hard work and harder ambition to become, by most accounts, the third-richest man in America. He went away to fetch a bride, then lost her at least in part because of the very particulars that made him and Pittsburgh rich: ceaseless work and the industry that shrouded even gentle folks' lives with stygian grime. And still he thrived, helping to establish (and own major pieces of) such corporate giants as Gulf Oil, Alcoa, Carborundum, American Locomotive, Standard Steel Car, Koppers, to say nothing of his expanding bank, one of the score largest in the nation. In due course he amassed personal wealth exceeded by only John D. Rockefeller and Henry Ford. In the process he came to dabble as gentlemen will in very expensive hobbies: travel and collecting precious things.

Having made indelible marks on the face of Pittsburgh and the body of American industry, Mellon entered national politics—he'd been an unseen player in Pennsylvania—only when allies forced President-elect Harding to name him Secretary of the Treasury. Like most people, Harding had never before heard of Mellon, whose name hardly appeared in the *New York Times* until his nomination. Be that as it may, the appointee stayed on for two more administrations, presiding over the economy during the booming twenties and certainly became the most famous and the most popular member of the Harding, Coolidge and Hoover cabinets, until the stock market crash of 1929. When he became Everyman's scapegoat and a political liability, he was named ambassador to Britain, a fitting post to crown his career as a public servant. Retired by the advent of President Roosevelt and the New Deal in 1933, he returned to Washington with the wherewithal of every sort needed to invent a national institution: money, skill, energy, influence, taste and will. The discipline, the wealth and the cerebral inventiveness were all developed in Pittsburgh and tested in its crucible of industrial business. In sum, the history of the National Gallery begins with the founder, and the founder began in Pittsburgh.

In 1785 one Andrew Mellon was born in County Tyrone in northern Ireland. He married, begat, joined the rising tide of immigration to America, and in 1818 joined a community of kin and kindred farmers in a town called Poverty Point, Westmoreland County, Pennsylvania. Andrew the immigrant brought with him a five-year-old son, Thomas, who found his way to college, read law and became a Republican. He went courting—if that verb can be pressed into service. "There was no love making and little or no love beforehand so far as I was concerned: nothing but a good opinion of worthy qualities" Thomas wrote in his dotage of his sixty-five-year marriage to Sarah Jane Negley. "If I had been rejected I would have left neither sad nor depressed, nor greatly disappointed, only annoyed at loss of time."

Her people had settled a place called Negleytown, and the newlyweds remained there. It was renamed East Liberty and got its own train sta-

In County Tyrone, Northern Ireland, the stone cottage that generations of Mellons called home undergoes restoration. In 1818 one Andrew Mellon left here for America and settled among his ilk in Pennsylvania, bringing with him a five-year-old son, Thomas.

tion when the Pennsylvania Railroad went through in 1852. In 1859 (the year a man in nearby Titusville drilled the world's first oil well), Thomas became judge of the Court of Common Pleas for Allegheny County. By then he was also an entrepreneur, a landed gentleman living in a white-brick house, a private banker, a man of parts and of canny discipline: When news came of Lee's surrender at Appomattox, Judge Mellon gavelled the courtroom to enough order to adjourn, then on his way to join the revelry outside he stopped to wind the clock.

Sarah bore nine children, two hale boys in 1844 and 1846, then over a span of six years two girls and a boy who died in childhood, then starting in 1855 four more. The survivors, all boys, were Thomas Alexander, James Ross, Andrew William (whose given names were originally William Andrew), Richard Beatty, George Negley and Samuel Selwyn. The eldest, T. A. and J. R. (to follow the family's nomenclature), started out in the lumber and coal business, and amassed a net worth of $100,000 by war's end. According to David E. Koskoff's lucid family history *The Mellons,* "By the mid-1860s [they] were pioneering in the vertical integration of the enterprises that would make their younger brothers [A.W. and R. B.] ... two of America's richest men." They divided Negley acreage into homesites, which they sold at a profit; they sold lumber for homes to the homesites' proud owners, at a profit; they financed the building projects through their own bank, profitably; and then sold the new residents coal with which to heat the houses, again at a profit. All this they did under the scowling eye of the patriarch, Thomas Mellon, who surrendered the office of judge but never the title nor the habit of judging. Humorless, bigoted and eccentric, as an old man he published a memoir so dour that his sons tried to snatch every copy from circulation. In it he preached that at fourteen he had come to revere Benjamin Franklin, "poorer than myself, who by industry, thrift and frugality had

become learned and wise, and elevated to wealth and fame." Perhaps the sons feared his adage: "The normal condition of man is hard work, self-denial, acquisition and accumulation [of property]; and as soon as his descendants are freed from the necessity of such exertion they begin to degenerate sooner or later in both body and mind."

A.W., born on March 24, 1855, was an "unplayful" child, his official biographer Burton K. Hendrick discovered. Perhaps this was his natural portion, given his birth soon after the deaths of two sisters, and then given, when he was seven, the death of his adored nearest older brother. "He was remote," Hendrick wrote in a tome commissioned by the family and never published, "a light-haired, blue-eyed boy, slight of figure and quiet, unassertive, even shrinking in manners... a rather uninteresting child." When his younger brothers sold fruit from a donkey cart, Andrew went along to keep strict accounts and balance the childish books.

As a schoolboy he developed the heavy cursive hand of the time—and the strongminded idiom of moral certitude: As he wrote in 1870, setting down his first surviving statement on the subject, "Art Gallerys [sic] are exhibitions of sculpture and painting held for the purpose of gratifying and instructing the community, and sometimes of procuring purchasers for the works exhibited. They are generally productive of good influences, as they help to refine the minds and characters of men and divert them from selfish and sordid enjoyments." The schoolmaster found nothing to correct in his expression, only occasional egregious spellings, all duly marked.

He went off to college at Western Reserve (now the University of Pittsburgh) where he did well academically. But shortly before graduation—perhaps the bulk of the learning was over—his father encouraged him to leave school, an option he gladly accepted in order to get out of making a valedictory speech. He went straight to work for T. Mellon and Sons, the bank his father had founded in 1870, the year that John D. Rockefeller organized his holdings as Stand-

Mrs. Thomas Mellon, née Sarah Negley, keeps her composure late in the course of her sixty-five-year marriage. Her husband, the immigrant Andrew's son, better known as Judge Mellon, poses for his banker's portrait at the age of eighty-two in 1895. They had nine offspring; six would survive childhood, including a second Andrew.

More a savvy entrepreneur than jurist, Judge Mellon has a real talent for banking. In 1870 he opens T. Mellon & Sons' Bank on the ground floor of this two-story building on Smithfield Street in Pittsburgh.

ard Oil. Several of A.W.'s brothers became very able businessmen; one retired as a mere millionaire at forty and devoted the rest of his life to play. But it was soon apparent to the patriarch that Andrew possessed a special genius for business.

As a banker Andrew excelled and the bank continued to expand, its wealth and stability assured by dedication to grim prudence, which the Judge so admired. A handsome man, A.W.

was the model of self-discipline, sitting perfectly square at his desk and barely shifting position from the start of business until noon with both feet flat on the floor, and not a hair, a thread nor a digit out of place. It was said he was never seen to stretch, lean back in his chair or, heaven forbid, discuss anything in the office that was not directly connected with business; "the Mellon bank was not a place for conversation or gossip but for toil." The Judge made Andrew his surrogate and sole managing partner in 1882 when he was barely twenty-seven, turning over the bank to him lock and stock. (Alas he did it via a document that was vague enough to trigger a family argument and litigation decades later.)

If Andrew's dedication to business ever lapsed, it was in the understandable cause of romance. Having taken charge of the bank, Andrew wooed one Fannie Jones, niece of a powerful steel man and politician. She accepted his proposal and they were engaged, when she caught a wasting illness and, a year later, died. The mourning swain threw himself into work, hardly to be distracted by the fair sex again (it appears) until the turn of the century. The Judge observed that if A.W. stayed home years longer than his siblings, "This may be possibly accounted for by an unhappy experience which he passed through.... Since then he has gone but little into ladies' society, and become more and more absorbed in business pursuits."

As an industrialist, Andrew Mellon was an American original. Unlike peers such as Andrew Carnegie who cornered steel or oilman John D. Rockefeller, he did not concentrate on a single industry. Rather he was an elemental capitalist, a banker, the man who put up the money that financed other men's businesses and fueled their

promising enterprises. Typically he loaned men money to found new companies or invent new processes, and took repayment in the new company's stock. By learning to judge who had the character to succeed and who didn't, by picking projects adroitly and backing only ideas of true promise, he became a driving force in several basic industries—including oil and metals—a major player in American industry in the period of its most explosive and dramatic expansion. Yet he was modest and exceptionally quiet, an almost anonymous player so far as the general public knew; his starring role was off-stage in specific industrial dramas.

One of the first men he backed came from the same side of the tracks and would rise just about as high in the financial world. In 1871 Henry Clay Frick was the chief bookkeeper in his grandfather Overholt's distillery (a concern in which Frick and Mellon would eventually share interests). A farm boy whose formal education may have added up to thirty months, Henry Frick perceived that the new Bessemer steel-making process could turn Pittsburgh into a boom town. That would mean new demand for the materials needed in steel production such as coke—coal dug from Pennsylvania mines and baked for two days in beehive ovens. Frick was determined to supply the coke and put together a small partnership to buy coal-producing land. When he sought a loan from T. Mellon and Sons, a lackey sent to check his bona fides reported that he had good lands and well-built ovens; that he was on the job all day and kept the books faithfully at night. The report said he

A year later an advertisement in the Commercial-Gazette *announces with maximum dignity the bank's services at a new location. By 1902 armed with a federal charter, the Mellon National Bank issues its own money (below) secured by United States bonds—the first currency Andrew Mellon signs.*

Four gay blades of the 1880s embark on the Grand Tour: mustachioed Henry Clay Frick holds a cane while cool-eyed Andrew Mellon (seated) takes the photographer's measure. Their companions are A. A. Hutchison and Frank Cowan.

"may be a little too enthusiastic about pictures but not enough to hurt." He got the loan—$10,000 for six months at ten-percent interest.

Mellon would live to tell Frick's biographer that Judge Mellon agreed to take a chance on Frick because his character impressed him. Perhaps he saw what a phrenologist prognosticated a few years later from the lumps on Frick's head: "You have more force, energy, vim, get out of my way, drive, push, energy, pluck than one man out of a thousand." More likely, A.W. remembered, "My father was pleased with the

type of statement which Mr. Frick furnished of his affairs in which everything was frankly set forth, the favorable with the unfavorable." The Judge acknowledged "that the loans being made to Mr. Frick were larger than Frick's material resources justified but that he was of a character to succeed."

Frick and Mellon, who was five years his junior, continued to do business together as long as they both lived. In good times they prospered and saved enough to ride out slumps that ruined many competitors. In bad times, Frick took

46

advantage of panics as he bought properties from men who found themselves strapped for cash. Decades later Mellon prided himself on the fact that his bank, run prudently so as always to be able to meet its obligations, weathered economic storms without failing a single depositor. It was in the wild and woolly business climate of these years that Andrew Mellon learned that "a [financial] panic was not altogether a bad thing"—as he counseled the President during what they both believed to be just another dip in the business cycle. Such a downturn flushed out the weak, the imprudent, the unfit and purged the system, he opined to Herbert Hoover after the stock market crash of 1929 tumbled the United States into the Great Depression.

Prospering together in kindred branches of commerce, Frick and Mellon "became intimate friends" as the younger man remembered. (Oddly there was no parity in how they addressed each other. Newsy personal letters that opened "Dear Andy" were signed "H. C. Frick." But then it is said that nobody including Andrew Carnegie called the coke king "Henry.") Until "Mr. Frick" moved to New York in 1905, Mellon wrote "we were accustomed to lunch together daily at the Duquesne Club in Pittsburgh. Our party of about eight usually included the late Judge James Reed, P[hilander] C. Knox until he went to Washington [as a member of the Senate], inventor George Westinghouse, my brother [R. B. Mellon] and several members of the Carnegie Steel Company." Furthermore, it appears that Frick instructed his friend in the delights of art, tutoring him in the ways of collecting, teaching him so well that the student perhaps surpassed the teacher. This instruction began in Pittsburgh, where Frick was already a patron of several local artists, and it continued abroad.

"In the early part of 1880, as neither of us had been abroad and the business horizon appeared clear," Mellon recorded, "we decided to make the trip together and included two business friends [A. A. Hutchinson and Frank Cowan], one a coke manufacturer and the other

a publisher of a daily paper." In June they sailed on the steamship *Abyssinia*, bound for Liverpool, and spent "a happy period" of five months on the grand tour. Landing in Ireland, they waved an American flag at Blarney Castle on July 4th. "Thence they jaunted, as boys on a lark," according to Frick's gentle biographer, "to Dublin, Belfast, Glasgow, Edinburgh, London, seeing all the sights, and presently crossed to Paris for a brief sojourn, followed by 'a dash across the continent' to Venice, their objective point." When the rival coke maker wanted to extend his trip into a world tour but lacked the ready cash, Frick accommodated him by buying his coal lands "greatly to the advantage of H. C. Frick & Co. and [to] the amusement of the young banker," i.e. Mellon.

It was in Europe that Andrew Mellon became an art collector, and shocked Pittsburgh society by bringing home his first picture, a single canvas for which he had paid the princely and unprecedented sum of $1,000. Quite possibly it was a landscape of the Barbizon school, which was the rage at the time and about the only art of transient value that might command such a price. In any case, the picture's identity has been lost long since along with the painting itself. Nevertheless that was one beginning.

Another beginning occurred at a ball the following winter when Mellon arranged for Frick to meet a young lady whom he married before

Still going strong in 1908, Thomas and Sarah Mellon send out this picture on a birthday greeting; he is 95, she 91.

As a bachelor in the 1880s and 1890s, Andrew Mellon (the younger) often tours Europe with fellow Pittsburghers. In Venice, Henry Clay Frick holds his daughter in his lap in the gondola on the right; Philander C. Knox, lawyer and politician, sits amidships with his wife and daughters at left.

In Pittsburgh, the Mellon Bank thrives in 1922, the year after its chief executive departs for Washington and starts signing U.S. currency as Secretary of the Treasury.

Christmas came again. (Frick would return the favor nearly twenty years later.) In the meantime, these lions of Pittsburgh took trips to Europe, and vacations at Pride's Crossing, Massachusetts, and summer jaunts to Bar Harbor, Maine, where that new toy the photographic camera recorded their diversions. They joined the South Fork Hunting and Fishing Club (whose dam collapsed in 1889 to cause the Johnstown flood). They continued to thrive in business. Frick made his enormous fortune in coke and steel, becoming Andrew Carnegie's partner, manager and troubleshooter at United States Steel. He also became a symbol of his time—admired by his peers and would-be aspirants, detested by the working class as it found a voice. For one thing, Frick invented company scrip and the practice of paying wages in paper redeemable only at the company store. For another, when confronted by union organizers in 1892, he fired a mine's entire work force and rehired only those who

pledged not to join the union. To back himself up he hired a small army of Pinkerton guards, and the upshot was the notorious Homestead Strike, which left dozens of goons and strikers dead. Frick, who nearly died himself from a would-be assassin's bullet later, settled in New York, built a mansion on Fifth Avenue and devoted himself to gathering the remarkable pictures and decorative objects that now adorn the Frick Collection.

If assorted zealots, anarchists and progressives considered the coke and steel king anathema, they hardly perceived Mellon at all. Andrew continued on through his middle years as a nearly faceless family banker (often sharing deals with his brother R. B. with whom he stayed exceptionally close). He remained the banker at the right place and the right time to exercise his keen sense of business and of men's character. Because of the nature of his work, he was rarely in the public eye, and the Mellon name remained unknown outside Pittsburgh except in business circles, where it earned a reputation for unquenchable acquisitiveness and unquestioned integrity according to the standards of the time. Many years later, a famous associate recalled an example in his memoir:

An inventor with an idea sought a loan without enough collateral to secure it. "I sometimes personally loan money on the security of character," Andrew responded, "and if you want to take $10,000 on that basis you can have it." Making slow progress, the man came back for more capital, then for major backing when he developed an economical way to produce a strong, rustproof alternative to steel. Mellon advanced the funds each time and, when the great breakthrough was at hand, he accepted without quibble the inventor's proposal to share the new concern fifty-fifty. Shaking hands on the agreement, the inventor told Mellon "You could have foreclosed upon me any time in the last three years and taken the whole business." The banker replied, "The Mellons never did business that way."

If that account of the founding of Alcoa seems apocryphal in its simplicity, the teller, former President Herbert Hoover, admitted as much. "But it accords with my knowledge of Mr. Mellon's character." Mellon backed people in whom he had confidence, and he was absolutely scrupulous, a man of his word—for fiscally sound reasons if not for emotional or philosophical ones. Nor was he a corporate sentimentalist. One of the men he backed was Dr. Heinrich Koppers, who revolutionized the chemicals industry by improving coke-making. (His ovens extracted such valuable gases from coal that coke soon became the byproduct.) Koppers was a German national, and when World War I broke out and the Alien Property Act made foreigners' assets forfeit, Mellon bought the Koppers company at auction for a fraction of its worth.

According to an associate years later, Mellon ran his bank as "a sort of revolving fund for the promotion of enterprises" including Alcoa, Gulf Oil, the Koppers chemicals empire, the bridge-

Another Pittsburgher who made good and left town: Henry Clay Frick in a flattering engraving.

building firm that became Bethlehem Steel, a web of Pennsylvania utilities, along with companies that sold railroad parts, locomotives, insurance and more, many of them concerns that provided each other's materials, services or markets. What was his net worth? It was "probably beyond knowing," reports a scholar who totted up family resources as of 1929. The total, according to historian Stewart H. Holbrook: industrial assets of $1.9 billion; banking and financial interests of $500 million. Banking alone paid $3.8 million in dividends in 1929 while industrial investments earned another $91 million. To find another index of Andrew Mellon's stature, consider what happened when he entered government and conflict-of-interest rules required him to resign other positions. "Surely the shiest of all American men of wealth," he resigned from the boards of fifty-one corporations—and most of these controlled other companies. In addition to commercial enterprises, he was an officer of the Carnegie Library, the Carnegie Institute of Technology, the Mellon Institute, Pittsburgh Maternity Hospital and the University of Pittsburgh.

Such were the talents, interests and powers that enabled Andrew W. Mellon to become a founding patron of the twentieth century's cultural awakening. ❧

The Man of Family

J udge Mellon's most successful son attended to the bank with remarkable single-mindedness well into his forties. Andrew rose early, ate a farmer's breakfast, worked through the day (less time for an agreeable lunch) and fetched home quantities of material to study in the evening. According to biographer Burton Hendrick, "He read few books, spent little time in outdoor sport, saw few plays and heard almost no music; business, tireless [sic] and unremitting, formed the consuming passion of his life." Before the word was coined he was a workaholic.

He visited Europe almost every summer (if not for five months at a stretch), often with Henry Frick and his family. Sailing with him one year on the *S.S. Germanic*, Frick struck up an acquaintance with a prosperous Briton and his wife who were chaperoning their only daughter home from a world tour that iced the cake of her finishing school education. By all accounts Nora Mary McMullen was a fetching girl, lovely, willowy and vivacious. Frick, a convivial traveler, made introductions all around

Fit for a fairy princess, Hertford Castle rises benignly over crofters' cottages in an idyllic engraving of the estate where Nora McMullen grew up, the baby in a family with seven brothers. Her father has the place on a long lease from the Crown; centuries earlier Henry VIII kept three of his wives here.

and the previously retiring Andrew Mellon was captivated. He pursued her; she refused him; he pressed his suit. Patient, experienced in biding time to his advantage, he was forty-four; she barely twenty.

Her father was a businessman whose interests included breweries in northern Ireland whence the first Mellons came to America. Alexander P. McMullen chose to live in Hertfordshire, indeed in Hertford Castle which dated back through Tudor times (when three wives of Henry VIII called it home), past the Norman conquest and all the way to the Roman occupation. A royal tenant, McMullen had it on a ninety-nine-year-lease for his own tribe of seven sons and Nora, the baby. Theirs was a lively, even rowdy, clan given to sports and affection the way Mellons were dedicated to business and reserve. (When Mr. McMullen read Judge Thomas Mellon's memoir, which Andrew must

have provided, he made no secret of the fact that he thought the old man odd.) In any case, Nora spurned Andrew in 1899 and relented in 1900.

The September wedding in Hertford, the market town and county seat straddling three rivers, was a hearty event. Many Mellons had voyaged from America, a special train brought guests down from London, and the village turned out as if for the daughter of the lord of the manor—indeed Alexander McMullen was the next best thing. A surviving newspaper cutting says the "very pretty" ceremony in the fifteenth-century church "was witnessed by a very large number of people. Indeed the streets between the Castle and St. Andrew's Church were quite gay with spectators, and great interest was taken… [reflecting] the respect and esteem in which the bride's parents are held in the town and neighborhood." The church was festooned with huge Kentia palms and all manner of white flowers. The vocal offerings included "The Voice That Breathed O'er Eden" and "O Perfect Love," solo by the rector, "and as they left the church the opening strains of Mendelssohn's 'Wedding March' burst forth from the organ…. After the ceremony a merry peal was rung on the church bells, and flags were floating all day from numerous buildings in the town and from the Castle both the Union Jack and the American Flag." At the Castle reception a Royal Artillery band played, speeches were made, toasts drunk all around.

Next day "Mr. McMullen's various employees and their wives, numbering about eighty, were entertained at the Castle. At a substantial repast," McMullen orated on "how pleased he was to … know that such a good feeling existed between employer and employed." There were "boating, bowls, and pillow-fighting," then a tug-of-war between teams of workers from two towns with the winners then being bested by the McMullen sons. "At the conclusion the men gave hearty cheers for their host and hostess … and for the absent son," who was off at the Boer War. Commentary on these goings-on by Andrew or kin has not survived; suffice it that the Mellons may not have seen the like before. Alas, surprise was the watchword for this marriage.

The newlyweds returned to America and rode the Pennsylvania Railroad to the edge of booming Pittsburgh and what had been founded as Negleystown: East Liberty, which was as much a Mellon feifdom as Hertford Castle was McMullen's. Nora looked out the carriage window and asked "We don't get off here, do we? You don't live here?" Indeed they were home.

From the old house on Negley Avenue, they soon moved to an undistinguished home on Forbes Street. It was about now—and perhaps to decorate this house in particular—that Andrew began to buy art in a more copious and systematic fashion. Starting in 1899 he had bought pictures as furnishings such as Troyon's *Cows in a Meadow* and other canvases which an eventual arbiter of art would say "have all mercifully dis-

The Mellons' house on Forbes Street.

appeared." Andrew became a familiar at the Knoedler galleries of New York, Paris and London. Late in 1901, for example, one partner wrote precisely and politely to confirm Mellon's receipt of a $43,000 consignment of paintings: (a Van Marche for $18,000, Mauve for $8,000, Jules Dupré for $5,000 and Corot for $12,000), and his return of a Maris watercolor. Charles S. Carstairs explained, "I want you to understand that it is our desire to do anything in our power

Serene gaze notwithstanding, Nora does not take kindly to Pittsburgh. "We don't get off here, do we?" she asks as their wedding trip ends in 1900. Andrew will write of married life in the dark house on Forbes Street (above), "we were devoted to each other and it seemed to me to be a state of happiness seldom reached." It seemed to her otherwise.

*One of the groom's better
buys during the early years
of marriage:* Herdsmen
Tending Cattle *(c. 1650)
by the Dutch artist Aelbert
Cuyp who anticipated
nineteenth-century land-
scape painters such as Joseph
Mallord William Turner.*

and trust you are satisfied. You should be, the paintings you have purchased are of the finest quality and worth every cent of the above prices." He assured his client that he could return any canvas at any time and be credited with the full purchase price. Meanwhile the dealer sent for his consideration a Diaz land-scape (for $3,200) like "the small Diaz belonging to Mr. Frick you admired so much." (Not that Mellon was just keeping up with his friend. In 1908 he bought a Turner for $72,875.67, tired of it a year later and sold it to Frick at a profit of precisely $10,000.)

Recovering her poise, Nora settled into domestic life with a will. She dismissed the housekeeper, meaning to manage the household herself. Andrew would record that "she did the marketing and managed everything beautifully. She had the English instinct of economy which appealed to my admiration but I made every-thing easy and smooth. She kept the accounts and paid the bills carefully. In the evening when not going out she would play or sing and some-times read the papers to me. We were devoted to each other and it seemed to me to be a state of happiness seldom reached. Of course there were at times trifling differences for the moment, but nothing to disturb our happiness." He called her

Norchen, she called him Andy.

Late in June 1901 Nora bore a daughter and gave her an old Scottish name, Ailsa. Barely a month later the little family went to summer at Hertford Castle. Back in Pittsburgh "through the winter of 1901 everything continued lovely," Andrew would write with nostalgia if question-able syntax. "We did not go out or entertain a great deal and I haven't much recollection of events during that period—however our life was all that could be wished." His effusive bride who loved the outdoors would write, "Today has been more perfect than any other day; every-thing is golden—golden—golden." But by and large, her home would be remembered as "very dark and the halls were very dark and the walls were very dark and outside, Pittsburgh itself was very dark."

During that winter Gulf Oil was being born, and Andrew spent many more evenings working in his study than listening to Nora play Chopin in the parlor. Beside that, she loved to ride but Andrew proved awkward on horseback. She cut a fine figure as a skater and he tried the diversion but had to give it up. She liked to dance and he even joined a dancing class though "it was a part for which nature had never intended him," his sympathetic biographer wrote. "She liked the theatre, and parties, and now and then Mellon let himself be taken from the fireside for such uncongenial diversions." But he did not much like going out in society, and the first families of Pittsburgh did not much welcome the foreign beauty who had snatched away their city's most eligible bachelor.

Still the Mellons seemed an enviable couple. They took long vacations, in Florida; California; Aiken, South Carolina, a new wintering ground for the smart set; Pride's Crossing, Massachu-setts; a few months in England every summer for a decade.

When Nora underwent surgery for an un-named condition the next year, he took a room in Roosevelt Hospital for the fortnight of her recuperation. They considered living in England half the year and surveyed an estate in easy reach

of both Windsor and the churchyard celebrated in Thomas Gray's *Elegy…,* somber Andrew's favorite poem.

And still he kept buying art, his taste possibly having changed with his family situation. Perhaps for decoration—Nora had no interest in pictures—or perhaps as his eye improved, in 1905 he purchased Cuyp's *Herdsman Tending Cattle* and a Gainsborough, the portrait of Mrs. John Taylor. In 1906 Carstairs, by now signing himself "Charlie," pens

My Dear Andy—"I am writing… to send you a photograph of one of the most beautiful Romneys you have ever laid your eyes on, a charming little girl. I thought of you the moment I bought it as a picture that would go straight to your heart. The dress is white, the sash and ribbons a pretty pink and the sky a lovely blue and the whole picture is full of light. The big blue eyes look at you in a frank childish manner most fascinating—I am reserving the picture for you and I would like you to cable me *Knoedler*

London "yes" or "no." The price is $50,000. It was painted just two years later than Mr. Frick's "Lady Hamilton" and is of Romney's first period. It is a portrait of "Miss Willoughby."… With love to Nora and dear little Ailsa.

Two years later Charlie Carstairs informed Andrew, "I hurriedly made up my mind to have an exhibition of Old Masters and included your beautiful Turner which from the dignity and character of the exhibition I knew you would be glad to loan me." Claude Phillips, an eminent English critic and curator of the peerless Wallace Collection "expressed most poetically the charm of your lovely Turner which I am so glad you possess. It is indeed a treasure to be proud of.… I have sold the two small Turners here in England, you will be pleased at not having to think further about them.… I wanted you so much to have them.… Give my love to Nora and Mrs. McMullen and kiss for Ailsa and Paul."

On June 11, 1907, Nora had borne a son

whom Andrew named simply Paul (to avoid the family habit of saddling boys with initials) and they returned again to Hertford Castle. The reason she "took my baby boy to Hertfordshire" was, as she would remember, "I wanted to nurse to life in him my own love for the green fields and the open sky. I wanted him away from the gray-smoke and dust-filled air of my husband's cold and grim estate." The family continued to travel widely and vacation regularly, but home was still and forever Pittsburgh.

Nora had seen herself

in the role of the mistress of the manor who lightens the burden of the peasant. I imagined myself as a link between the old world and the new.... I would go into my husband's American towns and plan and plant and win the love and affections of his people, and give them an heir that I would bring up good and kind and generous, a master of his fortune, not its slave.... My first great disillusion came when I learned that his people were not of his people at all. [He said] "They are foreigns, Huns and Slavs and such as that, and you can't do anything with them...."

By 1908 Nora lingered in England and wrote to Andrew from a place called Sunninghill Park:

The thought of those long dreary lonesome days and those silent preoccupied evenings almost kills me.... Why must that loathsome business take all the strength and vitality which you ought to give to me? Why should you only give me your tired evenings? Why should I give you all my strength and health and youth and be content with nothing in return? For I am not content and never shall be as long as I have to be second—always second, I am feeling so desperately lonely tonight I could almost kill myself. But I would rather be lonely here than in Pittsburgh.

In April of 1909, Nora confided in a couple whom both Mellons considered close friends, and Thomas L. Chadbourne carried the message to Andrew, who would commit it to paper:

Chadbourne asked did I know Mrs. Mellon was unhappy. I asked what he meant. He replied 'She tells me she wishes to leave you, that she has been unhappy for a long time and wants to be divorced.... Mr. Mellon, I would have more hope for the situation if the trouble were the result of a quarrel or a disagreement, but it seems so deep-seated that both Mrs. Chadbourne and I believe there is no possibility of changing her. We have both done our utmost before coming to you.'... It was a bolt out of clear sky to me.

Andrew responded by battening down the hatches. He handled the breakup of his marriage as carefully as any business matter. The team of lawyers he enlisted in his cause comprised Pittsburgh's best—all of the best including two perennial adversaries, so that Nora had to go as far as Philadelphia to find representation. Then Andrew's counsel countered her notion of a quick Reno divorce as not binding in Pennsylvania. If there were to be a divorce, it would be granted in the Commonwealth under a new law enacted by the legislature and signed by the governor with noteworthy speed. Under existing state law, either party in a divorce could demand

The Man of Family 57

Paul and his adored sister Ailsa with their mother. The divorce decree provides for her handsomely and gives her partial custody.

a jury trial, but hardly had *Mellon v. Mellon* been joined than that law was altered so that one party could block a public trial. As Andrew and Nora gathered their respective forces, it was clear that their differences were irreconcilable over publicity at least: She wanted all the public notice she could get while he wanted none at all if he could help it. And he could help a lot, given his wealth and influence. The subject of the Mellons' break up was somehow deemed not a matter of public interest in Pittsburgh where the local press embargoed the story, evidently out of deference to the powerful plaintiff. But some out-of-town papers had a field day, and the finer families of East Liberty sent servants down to the depot before breakfast to pick up copies like contraband.

Nosy neighbors aside, Andrew v. Nora got nasty enough to have been featured in a soap opera. He bugged the house with hidden microphones; she tore them out. He hired detectives to shadow her; she flaunted her independence by traveling with a dashing man. Andrew's team won one point when detectives in England discovered Nora rented a house as a "Mrs. Curphey" with one Captain Alfred George Curphey, a presumed English officer and gentleman who turned out to be a bounder. Andrew's team appeared to win another point by getting the case brought to a closed-door trial back in Pittsburgh on grounds of adultery rather than desertion as agreed. Nora's lawyers then won a major point in having the case grandfathered and thus exempted from the secrecy provisions of the new divorce law should she want an open trial.

Things were especially nasty in terms of one genuinely contested issue: custody of Ailsa and Paul. Once delivering the children to their mother aboard a steamer that would take them to England for a holiday, Andrew changed his mind and spirited them back to Pittsburgh. Guessing what was afoot, Nora jumped ship and gave chase, leaving her maids and luggage aboard to sail without her. On another occasion, Nora was forced out of the family mansion by burly men in Andrew's employ as the children watched. While the court was supposedly overseeing the issue of custody pro tem, nine-year-old Ailsa was torn screaming hysterically from her mother's arms and packed away to a strange house by a nurse. Three-year-old Paul took it more in his tiny stride, evidently because he simply did not understand what was happening.

The separation, begun in 1909, was resolved in 1912 when custody of the children was deemed to be shared equally. Nora received a substantial settlement—the interest from $1 million in trust funds—and left the detested city of her marriage for points north and of course for England where the children spent memorable holidays. Andrew remained in Pittsburgh for another decade where he continued working hard and making enormous amounts of money. There is more to the story of their hate and love, but that can wait. For now, the private tragedy of the marriage had two important results of eventual public import and relevance here:

First, it appears that Andrew Mellon's interest in pictures took on a different fervor when he became a bachelor again. Not to overstate the obvious, he began taking increased pleasure in the acquisition and enjoyment of art; increasingly art was something in which he took obviously sensual pleasure. It's a wonder, one said, that Andrew Mellon didn't take a mistress; it appears that by and large he was enamored of painted ladies—Gainsboroughs, Romneys and such.

He moved to an imposing red brick mansion built by a Jones & Laughlin Steel magnate,

a grand house with tall ceilings, large bedrooms, large baths, a handsome library full of books and a white-paneled dining room furnished in the eighteenth-century manner. As John Walker, a member of Paul's social set, recalled of Mellon:

Andrew Mellon buys this impressive house on Woodland Road in Pittsburgh where he lives comfortably and whence the children leave for boarding schools.

In the daytime the house on Woodland Road was as full of sunshine as the smoke of Pittsburgh's blast furnaces and steel mills permitted; but at night one had a general sense of gloom, the darkness broken by patches of light where reflectors on paintings illumined the muted colors of English and Dutch portraits and landscapes. I remember on one occasion seeing emerge from the shadows a frail, fastidiously dressed man with high cheekbones, silver hair, and a carefully trimmed mustache. He was most impressive in an aristocratic, patrician way. I found him, however, exceptionally silent, as I tried my best to convey my admiration for his collection. He was inarticulate on the subject of art. Even the names of the artists whose works he owned occasionally escaped him. But from the way he looked at his paintings, from the sheer intensity of his scrutiny, I knew that he had a deep feeling for what he collected, a relationship to his pictures which I have rarely found in the many collectors I have known.... He seems to have wanted paintings which would offer him an escape into an ideal world filled with civilized human beings, often portrayed in the midst of beautiful scenery.... In Pittsburgh where day after day he faced the smoke

and dirty fog which produced his wealth, he wished to dream of a pleasanter environment. His portraits of George IV and the Duchess of Devonshire by Gainsborough, of Miss Urquhart by Raeburn, of Lady Caroline Howard by Reynolds, offered imaginary companionship with people whose personalities did not jar and whose presence did not in any way affect his reticence.

Second, the children's bifurcated life had manifold results. Perhaps the most beneficial of them is in the duality of Paul's character, the son of both his parents. Memories of his childhood include "a sunny and imperturbable English summer landscape. There seemed to be a tranquility in those days that has never again been found." As an adult he became devoted to art, and the champion of the museum his father would found. In maturity, he loved art as intuitively as his father had, but more learnedly and systematically as well. He also manifested his mother's more romantic, poetic nature—a love of things British and the out-of-doors, a friendly noblesse oblige.

Though Andrew and Nora's parting seemed anguished and absolute, it became ambiguous. Almost immediately, according to some news re-

ports and then published biographies, there were hints at reconciliation. Once divorced, Andrew and Nora kept in touch with each other, at first doubtless because of their mutual interest in the growing children. After a decade, their contacts were frequent as they exchanged Christmas and birthday greetings. Andrew sent flowers when Nora was ill, biographer Hendrick wrote, and "talks over the telephone, telegrams and letters brought cheerful moments into the Secretary's life."

But in the spring of 1923 there came a turning point. Nora announced her engagement to one Harry A. Lee, a young Englishman who sometimes sold antiques on New York's Lexington Avenue. The news startled Mellon enough for him to write her about reconciling in no uncertain terms. Nora answered that it was what she had long desired, but now she wrote

If only you could have given me the faintest hope during all these years.... This is not a reproach, dear Andy. I have not the shadow of one in my heart for you. It is just a dreadful tragedy, at least for me.... Dear, dear Andy, even though I feel I have a mortal, inward, bleeding wound, still I am so grateful not to have died without telling you how much I have loved and missed you all these years. As long as I live it will always be the same. I shall try very hard to be brave and regain some peace when I am once more among my flowers. Think kindly of me sometimes and, if you can, write me.

The Tuesday before St. Patrick's Day he replied in spades, using the treasured diminutive:

Dear Norchen.
I have read your letter and it has grieved me deeply, while at the same time bringing solace and abiding comfort.
I have been sadly wrong but must tell you how it was that I did not speak sooner.... The old love was in my heart even while I was so obtuse and blind, and it makes me heartsick to think of you in all this time suffering so sadly alone. The past can not be brought back and we must now look to the future.

You have had more than your share of unhappiness and are entitled to brighter days.

I want to be helpfull [sic] to you now and always. You must look forward and not allow anything of the past to distress you. Interest in the farm [where she now lived], and garden will do much and your married life can become a happy and contented one.

For myself, aside from all else, the truth of our understanding remains, and is an abiding comfort in my heart. I shall be interested in your life and pray for your happiness....

God bless you, dearest Norchen,
Your ever loving
Andy

Her second marriage ended after five years and in 1928 Nora took back the Mellon name; friends never got used to calling her Mrs. Lee, she said. After her second divorce Andrew augmented her trust funds, increasing her income substantially. Indeed he was ever helpful. He gave her country houses near Hudson, New York, and in Litchfield, Connecticut. He bought her a thoroughbred stable, the four-hundred-acre estate called Rokeby Farms near Middleburg in the Virginia horse country.

When Andrew died a decade later, Nora braved Pittsburgh society's inevitable snubs and attended his public funeral. Four decades later she died, at the age of ninety-four, and was buried in a little private cemetery within fieldstone walls amid the rolling Virginia farmland, a place as green and golden as any in Hertfordshire. There lies Norchen beside her husband, Andy. ❧

A horsewoman, Nora lives for a few years at this farm in Virginia hunt country.

Mr. Mellon Goes to Washington

I n 1920 the Republican Convention couldn't pick a nominee, so the leaders met privately and chose a nice dolt who ran on his front porch, promised a "return to normalcy" and took sixty-one percent of the vote to beat a Democrat named Cox and running-mate Franklin D. Roosevelt. Naming a cabinet was harder work than campaigning, and Warren G. Harding managed to bring presidential appointments to a new low except in his choice of three able secretaries: Charles Evans Hughes at State, Herbert Hoover at Commerce and Andrew Mellon at Treasury. Hughes and Hoover were old pros in government and well known; Mellon utterly unknown except by the banking community and some powerful political conserva- tives. Yet within four years, the *New York Times* reported, moviegoers cheered loudest during news- reels when he appeared, and FDR soon quipped that Calvin Coolidge "would like to have God on his side, but he must have Andrew Mellon."

When he came to Washington in 1921, the capital city was still small but growing, still southern but increasingly cosmopolitan. The grand residential streets of Connecticut, Wisconsin and Massachusetts Avenues here and there boasted clusters of handsome mansions and townhouses. Yet

these boulevards also stretched more than a half-mile between intersections as they passed through farmland. In its choice precincts, the city had become architecturally distinguished as many affluent people from elsewhere built spectacular homes designed by the likes of Charles McKim, Stanford White and John Russell Pope. These residents were not just politicians and diplomats whose work required their presence here but also gentry who came to Washington because they liked it.

One neighborhood of grandiose homes had grown up around the junction of Connecticut and Massachusetts Avenues. Overlooking Dupont Circle itself was the stately 1900 home of Herbert Wadsworth, a man with agricultural interests in upstate New York, which became the Sulgrave Club. A block northwest of the circle lived Speaker of the House Nicholas Longworth and his wife, Alice, Teddy Roosevelt's daughter.

Up another block, a retired railroad president built a house where his daughter was married with President Taft in attendance, and where president-elect Franklin Roosevelt would stay before it became the Cosmos Club. Nearby was the 1897 house of another Civil War veteran, Major D. Clinch Phillips, a Pittsburgh glass manufacturer married to a Jones & Laughlin Steel heiress. When their doctors prescribed a healthier setting than Pittsburgh, they tried Washington—in the balmy winter of 1896— and built the house their son Duncan opened in 1920 as the Phillips Collection, a museum of "modern art and its sources."

One block east of Dupont Circle, on Massachusetts Avenue at 18th Street, the five-story McCormick had just opened, and here Andrew Mellon chose to reside, a renter for all his years in the capital. James M. Goode, an authority on local architectural history, has

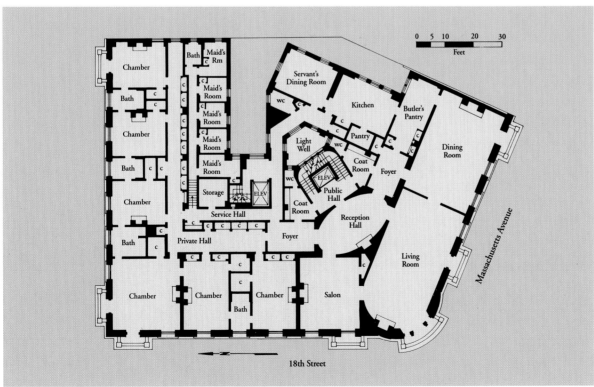

Welcome to the lavish McCormick and Andrew Mellon's living room. The floor plan shows a typical apartment with six connecting bedrooms, four full baths, two coat rooms with w.c. and self-contained servants' quarters.

called it unconditionally "the finest apartment house erected in Washington." Tastefully detailed, superbly designed and fastidiously built, this building's 11,000-square-foot apartments were the city's largest. At fourteen-and-a-half feet, the ceilings were the highest; at $600,000, the construction costliest. Restoration architect Nicholas A. Pappas, who recently rehabilitated the building as headquarters of the National Trust for Historic Preservation, says the McCormick uniquely combined opulence, cleverness, beauty and amenity.

Deft use of mezzanines provided the five-story building with eight levels of lower-ceilinged servants quarters. Each apartment had a laundry with gas-heated clothes dryer. Each had a walk-in refrigerator and built-in telephone conduits. Financed by heirs of Cyrus McCormick, inventor of the celebrated reaper, the Beaux-Arts residence was designed by Jules H. de Sibour, Paris-born son of a French count (and a mother from Maine) who was educated at Yale and the Ecole des Beaux-Arts.

In a building that had one apartment per upper floor, Mellon took the uppermost, the fifth, the only one with a narrow balcony running along the twenty-two windows fronting the streets. To call this a six-bedroom, four- and two half-bath residence is to understate the fact, because the servants' wing, complete with a dining room for the help, had five maid's rooms and two more baths. The formal entrance, reached by stairs or elevator, was a "public hall" flanked by coat rooms for gentlemen and ladies (each with its w.c.). The hall led to an oval reception hall which opened onto two "foyers," and a salon and the 24 x 45-foot living room. (The dining room was just 10 feet shorter.) The corridor serving the six connecting bedrooms ran 110 feet. The eight fireplaces were all set off by unique surrounds. The butler's pantry came with a walk-in silver vault just as a dressing room off the master bedroom boasted a little jewelry safe embedded in the wall.

Brother James came to see Andrew's digs and asked about the rent. The Secretary of the Trea-

sury said it was $25,000 a year, more than twice his $12,000 salary, and James warned, "Remember Andy, Father always said we should live within our income." In any case, Mellon's fellow tenants were hardly pinched. They included diplomat Robert Woods Bliss, who later moved to Dumbarton Oaks, which became a museum for his collection of pre-Columbian art; Sumner Welles, who soon moved across the Circle; Alanson B. Houghton, later ambassador to Great Britain and Germany; and in the littlest flat, oil-and-tools heiress Perle Mesta, the celebrated hostess and eventual ambassador to Luxembourg whom Ethel Merman burlesqued in *Call Me Madam.*

Here Mellon came to live in his accustomed style. He rose early, ate substantially and (in one departure from his Pittsburgh routine) embarked on foot for his office three-quarters of a mile away, usually walking home again for lunch. Of course he kept a car, a unique aluminum Standard said to have cost $40,000. (As one awestruck observer wrote in Pittsburgh, "It was not a particularly beautiful car, being some-

66

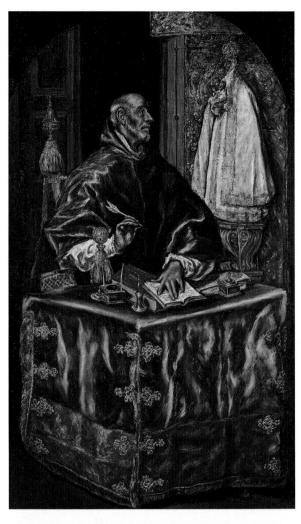

what angular, but obviously it was Mr. Mellon's car and traffic parted before it as the Red Sea parted for the children of Israel.") He continued to chainsmoke "rat-tails," miniature cigars at fifteen cents a box, to wear magnificent somber clothes, to collect pictures—albeit with new seriousness.

For at least forty years Mellon bought pictures mainly to decorate his homes. There were the Barbizon School landscapes at first, Cazin's *Moonlight Effects*, which he bought from Knoedler in 1899, the Troyon *Cows in a Meadow*, and Van Boskerck's *Sunset, Pulborough, Sussex*. During his marriage he had spent some $400,000 on pictures, not one of them worthy of his eventual National Gallery, according to its first chief curator. Yet his choices over time displayed a developing taste, and he adorned the apartment with pictures for his private pleasure.

His biographer noted that for the McCormick apartment he favored

the natural reproduction [i.e. portraits] of the kind of people from whom he had sprung and among whom, all his life, he found most congenial association. Thus the British and Dutch painters were the ones among whom he found himself most at home— the beautiful English ladies and proud gentlemen of the late eighteenth century and the very human faces of the Dutch masters. His apartment, when first set up, radiated with Gainsboroughs—"George IV as Prince of Wales" which had hung in the Pittsburgh house, a full-length "Duchess of Devonshire" and several others.

There were Frans Hals' imposing *Portrait of an Elderly Lady*, Henry Raeburn's demure and sensuous *Miss Eleanor Urquhart*, El Greco's exotically monastic *Saint Ildefonso*. Only a few Italian paintings hung here: the Filippino Lippi *Portrait of a Youth*, Luini's *Portrait of a Lady* and a small Madonna by Titian. In his bedroom were Trumbull's *Alexander Hamilton* and Gilbert Stuart's Vaughan portrait of George Washington. His piano held Vermeer's *Girl with the Red Hat* while Turner's *Mortlake Terrace* hung over the mantel

Mellon's flat is soon famous among socialites who covet invitations in order to see his paintings including Bernardino Luini's Portrait of a Lady *(opposite), El Greco's* Saint Ildefonso, *and Vermeer's* The Girl with the Red Hat. *All are destined for the National Gallery.*

Bernardino Luini, *Portrait of a Lady*, c. 1520/1525
Andrew W. Mellon Collection

El Greco (Domenikos Theotokopoulos), *Saint Ildefonso*, c. 1605/1614
Andrew W. Mellon Collection

Johannes Vermeer, *The Girl with the Red Hat*, c. 1665
Andrew W. Mellon Collection

Catherine Tatton, Memling's *Madonna and Child with Angels* and *Lacemaker*, a presumed Vermeer. One evening at dinner a guest from an embassy missed seeing the Medici portrait and asked its whereabouts. "Mr. Mellon has sent it away," she was told, "because he did not like it." The guest exclaimed "How wonderful! To be able to say 'take that Raphael away! I do not like it!'"

Mellon could have been a leading player in Washington's social whirl—if he had wanted. His friend Eugene Meyer, Federal Reserve Board governor and then owner of the *Washington Post*, entertained lavishly and when his wife needed an extra man at dinner she would invite the Treasury Secretary, daughter Katharine Graham remembers. Mellon was popular not only because of his official eminence, but his quiet charm, sense of humor and habit of paying back social debts with small dinner parties in his apartment with its array of art of which he was duly proud. As a cousin wrote "A.W. delighted in the sensation that his pictures made. He was as happy when the pictures were being admired as he was unhappy when attention was focused on himself."

While avoiding many official functions, he was a regular at White House poker games where, a scholar writes, "'the boys' would assemble, take off their jackets, snap their suspenders, light up their cigars, pour themselves a good belt of contraband drink, and play the night away.... He must have felt out of place in such a crowd, but he played there and ... he usually won. More often he played in polite company" with his colleague Ogden Mills, Nicholas Longworth and vivacious Alice. Her sister-in-law, Mrs. Theodore Roosevelt, Jr. recorded an immortal hand he played with future Vice President Charles Curtis. Someone opened with a full house, then:

Mr. Mellon drew a card. So did Charlie Curtis. I forget what the others did, but it didn't matter. The full house bet the limit, was raised by Mr. Mellon and again by Charlie. The rest couldn't throw in their

in the private sitting room. His first major buys after coming to Washington, including Hoppner's *Frankland Sisters* and two Turner landscapes, hung in the apartment.

For a time his drawing room boasted Raphael's *Giuliano de'Medici* who had, he felt, an evil face; "It seemed to me a strong work but not particularly attractive for a private living room," as he told Frick's daughter. So he sent it back to the dealer (under terms of his standing agreement to return anything for full credit) in a transaction that got him Gainsborough's *Miss*

hands fast enough.... Mr. Mellon raised; Charlie raised. Mr. Mellon raised again, refusing to believe he was beaten. Charlie raised back. Mr. Mellon, remarking that he always had to pay for his experience, called and laid down four queens. Charlie had four kings and an ace. At the end of the evening Mr. Mellon, a gentle, shy man, laid forty cents on the table. "That's all I have left," he said in a soft voice.

The softness of his voice became legendary; a sorry orator, he often could not be heard by his audience and at best read his prepared texts woodenly and verbatim. On one occasion, he lost his place, gave up trying to find it, and closed with the simple peroration "That's all." On another, while reading remarks at a ceremony dedicating a predecessor's statue in Washington, he lost his place for so long that the Marine honor guard thought he was done and retired the colors. (Some said his voice and aversion to public speaking were the liabilities that kept him from entertaining the idea of running for president himself.)

As late as 1926 Mellon still said that he was buying art for his own sake. He wrote an English lady, "I have only those paintings and a few tapestries which I have acquired from time to time when I had suitable places of residence. I have not had occasion to consider acquisition of such for public purposes." Not that he was able to acquire all he wanted for private enjoyment. He had coveted Sir Thomas Lawrence's *Red Boy* but refused to pay the asking price near $1 million. And he missed Gainsborough's *Blue Boy* which went to California collector Henry Huntington who loaned it to him on its way to the coast.

For some time Mellon had bought largely through Knoedler & Company, dealing first with Roland Knoedler himself, then in turn with Charles Carstairs, Charles Henschel and Carman Messmore. It was Messmore who acquired a spectacular Rembrandt self-portrait, which had been owned for generations by a noble Scottish house, and offered it to Mellon at a price that got his Irish up. The picture showed

The 'McCormick Collection' (as it might have been called but wasn't) reflects the tenant's fondness for classic portraiture. It includes works from many eras and parts of Europe, yet the subjects are usually aristocratic personages: Filippino Lippi's Portrait of a Youth *was painted in Florence about 1485; Goya's Spanish* Marquesa de Pontejos *and Gainsborough's English* Miss Catherine Tatton *were both done in the 1780s.*

Filippino Lippi, *Portrait of a Youth,* c. 1485
Andrew W. Mellon Collection

Francisco de Goya, *The Marquesa de Pontejos,* probably 1786
Andrew W. Mellon Collection

Thomas Gainsborough, *Miss Catherine Tatton,* probably 1785
Andrew W. Mellon Collection

the artist at the age of fifty-three, seated in a manner that belies composure, his hands in his lap, a black cap on his head; bankrupt and without property, an utter failure according to the tenets of burgher culture, he has ten years to live. As John Walker would write, "There exists no painting more pitiless in its analysis or more pitiful in its implications."

Messmore got the picture by a stroke of luck and offered it to Mellon for $600,000. When asked what he had paid for it, Messmore told

Ailsa Mellon about the time of her engagement to David K.E. Bruce.

him frankly $250,000, a price that dampened Mellon's enthusiasm. After weeks of hearing nothing, Messmore took the painting to Washington, presented himself at the apartment and hung it in the dining room; Mellon returned home for lunch, bade his guest join him, and made no mention of the picture that looked down upon the meal. Weeks later he advised the dealer "I will buy the Rembrandt, but not at the price demanded. You will have to make a considerable reduction." The counter offer seemed to save the buyer's face more than his cash. Mellon proposed to allow the dealer less than a 100-percent markup by paying $475,000 and returning a Pieter de Hooch he'd bought for $65,000 and tired of. In short he bought the Rembrandt for ten percent off the asking price.

In 1931, Mellon bought one painting directly from a private owner, something he rarely did before and never did again. The political climate in Spain was deteriorating and an American diplomat's wife learned that Goya's portrait of the Marquesa de Pontejos might be bought from her descendants who were preparing to flee the country. Mellon's principal aide at the Treasury negotiated by transatlantic phone, but the transaction was nearly voided by the Spanish government. Knoedler's had to send a man from Paris to get an export license, grease some palms and get the painting out before new laws were enacted to protect the country's cultural patrimony. Mellon got his Goya only after the provisional government asked the advice of muralist José Maria Sert, who replied that the painting "would be the best ambassador Republican Spain could send to the Republican United States." Knoedler's work ended up costing Mellon what he would have paid as a commission. Thereafter he stayed out of private deals, as he always stayed out of auctions.

Mellon's children came of age during his years at Treasury. Paul, who had been sent off early, was a schoolboy at Choate in 1921, and vacationed with his father in Washington. Ailsa, recently graduated from Miss Porter's School, soon made her home with Andrew, her corner bedroom in the apartment adorned by the Reynolds portrait of Lady Caroline Howard. She often presided as hostess at his dinner parties for a dozen guests. Otherwise she engaged in the social whirl and dated royalty, accompanied by a chaperon from Pittsburgh. Called "a great horsewoman," she had an English accent and was very reserved, as aloof a young woman as she was sought after. When she accepted a suitor, social arbiters said it was the most awesome event in Washington since Teddy Roosevelt's daughter Alice was a bride twenty years earlier.

One spring Saturday in 1926 the Bishop of Washington solemnized the exchange of nuptial vows between Ailsa and David Kirkpatrick Este Bruce in the Bethlehem Chapel of the Cathedral of St. Peter and St. Paul, the then-unfinished neo-Gothic Episcopal seat overlooking Washington from the promontory of Mount St. Alban. The guest list suggests less a wedding than the ratification of an international alliance: The President and Mrs. Coolidge with two military aides; Vice President and Mrs. Dawes; five Supreme Court justices; five cabinet members; the secretaries of War and Navy; seven under- and assistant secretaries; eleven senators; the Speaker of the House and four members; six assorted "honorables"; thirteen foreign ambassadors and ministers; one general of note (John Pershing); and five individuals bearing the simple honorific of Mister—plus wives. The Chapel's capacity limited attendance to "official society, the members of the Bruce and Mellon families, and a few intimate friends." Private citizens accounted for barely half of the three hundred in the Chapel; the reception at the Pan American Union was attended by two thousand.

Wrote the *Washington Times* with breathless reverence and quaint usage, "Hoping for a glimpse of the bonny bride and all the distinguished personages assembled to do her honor, crowds of interested spectators from every class lined the curbs without the Cathedral Close, but none save the wedding guests were allowed within." A second page-one story enthused

Father of the bride strolls with newlyweds Ailsa Mellon and David Bruce at their summer home on Long Island.

Gifts of a fabulous value, unequalled by any collection of precious stones and metals and art in all the history of this Capital are crowding the special apartment rented by the Mellons to house the wedding gifts…a priceless sideshow to the nuptials…. Gifts, the price of which most men strive a lifetime for, are trinkets in the collection, and more are pouring in. They come from Presidents and Ambassadors, from the great captains of American industrial organizations, from Senators and Cabinet members, and most important of all—from Andrew W. Mellon himself. Ten million dollars is the cash dowry he is said, in circles that rumor, to have settled upon the bride. Added to this are numerous smaller presents, such as a $100,000 string of pearls and other jewels which he is said to have presented to his daughter. A veritable army of Secret Service men is guarding the treasured collection of gifts, scrutinizing every man and woman and child who comes near the apartment, and watching even each other.

Federal agents chauffeured the bride to the church as well.

The groom, brilliant, charming and able David K. E. Bruce, was attended by ushers who included two Mellons (brother Paul and Uncle Richard), a future senator from Maryland, and Macgill James, later assistant director of the National Gallery. Certainly his father-in-law settled some wealth on David—$2 million says one family friend—when he married Ailsa; he came from a family with social and political pedigrees if not money, and he would bring it great distinction. Scion of an old Baltimore clan, David was the son of a sitting senator from Maryland. He entered Princeton in 1915, then dropped out two years later to serve in the field artillery with the AEF in France where he won a battlefield commission. After finishing Princeton, he studied law at both the University of Virginia and University of Maryland, then ran successfully for the Maryland legislature. Now he was a fledgling diplomat and as soon as the honeymoon was over he took his bride to Rome, where he was posted as a $2,500-a-year vice consul embarking on a career that would be nothing short of spectacular. After two years, he left the Foreign Service for banking—with Bankers Trust in New York, then W. A. Harriman and Company.

When Andrew Mellon was dispatched to London as ambassador, the Bruces followed, Ailsa as his official hostess, David as a stalwart friend. During the next decade Bruce tried his hand at several things. He became a gentleman farmer in Virginia, wrote a history of the presidency, dabbled in the parachute business and ran a tobacco plant—the while advising and assisting Mellon in many areas, especially later when it came time to establish the Gallery. It is said today by one who knew David intimately, that he must have married Ailsa out of respect and affection for her father.

David was brilliant, outgoing and charming; Ailsa intellectually undisciplined, imperious and painfully shy. He was destined to rise even though the marriage lost its sheen. In 1940 he went to Britain evidently to represent the American Red Cross, but within a year was a London-based army colonel organizing the Office of Strategic Services (a.k.a. OSS or "Oh So Social" as the CIA's precursor was known both intimately and enviously). Before the war ended he was chief of European operations; after it he pursued a career that no other modern American diplomat has matched in terms of eminence and geographic breadth of posts. David K. E. Bruce would serve as Truman's ambassador to France, Eisenhower's to West Germany, Kennedy's to Great Britain, Nixon's first envoy to the People's Republic of China and Ford's representative to NATO.

In the meantime, Mellon came to rely heavily on him in private matters, as he relied on a group of capable men at the Treasury in handling public business. There were: the cherubic Ogden Mills, holdover Assistant Secretary and Mellon's eventual successor; the professorial S. Parker Gilbert, an expert on German war reparations whom Mellon named Under Secretary and who later became a J. P. Morgan & Company partner and Bankers Trust director; the polymath Huntington Cairns, who started out freelancing as Treasury's official "censor" of art and books presented to customs officials for import. Finally there was David Edward Finley, a young lawyer and former aide of Eugene Meyer at the Federal Reserve Board.

In the early years at Treasury, Finley became Mellon's personal aide, confidential assistant, ghost writer and all around factotum. Whatever papers reached the Secretary's desk got there after Finley vetted them. Whatever left the desk was at least scanned by Finley's eye if not written by his hand. Finley attended Mellon's dinners and checked the seating chart for Ailsa's marriage. When Mellon went to London as ambassador, Finley went with him, as an Honorary Counselor on the Foreign Service payroll at a dollar a year. It was Finley who negotiated the Goya purchase. And Finley who bought a picture in London to save Mellon from breaking his promise to himself not to buy art while he was ambassador. In short he had long since become indispensable, and as familiar as a son. 🐝

Secretary Mellon at home at the McCormick— beneath A View on a High Road *by Meindert Hobbema, one of the Dutch masters who inspired England's great nineteenth-century landscape painters. In the background is Cuyp's* Herdsmen Tending Cattle.

Capital Builder

M ellon's real political experience amounted to having personally underwritten a GOP campaign deficit of $1.5 million. Coming to Treasury like a savvy entrepreneur taking over a company, as the new CEO he invited division heads appointed by the Wilson administration to stay until he learned the ropes, and he essentially continued Wilsonian policies. At first the outsider, in due time he ran Treasury like a corporation and the economy like a cartel as he became a commanding figure in the capital. He was soon called the greatest Secretary of the Treasury ever, though few people could name his predecessors or say what they had done to be less great. The fact remained that men-in-the-street now knew who the Treasury Secretary was, and they believed he was the alchemist of the rising prosperity they were enjoying so prodigally as the twenties roared.

Greatest or not, Mellon was undeniably a most durable Treasury boss. Before he was done he would serve for eleven years, longer than any other before or since save Albert Gallatin (1801–1814). Uniquely, he would serve under three presidents (Harding, Coolidge and Hoover); and despite an

Around the century's turn, Washington boasts prolifer-ating telephone poles, federal offices scattered all over town and (on the Mall) this railroad station where President Garfield was shot in 1881. The chaos prompts two reform efforts—to beautify the city and get the government organized—which ulti-mately lead to this site's choice for the National Gallery. (A brass star in the station floor marked the spot where Garfield fell; it was offered to the Gallery and declined.)

impeachment threat he stayed in office until he was appointed ambassador to the Court of St. James's at the age of seventy-six. He was also blessed by circumstance as he directed the Treasury during boom times when the economy responded to simple stimuli in classic ways. Business principles would apply, and if a healthy business could not long survive in the red, neither should a government tolerate a perennial deficit. Tightening the nation's fiscal belt, he brought an end to the recession that began in 1920. Declaring war on the debt incurred during World War I, he cut it substantially by advocating lower taxes and thus freeing private capital for investment that enlarged the tax base (all according to prevailing pre-Keynesian wisdom). As it happened, the economic engines of the world were geared up for expansion at breakneck speed, and America's economy led the rest—with Mellon at the throttle.

For all his laissez-faire philosophy, Mellon was not averse to helping his own—to doing good close to home and where it would be appreciated. For example, Treasury oversaw tariffs such as the duties on certain bronze imports, and during Mellon's watch it came to take a benign view of belfries, which were no longer regarded simply as habitats for bats, but instead as "bonded warehouses" for imported bronze bells. This exempted the owners from the stiff duties they would have to pay if the bells were hung and rung elsewhere. This nicety of regulation benefitted anyone who had occasion to raise a new steeple, namely persons apt to be prosperous in the first place and Christian in the second, like Mellon himself. Of wider importance, the Secretary of the Treasury was empowered to grant tax exemptions, and it was hardly coincidence that in Mellon's time these were enjoyed by citizens who gave $10,000 or more to Republican campaign chests.

It also appears that Andrew Mellon profited personally from decisions he made in government—as may have been more common in those times. During his tenure he solicited advice from the Internal Revenue director (his

subordinate) on ways to reduce his personal tax liability. He had an Internal Revenue agent assigned to prepare his own returns, and then hired the agent away from Treasury to work on his personal staff. Historians say that while he was representing the United States in Britain, he negotiated pacts involving the Middle East that directly and substantially benefitted Gulf Oil, the family's company. Finally, while he was a cabinet officer, he bought fabulous pictures from Russia's Hermitage, treasures the Bolshevik government was eager to cash in for hard currency to finance development. Eventually these complex transactions, handled secretly by agents in Leningrad, Berlin, London and Moscow, secured twenty-one pictures for $6.7 million.

Deficit reduction and extracurricular activi-

transformed the city. The District of Columbia was largely rural when Mellon came. Sixteenth Street did not yet reach the Maryland line, nor East Capitol Street the Anacostia River. He iced the cake of its greatest peacetime transformation, which had begun a score years earlier.

The grand ceremonial expanses designed in 1791 by French engineer Pierre L'Enfant had long since been put to baser uses. The tract at the foot of Jenkins Hill, which L'Enfant called "a pedestal awaiting a monument" before he placed the Capitol there, accommodated a railroad yard and the depot where President Garfield had been shot. Westward lay a warren of barrackslike buildings thrown up as temporary offices during World War I, and pastures, woods and swamp giving way to the Potomac. Pennsylvania Avenue, meant to have been a ceremonial boulevard between the Capitol and the White House, was a common commercial street. At Seventh Street NW, then the city's main northbound artery, the Avenue boasted Center Market, the city's largest with stalls for one thousand vendors and parking for three hundred wagons when Mellon came to town. By the time he left, Center Market was doomed at his direction to be replaced by a unique and imposing monument to the past.

Though the city had been planned before the government moved in with its complement of 130 clerks and staffers in 1800, much of the original plan had been forgotten. By 1901 the "city beautiful" movement blossomed across America and Senator James McMillan of Michigan established a Parks Commission that would oversee the capital city's metamorphosis into a "civic work of art." The Commission included giants in their fields: architects Charles McKim and Daniel Burnham (who designed Chicago's spectacular World's Fair), landscape architect Frederic Law Olmsted, Jr., sculptor Augustus St. Gaudens. Together they drafted the so-called McMillan Plan, which resurrected major features of L'Enfant's grand scheme, especially downtown and from Capitol Hill to the Potomac along what became the Mall.

Pennsylvania Avenue at 12th Street hardly measures up to the ceremonial boulevard envisioned in Pierre L'Enfant's grand design for the Seat of Government. The Federal Triangle project, directed by Treasury Secretary Mellon, would start setting it aright.

ties notwithstanding, an enduring accomplishment may be the least appreciated. Mellon's Treasury revamped America's paper money by designing look-alike bills in every denomination. This saved more than $1.5 million annually in labor, paper and ink since the new currency was one-third smaller than the old and the bills would last longer. An adoring biographer, Philip H. Love, wrote: "Inspired by his natural Scotch [sic] belief in economy, these thrifty bills, which run from $1 all the way up to $10,000, are distinctly Mellonistic both in design and in size"— neoclassical and smallish respectively.

If his most neglected achievement was literally making new money, his most concrete project was the remaking of downtown Washington with a positively augustan building program that

Center Market, the city's oldest and grandest, is doomed by the Federal Triangle plan. It is to be razed for a new Justice Department, until architect John Russell Pope argues that this important site with its intersecting north-south axis deserves a unique government building—the National Archives—which he then designs.

There was growing momentum for progress in terms of the look and layout of the city, but there were also awful obstacles to overcome, such as those rail yards below the Capitol. Architect Burnham persuaded Alexander Cassatt, painter Mary's brother and president of the Pennsylvania Railroad, to move his eyesores from the Mall and cooperate in the building of a shared terminal, Union Station, at a less intrusive site northwest of the Capitol. In turn the growing popularity of the idea of urban beauty led Congress in 1910 to establish a Fine Arts Commission to advise "upon subjects within the domain of the fine arts"—including architecture and planning. All this momentum found one culmination in what became Mellon's Federal Triangle project, a new "comprehensive" government center in the area bounded by Pennsylvania Avenue, Fourteenth Street and Constitution Avenue, the Mall's new boundary.

By the 1920s, 60,000 federal employees were quartered higgledy-piggledy in offices all over town, and efficiency was something devoutly to be wished. Succeeding Harding on his unexpected death in 1923, Calvin Coolidge proposed an ambitious building project, which fell to the Treasury Secretary to oversee. (When that famously terse President discussed this or anything else with the laconic Mellon, a wag wrote they conversed "almost entirely in pauses.") Mellon had to conceive the legislative authority to build what Fine Arts Commission Chairman Charles Moore called "the greatest group of public buildings ever constructed at one time in the

history of the world." If by greatest he meant biggest and dearest he was not just whistling hyperbole. America had a population of 120,000,000; the scheme's costs came to $116,246,472 or 98 cents a person, and Mellon was in charge.

He explained the grand plan in a Founder's Day speech at the Carnegie Institute in Pittsburgh by first quoting Coolidge:

If our country wishes to compete with others, let it not be in the support of armaments but in the making of a beautiful Capital City. Let it express the soul of America. Whenever an American is at the seat of his Government, however traveled and cultured he may be, he ought to find a city of stately proportion, symmetrically laid out and adorned with the best that there is in architecture, which would arouse his imagination and stir his patriotic pride....

Pennsylvania Avenue had become an eyesore of hotels, souvenir shops, tattoo parlors. "Certainly there is no avenue of corresponding

importance in any capital which can compare with it in sheer ugliness or lack of architectural dignity," Mellon averred. That was why Congress had authorized this huge buildings project. It would comprise a new Commerce Department, Bureau of Internal Revenue head-quarters, National Archives, Department of Labor and several others. Mellon felt that the "placing of these buildings is a great responsibility, for on [it] hinges the future development of Washington." No more federal offices would be built on the Mall, which would become a park; instead a new government center would rise in the triangular area east of the White House/ Treasury compound below Pennsylvania Avenue.

The Federal Triangle would consolidate government operations, increase efficiency and improve economy, Mellon believed.

At the same time the [adjacent] Mall will present the spectacle of a great park bordered on one side by the new boulevard [Constitution Avenue] lined with beautiful buildings, and on the other side by a wide

Having helped feed the city since 1801, the Market has grown to some 1,000 stalls which cater to the carriage trade and hoi polloi alike.

park-way of greensward with its four rows of trees, its drives and walks, statues and reflecting pools, all arranged in such a way that long vistas will be opened up for views of the Capitol in one direction and of the Washington Monument and Lincoln Memorial in the other.

The city had grown, Mellon noted, from a population of 75,000 during the Civil War to half a million.

But so long as it remains chiefly a seat of government, it will retain its unique character among the cities of the country. More and more it will be visited by people who will go to Washington because of its beauty and their feeling of pride and personal ownership in the nation's Capital.

The city of Washington, as President Coolidge has said, [should] express the soul of America. We do it well, therefore, to give it that beauty and dignity to which it is entitled. In doing so we are not only carrying out those plans which Washington made so long ago for the city which he founded but, at the same time, we are justifying that faith which he had from the beginning in the future greatness of America.

Yes, Mellon was a booster, and it is hard to believe that when he waxed so poetic about the new government buildings and the city at large, he did not also ask himself what he could do for his country's capital. Indeed it was during his tenure in the office overlooking the Mall and while supervising the Federal Triangle that he nurtured the plan for the Gallery. "He had begun to think of a national gallery in Washington before President Harding summoned him there to be his Secretary of the Treasury in 1921," the *Washington Post*'s White House reporter confided immediately after Mellon's death. Revealing an off-the-record interview several years earlier, Edward T. Folliard wrote that the idea

took concrete shape when he was in the Treasury. He used to stand at his office window on the second

floor of the Treasury Building and look down toward Potomac Park and the Mall. In the years ahead he was to be responsible for the great building program in the Federal Triangle... and in thinking about this he began to think more and more about a national gallery of art.

The Federal Triangle comprised seventy acres, would contain twelve enormous federal buildings and would have a huge and lasting impact on Washington. It gave the city a government core as classically derived as any on earth—and perhaps the most dehumanizing, some argued. The Bauhaus school, which championed blocks of grimly plain office buildings, was on the rise and its exponents carped about the Tri-

angle's "facadism." One pronounced it a complex of "brutal stone masses built in an eclectic style as boring as it was massive and unoriginal." Suffice it that the smart set overlooked a motive in what they took for architectural madness, and indeed the Triangle plan bowed to tradition: government centers have often been intended to impress—not to seem of ordinary scale, but to awe the citizens who visit or bring their business to them. This is not a "democratic" notion of Jacksonian egalitarianism, but an even older one that had been invoked when the Capitol was built, to say nothing of the great capitals of Europe.

Furthermore, given the pendulum swings of taste, the merits of neoclassical architecture now seem clear once again. In 1990 the *New York*

Times' architecture critic praised Mellon's project:

Designed by several of the nation's best, if most conservative architects, the Federal Triangle is one of the great collaborations of the twentieth century. With its blocks of similar but not identical classical buildings forming a handsome and lively rhythm on the streets, it is a true triumph of urbanism. For years it was politely tolerated but never really admired; now, with the resurgence of classical architecture, everyone from architects to bureaucrats has begun to speak of it as if it were a six-block version of the Parthenon.

If one building stood out from the rest, it was that which had the densest cluster of columns, the most complex entablature, the most richly sculpted pediments, the most manifestly layered roof and corner treatments. This was the National Archives building as designed for the site of the old Center Market by John Russell Pope, the outstanding exponent of neoclassicism in America and of whom much more later.

The Triangle consummated the McMillan Plan's design for Washington by providing a precinct for government offices. This helped clear the Mall, which was defined by Constitution and Independence Avenues, and was dedicated to special uses—recreational space and open vistas punctuated by monuments and a few monumental buildings. If Jenkin's Hill had been a pedestal awaiting the Capitol, the Mall that Mellon's Triangle helped to create was a verdant expanse awaiting a few edifices of unique dignity. In time, Mellon's gallery would provide two of them.

But long before he or the Federal Triangle was finished—in fact the year before construction began—the world turned upside down. In 1929 the stock market crashed and the economy he had been superintending so traditionally began its long, slow slide. Herbert Hoover was president, the third "to serve under Secretary Mellon" as the saying went, and the one who served least comfortably. At first Hoover accepted Mellon's bitter prescription for recovery. A good old-fashioned financial panic was not an altogether bad thing, the Secretary said, "It will

purge the rottenness out of the system. High costs of living and high living will come down. People will work harder, live a more moral life. Values will be adjusted, and enterprising people will pick up the wrecks from less competent people." Needless to say, that didn't sit well with many voters whatever their competence. In his memoirs, published thirty years later, Hoover wrote of Mellon: "He was in every instinct a country banker. His idea and practice had been to build up men of character in his community and to participate in their prosperity. He had no use for certain varieties of New York banking, which he deemed were too often devoted to tearing men down and picking their bones. When the boom broke he said 'they deserved it.'" Whether those specific words were uttered in public, people knew where Mellon stood and not only resented his philosophy but made him the scapegoat. His popularity fell as fast as it had soared early in the decade.

At about the same time, voices on Capitol Hill—variously those of progressives, crusaders and opportunists—were once again raised against the Pennsylvania Croesus for some of his public policies and private acts. Now they grew louder. Wisconsin's Senator Robert La Follette, Jr. had continued his father's Populist opposition to all Mellon represented, and now a freshman firebrand, Congressman Wright Patman, called for his head on the block of impeachment proceedings. Mellon was accused of misdeeds from war-profiteering to not enforcing Prohibition strenuously (since he'd had a piece of the Overholt distillery). By the time the 1932 elections loomed on the national agenda, Mellon was perceived as the villain who had single-handedly caused the Depression that was spiraling out of control. Hoover moved diplomatically and deliberately to bring someone else to Treasury's helm through the sound expedient of kicking the elder statesman upstairs. Someone of his experience was actually needed in London to consult regularly with Europe's equally beleaguered finance ministers as the industrialized world slipped into economic limbo. ✣

These railroad tracks on the Mall intersect what would become the Rotunda of the National Gallery. From the Baltimore and Potomac station, passengers transfer by cab to Capitol Hill's depot for the Baltimore and Ohio line, a subsidiary of the Pennsylvania Railroad. Mary Cassatt's brother, president of the Pennsylvania, agrees to merge the two separate depots into one new Union Station. As soon as it begins operation in 1907, demolition crews attack the older depots.

Mr. Mellon's Foreign Affairs

Having overseen the nation's finances during the decade of astronomic boom, after the bust Mellon was banished to the Court of St. James's. It might have been an occasion when he used a pet homily: "No good deed goes unpunished." The posting as ambassador in 1931 was fortuitous, about the only job that wouldn't seem a dismissal, and the move to London was nearly a homecoming. Mellon had spent holidays in England almost annually for fifty years. He had friends there, and by his legally lapsed marriage he had kin with whom he was still in touch. In London he was near the National Gallery, which inspired and refreshed him, and which he haunted whenever time allowed. "Everything there appealed to him: the size, the installation, the high level of quality," David Finley wrote later. As another associate put it, "It was this Anglophilia which, outside his business, molded his life; and it was the National Gallery in Trafalgar Square which always remained for him the ideal museum and the model" for Washington.

To enhance his official residence in Prince's Gate, he took all his best paintings that could travel safely. At home someone had suggested that the English "might be embarrassed to find their

The Right Worshipful, the Mayor of Southampton Fred Woolley, wearing the symbols of his 500-year-old office and escorted by a mace bearer at each hand, welcomes the new Ambassador to the Court of St. James's when his ship comes in on April 16, 1932.

ancestors on the walls of the American embassy." Finley, who looked into the matter before embarking, got this assurance from the British ambassador: "The only embarrassment Mr. Mellon will suffer will be in refusing to buy more paintings of British ancestors."

Reining in a fifty-year habit, Mellon forswore buying art for the duration. "Buying a good painting takes time," he said. "And I shall have no time to give to such matters." He broke the promise in spirit just once, when David Bruce learned that a canvas of unique historical significance might be had. So that the letter of the promise would remain unbroken, the Ambassador gave David Finley the cash, and his Honorary Counselor bought the anonymous portrait said to be of Pocahontas in Jacobean dress during her brief London sojourn as John Rolfe's wife.

Mellon's arrival in London followed by one year the conclusion of a spectacular feat of international collecting that had been handled by Knoedler's, with whom he had done business for decades. This dealer had served him well as his taste developed, and history intervened to let the firm mediate the great leap in Mellon's career as an art buyer—the one that made his collection worthy of becoming the basis for a museum of international importance. It was Knoedler's that arranged for Andrew Mellon to buy the lion's share of the paintings that the young Soviet government would sell from the czars' fabulous collections at the Hermitage in Leningrad.

A few years earlier rumors began to spread through art circles in Europe and America that the czars' art might come up for sale—at imperial prices. The Kremlin was broke, the ruble not convertible on international markets; Moscow needed hard currency to buy materials and machines to modernize Soviet industry and agriculture in pursuit of the Marxist dream. A rare source of capital lay in the imperial art collections. American entrepreneur Armand Hammer tried to start the bidding on art, but surprisingly (in view of his other successes) failed at first. Multinational oil magnate Calouste Gulbenkian

made the first few clandestine purchases but then uncharacteristically let the secret slip out when he tried to recruit a Berlin dealer to do his buying in Moscow.

Well-traveled and well-connected in Russia, the dealer named Zatzenstein (a.k.a. Katzenstein, a.k.a. Matthieson) was the selfsame expert whom the commissars had previously asked to appraise some art when it was clearly not for sale. His clients simply wanted to know what they had fallen heir to. In any case he had nothing near the necessary capital had anything been for sale. When Gulbenkian asked him to be his agent, Zatzenstein realized the situation had changed and decided he could do better with other partners. Seeking associates who had capital but lacked his access to Soviet insiders, Zatzenstein approached Colnaghi's, the old London gallery which was also short of ready cash. In the past Colnaghi's had cooperated with Knoedler's, and now they went to the rival firm because Knoedler's had one priceless asset in the

Accompanying his daughter and official hostess Ailsa Mellon Bruce, the Ambassador prepares to appear at the court of King George V. Mr. Mellon wears trousers, not the knee britches called for by custom, lest he offend sensibilities at home.

commissions; Mellon got his pick of art that no one else could even bid on. The prices were high, but as one art sage said "When you pay high for the priceless, you're getting it cheap." The situation was complex, since the Russian authorities would only discuss a few pictures at a time. It was even dangerous for some, such as the Hermitage curator who disappeared after arranging one of the first sales. Word came back that he had been liquidated—not for selling a national treasure, but for letting it go too cheap.

The deal was sealed by April 1930, when Knoedler partner Carman Messmore wrote Mellon

It is understood that you have authorized us to purchase for you certain paintings from the Hermitage Collection in Petrograd [Leningrad] and that if you decide to retain them you will pay us a commission of 25 percent of the cost price. In the event you do not wish to keep any of them, it is understood that we will sell them for your account, and pay 25 percent of the profit on the price we receive for them. We have shown you reproductions of the paintings which we decided to purchase from the above Collection, and it is understood that we will acquire them at a price at which we consider they can be disposed of, should you not care to retain them, of approximately 50 percent profit.

Implicitly it appears that Mellon would provide funds to the little cartel in its Russian adventures. Explicitly it seems the group had the advantage of offering virtually cash deals. In the case of Van Eyck's *Annunciation,* as a Finley associate wrote later, one Knoedler partner advised another in America, "'Mr. Mellon says go ahead and buy the picture as cheaply as you can and he will send the money to our account... in London.' A few days later in Berlin [the Soviet official] received his check and delivered the painting. Nothing from Russia was ever fully paid for until delivered, though there was often a 10 percent payment on reaching an agreement."

These transactions involved as strange a group of bedfellows as politics ever arranged. There were the three dealers who were mutually

patronage of a peerless client. And Mellon had all the liquidity anyone could desire.

Thus was forged a chain of participants who all enjoyed established relations with their immediate neighbors, and knew them well enough to be aware of risks and act with appropriate caution. It was a win-win-win-win situation. The Russians got hard currency and a degree of confidentiality since the agents and buyer had nothing to gain from publicity except competitors; Zatzenstein as point man and Colnaghi's and Knoedler's as middlemen all got agents'

suspicious yet interdependent and whose cooperative monopoly pro tem guaranteed their silence. There was the single manifold seller, the bureaucracy of the Soviet Antiquariat, which could enforce a vow of silence among its own by the most extreme measure. There was the sole client, ever the hard bargainer. If Mellon had not insisted on such liberal escape clauses in his deal with Knoedler's, and had Knoedler's in turn not pressed the Soviets for the lowest possible prices, more pictures might have come to America. Mellon did not get two Leonardos and a Giorgione, for example, because he thought the prices were too high. Be that as it may, between June 1930 and the following April, Mellon bought an astonishingly fine group of old master paintings out of the Hermitage holdings. If he did not get all the choicest pictures in the czars' patrimony—Gulbenkian got a few and Hammer got others—Mellon acquired a matchless score of them. Furthermore, he

enjoyed the chase and achieving what it implied for the National Gallery, as letters to Paul reveal.

Andrew Mellon wrote in a hand that seems even less imposing than his famously soft voice. His nib must have been as thin as his smile, but it raced across fine bond paper with complete legibility, only occasionally joining two words with an accidental ligature. It is the hand of a man who reveres accuracy and precision even while passing on family chat. On paper he was correct and formal, yet more expressive than we moderns might expect. And clearly he was committed to the idea of a National Gallery which was sufficiently old hat *en famille* to be identified by verbal shorthand. Thus on November 2, 1930, he tells Paul that Nora has been ill and then:

I have received two more of the Russian paintings, a Velasquez and a Rubens making twelve in all so far. Have not made up my mind whether I shall allow

any of them to be [re]sold. The trouble is that they all seem to be of high quality and quite low in cost. While I can make good profit on any that I may let go to be sold I am reluctant to do so, notwithstanding the large cash investment which the purchases are requiring during these hard times. I am still expecting more of them to come as for some reason [the Soviet authorities] only decide to sell one or two at a time with long intervals between when nothing is doing. As ever, with love, Father.

The following February, in a typed letter, he writes about Nora's continued house-hunting in horse country, then:

I have lately acquired three more of the Russian paintings. They are among the most important if not the most important of the Gallery.... They will not arrive for several weeks but I am not bringing them to Washington as for the present I do not want it to be known that I have them. If they do not come up to expectations when I see them I will have Knoedler dispose of them. With my love, as always, Father.

On April 15, 1931, he writes Paul at Cambridge

I hope you are having some time to spend at The National Gallery [London] as it will be useful to you to have some knowledge of the important pictures in the gallery in view of the contact you will have with works of a similar character in the near future.

I have gone deeper into the Russian purchases—perhaps further than I should in view of the hard times and shrinkage in values, but as such an opportunity is not likely to again occur and I feel so interested in the ultimate purpose [that] I have made quite a large investment. However I have confined myself entirely to examples of ultra quality.

The whole affair is being conducted privately and it is important that this be kept confidential ....

In all, he finally bought twenty-one masterpieces for $6,654,000, a huge sum even in those days. Among the finest: Botticelli's *Adoration of the Magi* is a Renaissance icon of the new pla-

tonic order painted during the time of Lorenzo de' Medici. Raphael's *Alba Madonna,* for which Mellon paid $1,116,000, thus became the world's most expensive picture. A second Raphael of immaculate provenance, the powerful *Saint George and the Dragon,* is a tour de force of elegance, action, draftsmanship and composition smaller than a sheet of typing paper. Perugino's *Crucifixion,* also in perfect condition nearly five hundred years after its execution, is one of the painter's finest surviving works. Titian's *Venus with a Mirror* remained in the artist's family and one other until sold to Nicholas I.

There were four Van Dycks, which under scrutiny grew to five, then shrunk to four again, although a different quartet: *Philip, Lord Wharton, Portrait of a Flemish Lady* and *Susanna Fourment and her Daughter* all proved to be as

advertised. However research would reveal that *William II of Nassau and Orange* was by Van Dyck's follower, Adriaen Hanneman, and was not a likeness of the king but Henry, Duke of Gloucester. Then again, *Isabella Brant,* a portrait of Rubens' wife, was assumed to be by Rubens, until ascribed to his pupil Van Dyck, who had given it to the master as a token of gratitude.

Also there were five accepted Rembrandts: *A Woman Holding a Pink, Joseph Accused by Potiphar's Wife, A Turk, A Polish Nobleman* and *A Girl with a Broom.* There were Veronese's *Finding of Moses,* the Van Eyck *Annunciation,* Hals' *Portrait of an Officer* and *Portrait of a Young Man,* and Chardin's *The House of Cards.*

In ones and twos, via Berlin or London, these reached Washington where Mellon inspected them in the very secure privacy of a

Mellon's Hermitage purchases include icons of western art, among them an Annunciation *(opposite) by Jan van Eyck, and an* Adoration of the Magi *by Botticelli. The works will hang in Washington's National Gallery, a project that Mellon must have had in mind during his ambassadorial term.*

Jan van Eyck,
The Annunciation,
c. 1434-1436
Andrew W. Mellon Collection

Botticelli, *The Adoration of the Magi,* early 1480s
Andrew W. Mellon Collection

Legacy of the czars, the Hermitage sells Mellon an astonishing array of European masters representing major schools. Witness this trio: House of Cards *by French realist Jean Siméon Chardin (lower left); the* Crucifixion, *an all-important altarpiece by Italian Renaissance master Pietro Perugino (top);* Philip, Lord Wharton *by Anthony van Dyck, darling of English nobility during the reign of Charles I.*

Perugino, *The Crucifixion with the Virgin, Saint John, Saint Jerome and Saint Mary Magdalene*, c. 1485
Andrew W. Mellon Collection

Jean Siméon Chardin,
The House of Cards, c. 1735
Andrew W. Mellon Collection

Sir Anthony van Dyck,
Philip, Lord Wharton, 1632
Andrew W. Mellon Collection

*The Romanovs admired
Dutch masters hugely, and
Mellon buys Rembrandt
portraits that are signed
and dated:* Woman Hold-
ing a Pink *and* A Polish
Nobleman. *He also buys
Frans Hals' prosperous
subjects,* Portrait of a
Young Man *(lower left)
and* Portrait of an Officer.

Rembrandt van Rijn, *A
Woman Holding a Pink,* 1656
Andrew W. Mellon Collection

Rembrandt van Rijn,
A Polish Nobleman, 1637
Andrew W. Mellon Collection

Frans Hals, *Portrait of a
Young Man,* c. 1645
Andrew W. Mellon Collection

Frans Hals, *Portrait of an
Officer,* c. 1640
Andrew W. Mellon Collection

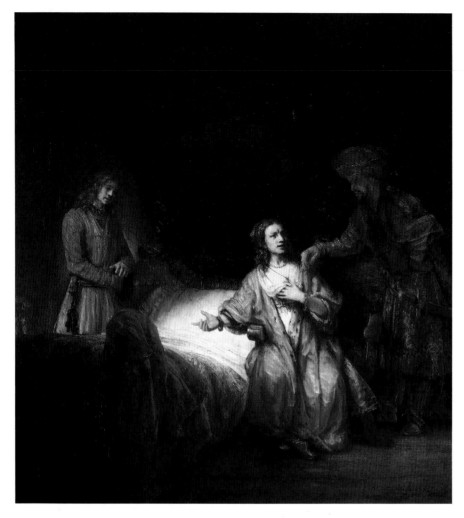

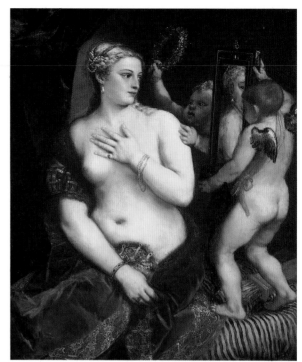

Hermitage pictures show legend and fantasy as well as portraits. Rembrandt's Joseph Accused by Potiphar's Wife *depicts an episode from Genesis— possibly with the artist's son posing as the seduced servant. Rembrandt's* A Turk, *wearing the same sort of turban as Potiphar, is likely a Dutchman in* *costume painted for Amsterdam's cosmopolitan market. Titian's* Venus with a Mirror, *done when the Venetian was in his late 60s, offers a Renaissance vision of classical Rome's deification of love.*

Rembrandt van Rijn, *Joseph Accused by Potiphar's Wife,* 1655
Andrew W. Mellon Collection

Titian, *Venus with a Mirror,* c. 1555
Andrew W. Mellon Collection

Rembrandt van Rijn, *A Turk,* c. 1630/1635
Andrew W. Mellon Collection

Adriaen Hanneman, *Henry,
Duke of Gloucester,* c. 1653
Andrew W. Mellon Collection

Sir Anthony van Dyck,
Portrait of a Flemish Lady,
probably 1618
Andrew W. Mellon Collection

Great paintings remain
great though attributions
change. The young man,
presumed to be William II
by Van Dyck, wears the
wrong decorations and
clothes for the time; he turns
out to be Henry, Duke of
Gloucester *by Adriaen
Hanneman. Peter Paul
Rubens painted his own
wife many times and the
sympathetic portrait of an
ill and aging* Isabella Brant
(above) was assumed to be
his last of her. Now scholars
assign it to Rubens' gifted
pupil, the prodigy Anthony
van Dyck who made it a
gift of gratitude when he
left Rubens' Antwerp
studio. Likewise Van Dyck's
Portrait of a Flemish Lady
*was believed a century ago
to be his teacher's work.*

Sir Anthony van Dyck,
Isabella Brant, c. 1621
Andrew W. Mellon Collection

*Mellon's gallery also gets
Italian masterpieces via
Leningrad and the Hermi-
tage. These include
Raphael's* St. George and
the Dragon, *a gem of
classicism in perfect condition, and Paolo Veronese's
lushly decorated* The
Finding of Moses.
Susanna Fourment and
Her Daughter *(opposite) is
one of five Van Dyck
portraits that Mellon buys
for his eventual museum.
Another donor will give
eight and four other
benefactors one or two each,
making the National
Gallery one of the richest
repositories of Van Dycks
anywhere.*

Raphael, *Saint George and the
Dragon,* c. 1506
Andrew W. Mellon Collection

Veronese, *The Finding of
Moses,* probably 1570/1575
Andrew W. Mellon Collection

storage crypt beneath the Corcoran Gallery of
Art. He never availed himself of the no-ques-
tions-asked return agreement with Carman
Messmore; despite caveats expressed to Paul, he
kept all the pictures he bought. And he visited
the Corcoran cellar regularly, no doubt as his
plans evolved for a national gallery built around
what he would call the "nucleus" of pictures
from the Winter Palace.

The coup of buying the czars' art was accomplished without the participation of the most
imperial of all dealers of the time. This figure
was kept out of the picture by the Russians
themselves for the very reason that he was such a
colossus: He only bought to resell at a substantial profit, which meant Russia would not
receive full price, whereas the commissars
believed (mistakenly) that the cartel arrangement was tantamount to selling to Mellon at the
maximum price.

Nevertheless, as Mellon rose in stature as a
collector, it was inevitable that he would do
business with the ne plus ultra dealer, Joseph
Duveen, who bestrode the art world on both
sides of the Atlantic. Lord Duveen of Millbank
was one of the liveliest opportunists of the
ancien regime, a man variously called a "loving
buccaneer," "exalted middleman" and much
worse. Mary Berenson, wife of Duveen's sometime colleague and sometime antagonist Bernard
Berenson, once mused "Oh Joe is wonderful.
He's like champagne." To which the eminent
connoisseur retorted, "More like gin."

This was the dealer to whom Mellon turned
more and more after the Hermitage purchases.
In turn the elegant rascal, who counted Frick,
Carnegie, Kress, the Wideners and cotillions of
the nouveau riche among his clientele, devoted
more of his remarkable energies to Mellon. In
the end they struck a bargain of mighty dimensions, one of the biggest deals in the annals of
cultural commerce. The journey leading to that
acme is worth recounting.

It began in London in 1921, according to an
incredible anecdote, with an encounter at

Claridge's where Mellon was staying in third-floor rooms and Duveen kept a suite on the fourth. But in order to engineer a meeting, the great dealer had moved to the second floor, it was reported, so that he could board an elevator at just the right moment and feign surprise at seeing the great American.

"How do you do, Mr. Mellon?" he said, and introduced himself, adding, as he later recalled, "I am on my way to the National Gallery to look at some pictures. My great refreshment is to look at pictures." Taken unawares, Mellon admitted that he, too, was in need of a little refreshment. They went to the National Gallery together, and after they had been refreshed, Mellon discovered that Duveen had an inventory of Old Masters of his own ....

So wrote the deft essayist S. N. Behrman in his profile of Duveen which appeared first in *The New Yorker* and then as a book, a biography that displayed all its subject's sheen but little of his sleaze. Behrman portrayed Duveen as an impresario of great events when he was more accountably a gifted merchant whose ethics appear to have been protean or absent. In this instance, Behrman said, Duveen knew when to wait for the elevator because his valet had been called by Mellon's valet after the latter helped Mellon put on his coat to go out. Indeed, another student of dealers' ways reported that Duveen employed one Bert Boggis as his major domo, formerly a merchant mariner who packed a pistol and marlinespike in his tails, and who bribed Mellon's minions to pass on all sorts of information. He boasted that when Mellon was at Treasury the contents of his wastebasket reached the train to New York in the time it took the Secretary to walk home from the office.

In any case, Mellon knew Duveen from New York at least two years before the elevator incident (if that is not apocryphal). Henry Frick introduced them—as he had introduced Mellon to Charles Carstairs at Knoedler's—telling Duveen "This man will some day be a great collector." As early as 1919, and without fanfare or

special emphasis, Mellon had recorded in his diary meeting Duveen. They were destined to do business together, because when all was said and done, Duveen had the greatest store of great old masters on the market, and Mellon would become his greatest customer.

Lord Duveen, born plainly Joseph Duveen in 1869, knighted and then made Baron of Millbank, was a flamboyant Edwardian by all accounts. Beyond that, reports differ. Behrman called him "the most spectacular art dealer of all

Sir Anthony van Dyck,
*Susanna Fourment and
Her Daughter*, c. 1620
Andrew W. Mellon Collection

Dealer Joseph Duveen—a presence on both sides of the Atlantic. He and Mellon share deep admiration for London's National Gallery (below), the museum that inspired Washington's National Gallery overall and in many details.

that bygone country of the gilded age, Albion America. Kenneth Clark wrote:

Duveen gave us a grand dinner in his house. It was large and pretentious, and on the walls were copies of English eighteenth-century full-length portraits of the kind that had made his fortune, men in red coats, women in large hats. All his richest clients were present, the men in white ties and creaking shirts, the ladies so weighed down with jewelry that a few of them (no one will believe this but it is true) brought pieces of jewelry in their hands and laid them down on the dinner table. This could have happened in the Middle Ages. We dined on a blue and white Sèvres service made for the Empress Catherine of Russia. Since my boyhood I have had a mania for ceramics and I expressed my delight to Lady Duveen. She replied, "Yes, it is nice. And we don't get it out every day, I can tell you. The last time we used it was for Mr. Ramsay MacDonald." After dinner I said to my host (whom one had to address in his own language): "Marvelous that Sèvres service. Privilege to eat off it." "Sèvres service," said Lord Duveen, "Sèvres service? Nothing. Eat off it every day." That was the real Duveen. After dinner we adjourned to the drawing room, also hung with copies of English portraits. A large soprano from the Metropolitan Opera, swathed in pistachio-colored satin, accompanied by a small orchestra, sang pieces of Puccini at the top of her voice. Nobody paid the slightest attention. Duveen

time," the one who "by amazing energy and audacity transformed the American taste in art." Others said he was a conniver and a charlatan. To put the kindest light on it, perhaps the truth about Duveen depended in part on the geography. Witness the London National Gallery director's delicious yarn about an evening in

was regal. In London he might be a clown; in New York he was a king.

When he needed a building to accommodate his elegant business in New York, Duveen commissioned a copy of a section of a Louis XV ministry on the Place de la Concorde for his million-dollar Fifth Avenue gallery. When the British Museum in London needed a new wing to house the Elgin Marbles, Duveen made it his gift and commissioned John Russell Pope to design it. He would do anything for his clients (and even insult rich upstarts into becoming his clients). He wrote letters of introduction for them, made hotel reservations, recommended architects "to build them houses," Behrman wrote, "and then saw to it that the architects planned the interiors with wall space that demanded plenty of pictures. He even selected brides or bridegrooms for some of his clients and presided over the wedding with avuncular benevolence."

In a controversial book accusing Duveen and Berenson of collusion, British journalist Colin Simpson reports that Duveen met Mellon as early as 1913 and introduced him to collectors in London and Paris. In the next decade, Simpson writes,

Mellon spent over $3 million at Duveen's. They invited each other to their daughters' weddings and Joe made many of the European arrangements for Ailsa Mellon Bruce's honeymoon. The relationship suffered a setback in 1927 when Mellon came to suspect that Joe had an "inside" source of information on his affairs. He was correct. His valet, Flore, and butler, Tom Kerr, were both on [major domo] Bert Boggis' payroll, but Joe's greatest source of information was the Paris representative of the Morgan Bank, Theodore Rousseau. He was a close friend of Joe's while Mellon used him as a sounding board and confidant whenever he was in Europe. Mellon particularly enjoyed discreet candlelit dinner parties, complete with equally discreet feminine company, which Rousseau was adept at arranging, for Mellon in Paris was not the shy, austere, almost ethereal figure he appeared to be elsewhere. Unhappily Joe let slip that he was aware of these assignations and Mellon jumped to the conclusion that the information had come from his valet; for a few months he treated Joe with unaccustomed coldness.

London's National Gallery displays landscapes in the best Victorian manner—by the acre.

Raphael, *The Niccolini-Cowper Madonna*, 1508
Andrew W. Mellon Collection

that in good time it would offer traveling shows, concerts, study collections and other novel programs. "Mellon was entranced," wrote Simpson. "He was to tell Theodore Rousseau a few days later that 'Duveen showed me what a government could do with a museum if it wished.'"

Certainly Duveen stirred the pot. As late as 1936 he would ask Kenneth Clark for information about his National Gallery's by-laws, organization, maintenance, operations, etc.; this in order to help with the "contemplated new National Gallery, Washington." But at best, I believe, Duveen cultivated Mellon's dream which seemed as much the old gentleman's own as a dream can be. Surely Mellon began thinking about a National Gallery long before 1928. He had frequented London for a half-century by then, and haunted the museum in Trafalgar Square. As Treasury Secretary he had been embarrassed by Washington's paucity of cultural amenities when visiting French dignitaries asked to see America's great art treasures; the best place to take them was his own apartment. By 1927, as his son Paul remembers, he had told his children about his idea of a gift to the nation. And David Finley writes that in that same year he told Mellon of being tempted by an offer to join a New York law firm, but that Mellon prevailed on him to stay in Washington, revealing then his intention to build a National Gallery and appoint Finley to run it.

About this time also, Mellon made his first major departure from august portraits and sublime landscapes when in 1928 he bought his first Raphael Madonna from Duveen. The *Niccolini-Cowper Madonna* is a picture of first-magnitude importance to art historians and the kind of stellar painting that a national museum must have—even one founded by a collector who previously avoided religious subjects.

Clearly Duveen was self-serving, self-centered, devious, vain, manipulating, flattering, smart and successful—among many other things. During the Depression, John D. Rockefeller, Jr., offered him much less than the asking price for three marble busts, hinting that a dealer might

(No less than the National Gallery's first chief curator would share the belief that Mellon's man sold information to Duveen, and continued to do so in later years when he worked in the Gallery director's suite as a doorkeeper.)

No one denies that Duveen influenced Mellon's National Gallery idea, feathering his own nest in the process. Simpson writes that Duveen and Mellon visited the National Gallery on Trafalgar Square in 1928. Duveen said "this will be my memorial" since he was becoming a trustee of the London museum, and he forecast welcome the $1 million in cash he would pay. Behrman writes that Duveen was outraged at the suggestion and in his reply "managed to convey the suggestion that if Rockefeller was in temporary financial difficulty, he, Duveen, was ready to come to his assistance." On another occasion when a would-be collector offered full price for a Rembrandt, Duveen refused to part with it because the man owned no other old masters and "the Rembrandt would be lonely."

When Duveen spoke of great paintings he called the greatest of them "Duveens" because he had bought, owned and sold them at one time or another. If it had ever been his, it was a "Duveen" forever. An oft-told anecdote reports Duveen standing before a "Duveen" he had recently sold—Van Dyck's *Marchesa Balbi*—and "expatiating enthusiastically on its wonders to the new owner. A beam of light from the setting sun suddenly reached through a window and bathed the picture in a lovely light. It was the kind of collaboration that Duveen expected from all parts of the universe, animate and inanimate." The story goes on, "'My pictures, Duveen,' Mr. Mellon replied, with the trace of a smile, as though acknowledging the dealer's cosmic partnership, 'never look so well as they do when you are here.'"

Duveen was ever the opportunist. When the Nazis became arbiters of taste in Berlin, he worked "under cover of an English firm of unblemished Aryan genealogy, [which] ... in turn employed a similarly impeccable Dutch concern" and shipped back to Germany cheap German art in return for "decadent" Italian pictures by Fra Filippo Lippi, Raphael and such. A mercenary connoisseur, Duveen was to old art what F. W. Woolworth was to new sundries. He kept enormous inventories of pictures and objects, often needing to make labyrinthine financial arrangements just to stay solvent. Called "the world's greatest borrower," in 1908 he was $17 million in debt. His creditors included a Who's Who of American bankers who profited from the relationship as much as he did. Mellon, for one, liked to live with a painting before buying

Sir Anthony van Dyck, *Marchesa Balbi*, 1622/1627
Andrew W. Mellon Collection

it, and often kept consignments from Duveen for many months, during which time Duveen found he had ready credit in Mellon's banks. Thus he had the use of Mellon money—for which he paid going interest rates—while Mellon had the use of the pictures gratis until he decided to pay up or send them back.

Be that as it may, in the end Mellon bought dozens of the very finest "Duveens" for his Gallery, and his lordship made the grandest sale of an already princely commercial career. ❧

A Taxing Case

Andrew W. Mellon, former Secretary of the Treasury and Ambassador to Britain, defends himself against charges that he has cheated on his taxes. The accusations, brought by the Roosevelt Administration and seen as politically motivated, are nonetheless serious in terms of possible penalties. The case harms both Mellon's health and his reputation.

Roosevelt beat Hoover predictably and soundly in 1932 (if by less than Harding-Coolidge beat Cox-Roosevelt in 1920) and this brought the recall of ambassadors from the blue-ribbon capitals. A fortnight after Inauguration Day, Andrew Mellon presented himself at the White House to turn in his credentials and retire after twelve years of public service. Whatever their politics, the President and the Ambassador were both gentlemen and their meeting was cordial. Mellon even came away complimented, however briefly, by the famous Roosevelt charm as the Hyde Park squire asked his advice on how to stem the deepening economic crisis. As Paul remembers it, his father left the White House convinced that FDR was about to do something right! He had asked the old entrepreneur his opinion of a bill that would provide insurance for bank deposits. It would spell disaster, Mellon answered certainly, by encouraging bankers to be less prudent; he believed it should be vetoed—and thought the president had been persuaded. He was aghast days later when Roosevelt not only signed the bill into law but crowed about its promise to do just about anything but slice bread.

Then out of the blue in 1933, Congressman Louis T. McFadden raised alarums about his fellow Pennsylvanian's tax returns for 1931. The Bureau of Internal Revenue read about it in the papers and on the basis of press reports embarked on a fishing expedition. Then, in a surprising move, Attorney General Homer Cummings told a press conference that Mellon was suspected of cheating on his taxes, and Mellon got to read that in the papers. Contrary

Art dealer Charles P. Henschel, president of M. Knoedler and Company, is one of the experts to testify in Mellon's behalf before the Board of Tax Appeals.

to standard practice, and using inflammatory words, Cummings announced the matter before an indictment was delivered, nay the day before the case was presented to a grand jury. Answering that slap of the gauntlet, Mellon called it partisan persecution and challenged Cummings to prove his point or bite his tongue. The two continued to feud in print, though to infer that charges and counter charges flew thick and fast is to misread the pace of events in the extreme. Charges came as slim as the accused and as slow as the taxman ever is to admit a mistake.

Let it be said that the new administration

was looking to set an example, if not to sacrifice a lamb. Roosevelt's crusaders believed they had a clear mandate to steer new courses as the nation (and world) slowly gyred down into a stagnant economic sump. Some laid the whole disaster at the feet of the moneyed elite (save "traitors to their class" as gentlemen-reformers like FDR were called). Further, New Deal visionaries did not concede that a taxpayer had the right to lawfully minimize his tax liability. According to John Morton Blum's definitive edition of the diaries of Roosevelt's Secretary of the Treasury and Hudson Valley crony, Henry A. Morgenthau, Jr.: "The administration wanted to change the [tax] law precisely because, as it stood, it enabled these [wealthy] men to reduce their taxes." Strange as it may seem today, the new Treasury Secretary thought it immoral (and illegal) for wealthy taxpayers to continue "exploiting loopholes in federal revenue statutes and inventing tax-saving devices." Morgenthau and company were especially outraged because these wealthy people could afford to buy the necessary legal advice and (presumably) also could afford to pay more taxes. In turn, Blum wrote, the targets of Morgenthau's wrath "felt that the Administration was persecuting them because they were rich and because they were, with few exceptions, Republicans."

"To plead the government's case before a federal grand jury in Pittsburgh," Blum reported, "Morgenthau recruited Robert Jackson, who reported that the Republican press was accusing him of ruthless tactics. 'You can't be too tough in this trial to suit me,' the Secretary said. Jumping up, Jackson replied: 'Thank God I have that kind of boss.' 'Wait a minute,' Morgenthau went on. I consider that Mr. Mellon is not on trial but Democracy and the privileged rich [are on trial] and I want to see who will win.' In court Mellon won," according to the scholar.

That is, the case went to a federal grand jury composed of laborers, mechanics, farmers, craftsmen, and three others who wore white collars. They heard five witnesses, deliberated for five hours and on May 8, 1934—a year after Mc-

Fadden's original salvo—declared the evidence was not sufficient for an indictment. Mellon, who had called the charges "impertinent, scandalous and improper," now declared he had been vindicated: "I am of course gratified. The fact that the grand jury reached a sound conclusion, notwithstanding the unusual methods pursued in my case, is proof of the good sense and fairness of the American people." Public opinion, for the moment, seemed on his side as editorial writers across the land applauded the jury's decision. The case was "the cheapest kind of political claptrap," said the *Cheyenne Tribune Leader*. The *Portland Oregonian* opined "The large outstanding fact is that a grand jury of such men as have little reason to love the rich tossed the Government's complaint into the discard."

But it did not end there. Internal Revenue went back to its adding machines, decided that Mellon underpaid his taxes for 1931 by $2,050,068 and accused him of tax fraud. He was assessed for that amount plus fifty percent in penalties and interest for a grand total of $3,075,103. Mellon replied that he'd actually overpaid for 1931 and was owed a refund of $139,034. Internal Revenue demurred and the matter ended up before the Board of Tax Appeals, which conducted a proceeding that resembled a trial. Though doubtless he might have preferred to see the matter drop, Mellon got his days in court at hearings in Pittsburgh and Washington. He took the stand for extended periods, demonstrating a firm grasp of the issues and details ex post facto—though revealing the hardly surprising news that he didn't do his own tax returns, which were prepared by a corps of accountants. "I don't know what I'm worth," Mellon testified. "I've never kept track for the simple reason that I never thought it was important to know. What's really important is that the money is at work, creating work."

At issue were two matters in particular. One involved Mellon's sale of a big block of stock, at a substantial loss, to a bank which then sold the stock to an umbrella corporation established by Mellon's legal wizard, Donald D. Shepard, for

Seeming relaxed, cogent, and candid, Mellon bides his time during the tax case in which federal authorities claim he owes more than $3 million in taxes and penalties. His reply: He had overpaid for the year in question.

the benefit of Paul and Ailsa. The other involved the A. W. Mellon Educational and Charitable Trust. Incorporated on the last day of 1930, the E&C Trust had received an initial gift of $10,000, then some of the Hermitage paintings, valued at $3,241,250. Later the Trust received paintings worth another $25 to $40 million. All these assets were destined, according to a deed filed in October 1935, to benefit the "National Gallery of Art of the United States." But Internal Revenue argued that Mellon had not relinquished control of the pictures and should not be allowed tax deductions for their value. In the course of the proceedings, the agency went so far as to suspend the Trust's tax exempt status briefly. (Having already provided for his children and Nora, Mellon left most of his estate to the Trust, which was eventually worth about $130 million and had a life of its own for fifty years.)

During the "trial" phase of the tax case, defense attorney Frank Hogan detailed the Trust's purpose. It was the vehicle through which Mellon intended to found, build and endow a national museum that would coexist with the Smithsonian's National Gallery. Hogan's report got major newspaper play, especially in Washington, as did his litany: "God did not place in the hearts and minds of men such diverse and

Joseph Duveen chats with Mellon during a recess. He testifies that Mellon's art collection is the finest in the universe. Testimony makes clear for the first time that Mellon intends his priceless array of pictures to be the core of a museum he plans to give to the United States.

opposite traits as these. It is impossible to conceive of a man planning such benefactions and at the same time plotting and scheming to defraud his government."

The star witness—or the most entertaining performer on the stand—was Joseph Duveen who testified for the defense but did the cause little good besides provide comic relief for all. In testimony that became downright bombastic, he confirmed that Mellon had long since been planning to build a national gallery to receive his fabulous paintings. Duveen left no doubt about his opinion that the collection had only been possible through his own good offices, and went so far as to say "I consider the Mellon collection of pictures the greatest collection ever assembled by any individual collector."

Duveen did not hesitate to correct gross misconceptions about great art on the part of the woeful prosecutor, Robert Jackson: "Really my dear fellow, art works do not rise and fall in value like pig iron.... They have a value and that's all there is to it." Regarding a Van Eyck portrait in Mellon's collection, he condescended, "perhaps you don't realize that there are only three small Van Eycks in America, and they can't compare with Mr. Mellon's Van Eyck." He even conceded that he had netted only $85,000 when he sold a Raphael for $836,000, thinking it "'a very low price. But Mr. Mellon thought it was a very high price. One day after lunch I gave way,'" quoted *News-Week,* adding: "Duveen beamed at Mellon. The banker stopped chewing gum long enough to wink at Duveen." In sum, the dealer's testimony was an exercise in self-promotion. He virtually claimed credit not only for selling Mellon the pictures that would allow him to create a worthy national gallery, but for conceiving the idea and even recommending its preferred location: "By the obelisk, near the pond." The remark brought the house down when the audience realized he meant the Washington Monument and Reflecting Pool.

Otherwise there was little to laugh about. When the hearings ended in 1935, the Tax Appeals Board recessed to consider the matter at

a glacial pace, and prosecutor Jackson declared ominously that the case was far from over. He might have seemed a mean-spirited crusader for the new order (or at least the New Deal), but Jackson was never to be taken lightly. Later a Supreme Court Justice, after World War II he prosecuted Nazi war criminals at Nuremberg. In fact, no new dramatic charges arose while Mellon waited for another shoe to drop ... and waited ... and waited....

The tax case dragged along through 1936 as winter closed in, time marched on and Duveen told Mellon, "I am going to retire from business. You are ready to give your collection for a national gallery. This is a combination of circumstances that can never happen again." So it happened that the supersalesman made his grandest transaction, and Mellon expanded his collection for the National Gallery.

Worn down by the lingering tax case, at eighty-one Mellon was also distracted by the malaise that the Depression visited on America. For fourscore years he had lived and breathed the vital vapors of business and industrial enter-

prise; his cherished milieu was sick and he too fell ill. Unable to travel and examine the most precious of the treasures stashed in Duveen's *palais* at 720 Fifth Avenue, he sent David Finley to New York instead. He gave the aide instructions to bring back for his inspection "everything I thought good enough for the National Gallery."

Finley spent three days in a "velvet-hung room" at Duveen's while lackeys came and went bearing objects for his consideration. He returned with thirty paintings and twenty-one sculptures all bound for the drab basement of the Corcoran Gallery of Art where the Hermitage pictures reposed. But Mellon was too ill to travel the dozen blocks from the apartment, so Finley arranged for Duveen to rent a flat below Mellon's at the McCormick and turn it into a private gallery. Installing the pictures and sculptures there, and posting a round-the-clock armed guard, Duveen gave his client a key to the place so that he could visit at will. Mellon took advantage of the gracious access, even entertaining in the suite and coming down alone late at night in dressing gown and slippers to enjoy the masterpieces—all of which was reported back to Duveen.

In due course seller and buyer sat down to negotiate what was then the largest single art transaction of its kind. Finley writes that he was the only witness when the two principals hammered out the deal, "both enjoying the contest immensely. Lord Duveen asked astronomical prices. Mr. Mellon countered with lower ones [though Finley was far too polite to name numbers]. At one point Mr. Mellon said: 'Well, Lord Duveen, I think you will have to take all these things back to New York,' and Lord Duveen replied: 'Mr. Mellon, I would give you these things for the National Gallery rather than take them away.'" In the end, Mellon bought twenty-four of the thirty pictures that Finley had chosen, and eighteen of the twenty-one sculptures.

The works that changed hands in this sale of sales included spectacularly choice sculptures. There was the work that would be given premier status as number A1 in the Gallery's inventory. This was the *Madonna and Child,* a free-standing statue in painted and gilded terra cotta that was then regarded as a landmark Florentine work of the fifteenth century and is now thought to be by Donatello. Other masterpieces include Mino da Fiesole's superbly preserved twin marble reliefs *Charity* and *Faith,* Desiderio da

Mino da Fiesole,
Charity, 1475/1480
Andrew W. Mellon Collection

His last transaction with Duveen brings Mellon forty-two works of art in one fell swoop. Included in the package deal is priceless fifteenth-century sculpture such as Mino da Fiesole's pair of Charity *(above) and* Faith *(opposite); Verrocchio's fabulously armored* Giuliano de' Medici *(right); Desiderio's charming* Bust of a Little Boy *(above); and a polychromed Florentine* Madonna and Child .

Settignano's precious lifesized *Bust of a Little Boy,* Verrocchio's *Giuliano de' Medici* and Della Robbia's glazed terra-cotta reliefs of the *Madonna and Child.*

When it was over, Duveen was the richer by $21 million, according to S. N. Behrman. For his lordship, whether the Pygmalion of art appreciation in America or the P. T. Barnum of the cultural circus, this sale meant that he was finally out of debt—perhaps for the first time in his half-century career as a flamboyant dealer.

As for the merits of the Justice Department case, President Hoover would shed some light in memoirs published decades later:

While Mr. Mellon was in my Cabinet, the question of a certain site for a public building came up. After the Cabinet meeting he came to me and asked that particular site be kept vacant. He disclosed to me his purpose to build a great national art gallery in Washington . . . I urged that he announce it at once, and have the pleasure of seeing it built in his lifetime. He was a shy and modest man. The only reason he told me at all was that he wanted that site reserved.

Mino da Fiesole,
Faith, 1475/1480
Andrew W. Mellon Collection

Desiderio da Settignano,
A Little Boy, 1455/1460
Andrew W. Mellon Collection

Andrea del Verrocchio,
Giuliano de'Medici,
c. 1475/1478
Andrew W. Mellon Collection

Florentine 15th Century,
Madonna and Child,
c. 1425
Andrew W. Mellon Collection

He asked me to keep it in confidence. Had he made this magnificent benefaction public at that time, public opinion would have protected him from the scandalous persecution under the New Deal. He was accused of having evaded income taxes. I knew that in the years he was supposed to be robbing the government he was spending several times the amount charged against him in support of public institutions and upon the unemployed in his state....

He felt the wound to a lifetime of integrity and many years of single-minded public service. The whole was an ugly blot on the decencies of democracy.... At one time it looked as if this very old, feeble, and innocent man would have to stand trial for defrauding the government to which he had given years of able service, and before a people to whom he was passionately devoted....

Former Tax Commissioner Elmer Irey, who headed the Treasury's tax enforcement branch from 1919 to 1946, also supported Mellon retrospectively. "The Roosevelt administration made me go after Andy Mellon," the introduction to his autobiography reported: "I liked Mr. Mellon and they knew it, so the FBI took the first crack and got tossed out of the grand jury room. Bob Jackson was made chief counsel of the Internal Revenue Department and he said to me 'I need help on that Mellon thing. The FBI investigation was no good. You run one on him.'" When Irey balked, Morgenthau himself gave Irey marching orders: "The Secretary said 'Irey, you can't be ninety-nine-and-two-thirds percent on that job. Investigate Mellon. I order it.' Irey explained his belief that Mellon was innocent but Morgenthau's answer was 'I'm directing you to go ahead, Irey.' They failed again."

The "tax case" figures in the history of the National Gallery because of the spectacular canard it spawned—the story entered folklore that the gift of the National Gallery of Art was the price Mellon paid for Roosevelt's forgiveness of his tax debt. If that were the case it represented Uncle Sam's slickest deal since the Louisiana Purchase, because Mellon's gifts amounted to at least twenty times the amount

he was said to owe, penalties and interest included. In the cooler light of historical hindsight, it appears that Roosevelt's minions—Morgenthau in particular—were at best energized by reformist zeal run amok, or at worst stooping to the basest sort of partisan terrorism. Very recently the case was singled out as an unbridled abuse of executive power by former *New York Times* reporter David Burnham in his book *The I.R.S.: A Law Unto Itself.* In a *Times* article he wrote,

One of the most brazen instances of a political vendetta... was the Roosevelt Administration's attack on Andrew Mellon.

No historian has been able to determine why Mellon so enraged F.D.R., but there is speculation that the New Deal President saw the millionaire... as the symbolic enemy. Nor has a document emerged that directly links Roosevelt to the decision to go after Mellon.

Actually there is a smoking gun in the Hyde Park library. A short note written in FDR's hand refers to Mellon's 1930 [sic] income tax return: "Why not have Cummings read it and make it public." The note bears no date, but it clearly shows Roosevelt's personal involvement to the point of giving marching orders to Cummings. Also, a typed memo from FDR to the Secretary of the Treasury dated February 2, 1934, asks "How about the publicity which I understand I am authorized to give out about income tax returns?"

Those items notwithstanding, Burnham continues: "A Justice Department memo written about the case in early 1934 shared [Elmer] Irey's sentiment: the charges against Mellon were either invalid or could not be proved." Nevertheless the Administration filed charges and the case finally came to the Board of Tax Appeals. "At the time, the tax board, theoretically an independent agency, was housed within the executive branch and board members tended to side with the Government," Burnham continued. "But after weeks of hearings and after reading voluminous legal briefs, the board on Dec. 7, 1937, issued a

Back in private life, Mellon works at his desk in Pittsburgh, cuspidor at the ready.

ruling that rejected the most significant aspects of the charges. Mellon was found to owe $485,809—about one sixth of the tax agency's claim—but the board dismissed all the criminal and civil fraud penalties."

As the *Dictionary of American Biography* summed up, though the Appeals Board increased Mellon's tax fractionally on a technicality, "the result was considered a complete vindication." Finding in Mellon's favor, the Board ruled that he "did not file a false and fraudulent return with the purpose of evading taxes." But by the time that decision came down, the trial transcript ran 10,345 pages and Mellon could not savor the victory. He had died four months earlier.

Given the ordeal of the tax case, which might have humiliated, infuriated or soured a lesser man, why did Mellon go ahead with his plan to found, fund and erect the National Gallery? The easy answer is that he was at heart a philanthropist, the obvious one that he was a patriot. His generosity was well known around

Pittsburgh where he supported the University of Pittsburgh, the Mellon Institute, the Carnegie Institute, to say nothing of the usual gamut of local cultural organizations, health agencies and the like, in addition to many individuals. His patriotism was more subtly expressed, though certainly he went to work for his government at the age when most men retire and served a dozen years in strenuous jobs.

Once asked specifically about building the Gallery when he'd been treated so shabbily, Mellon said simply "I am not going to be deterred.... Eventually the people now in power in Washington will be dead and I will be dead, but the National Gallery, I hope, will be there and that is something the country needs." When a similar question was put by old friend and University of Pittsburgh Chancellor John G. Bowman, Mellon's answer reached beyond patriotism and philanthropy: "He looked straight at me for a rather long pause. 'Every man,' he said slowly, 'wants to connect his life with something that he thinks of as eternal.'" ❦

L FUNDS SOUGHT OF WEEK

antee Backed and Individ- Date.

$43,000 SUBSCRIBED

mittee Meeting tel Accommo- Be Ample.

half the $100,000 e fund already leming, chairman nance Committee, at efforts will be te the drive for eek.

was announced f Admiral Cary T. l chairman, 94 individuals had vith subscriptions to $4,000. This ment of bills as and both Grayson the sale of parade ough to repay the money advanced. substantial profit returns being do- ty.

emocrat, of West of a Congressional ec, meanwhile an- ents have been e additional seat- ies in front of the

ns Adequate.

r of hotel accom- ugural visitors, it meeting of the itality Committee esterday afternoon. large crowds ex- gar-Morris, chair- g and Hospitality t several thousand ed at the Housing rd Hotel for those hotel accommoda- . Rooms can be strict 6040.

a headquarters in d that four com- Conservation Corps new uniforms and hovels, spades and in the inaugural

eorge E. Allen. General Reception while announced the following per- m:

ee, Col. E. Goring Bouve, John St. C. Butcher, Louis Colliflower, Carl Cottrell, Clarence ert V. Fleming, thur Hellen, Thil- Frank R. Jelleff, Thomas E. Lodge, ason, Dr. William McConihe, Lowell ris, Newbold Noyes, Mrs. Eleanor Pat- F. Barrett Pret- rdson, Frank M. jr.: John Saul, W. Spaid, Marcy Sullivan, Merle kerman, Corcoran

National Art Gallery Site From Air

Airplane view of Mall, with site of Andrew Mellon's projected National Gallery of Art indicated by artist.
Key to picture:
1. Proposed site of $9,000,000 gallery, fronting on Constitution avenue and extending from Fourth to Seventh streets. Abandoned foundation of the George Washington Memorial auditorium occupies part of this site.
2. Area suggested to be reserved as part of gallery site. Sixth street would be closed from Constitution to Independence ave-

nues. The block from Third to Fourth streets would be reserved for future extension of the gallery building.
3. Site of Apex Building, construction of which was begun yesterday.
4. Public buildings in the Federal triangle.
5. National Museum, under Smithsonian Institution. The new art gallery would be under the Smithsonian also.
—Star Staff Photo by Elwood Baker.

ROOSEVELT TO ASK EARLY ACCEPTANCE OF ART GALLERY

Ratification by Congress of Terms of Mellon's Gift Expected Soon.

DONOR STAYS IN D. C. TO WORK OUT DETAILS

Beautification of Area, Without Marring Monument Vista, Is Seen.

President Roosevelt will seek early congressional ratification of Andrew Mellon's gift to the people of the United States of his famed art collection and of a $9,000,000 National Gallery of Art on the Mall.

With Congress opening today, the President is expected to forward to the Capitol shortly a recommendation that special legislation be enacted providing for acceptance of Mellon's offer, with its stipulations concerning maintenance, management and extension of the gallery.

Mellon himself will remain here indefinitely to keep close watch on development of the project and to be available to officials in charge of governmental phases of the undertaking. He has conferred already with President Roosevelt, Frederic A. Delano, chairman of the National Capital Park and Planning Commission, and with other officials.

Plans Prepared.

John Russell Pope, who has prepared elaborate plans for the gallery, will come here from New York later to join in the conferences. The Fine Arts Commission, which must approve the design, is familiar with the tentative plans but cannot act until Congress has approved the project by formal act.

The enabling act would authorize acceptance of the gallery and art collection by the Federal Government, provide for creation of a board of nine trustees to supervise the gallery and authorize the Smithsonian Institution to acquire the gallery as a unit.

The President has asked Attorney General Cummings to confer with Smithsonian officials with a view to drafting the proposed enabling act.

Mellon Would Name Five.

The act would authorize Mellon to choose five of the trustees. The other four, ex-officio members, the Vice President, the Speaker, the Secretary of the Treasury and the secretary of the Smithsonian Institution or some other official. Mellon's appointees would be subject to approval by the regents of the Smithsonian Institution.

Mellon also would reserve the right to select a director, curator and several other officials of the gallery, with approval of the institution.

Provision also will have to be made by Congress for abandonment of the George Washington Memorial project and transfer of its site to the new gallery. The memorial plan has been changed to embrace an auditorium for George Washington University in another location.

Mellon has said he is ready to proceed with actual construction of the gallery as soon as all preliminary legal steps are taken.

Would Beautify Area.

ONE KILLED, TWO HURT IN TRAFFIC

Unidentified Man Is Victim. Woman and Girl Are Injured.

An unidentified man was killed and two other persons were injured, one seriously, in traffic accidents in the Washington area yesterday. Meanwhile, a coroner's jury freed two drivers who figured in fatal accidents and inquests into two other fatalities were set for tomorrow.

The unidentified man, whose body was taken to Gasch's undertaking establishment in Hyattsville, Md., was killed when struck on the Washington-

City Without Boiler Inspector Due to Abolishment of Fees

Abolition by Congress of the method of paying the District's boiler inspector out of fees he collects and the dissatisfaction of that official with the straight salary offered has left the Commissioners with a problem.

As a result of the developments the boiler inspector, Price M. Greenlaw, who has held that position since August, 1927, has not been on the job since December 24, it was revealed today.

Salary Not Provided.

On Christmas eve, by special act of Congress, Greenlaw was stripped of the privilege of making collections. At the same time Congress has made no appropriation for his salary.

Apparently no one in the District government, except Greenlaw himself, knew just how much he earned, but the Civil Service classification for his job fixes the rate of pay at $3,200 a

The Commissioners have agreed to reappoint him at that figure, although they have no money for the purpose, and Greenlaw has indicated he is not satisfied with the sum.

Funds to Be Asked.

Engineer Commissioner Dan I. Sultan, under whose jurisdiction Greenlaw's job comes, said the Commissioners have agreed to take the money from their contingent emergency fund to pay the inspector until Congress can make some provision for his salary. Sultan said the appropriation will be sought in the first deficiency bill sent to the next Congress.

Greenlaw's job was the last District office for which the wages were provided out of fee collections.

His duties required annual inspections of high-pressure boilers and tanks, along with their initial instal-

MUNICIPAL-OWNED GARAGES SOUGHT

Dupont Circle Citizens Weigh Proposal Involving Financing Fee on Autos.

The construction of municipal-owned garages to eliminate all-night parking and to relieve the congested traffic conditions was proposed by William Clark Taylor yesterday afternoon at a meeting of the Dupont Circle Citizens' Association, held in the Mayflower Hotel.

In his resolution, which was referred to the association's Traffic Committee, Taylor urged that $5 a year be levied on each car to raise

The Compact

I n his rose-colored memoir, David Finley suggests
that Andrew Mellon planned his greatest gift more carefully, cogently and ceremoniously than a Medici

prince amassing the dowry for his favorite daughter. The campaign, prepared with the help of trusted sup-

porters Finley, Donald Shepard and David Bruce, was both thought out and implemented step by step.

Sites had been searched out and compared—by the Tidal Basin where the Jefferson Memorial now stands,

on the Mall near the Washington Monument or the corner at Fourteenth Street which Hoover had pre-

empted for the Commerce Department. The foot of Capitol Hill was chosen. Distinguished architects

were considered (among them Supreme Court designer Cass Gilbert), and John Russell Pope was selected.

Innumerable legal, civic and governmental obstacles were anticipated, studied and surmounted. Because

federal legislation would be necessary to complete elements of Mellon's plan, the linchpin was to present

*In the first days of 1937,
newspapers across the land
report that Mellon intends
to give the people of the
United States a very pre-
cious gift—the National
Gallery of Art. Nobody
covers the story with more
gusto than the Washington*
Evening Star.

the fullborn idea to the President, and that became an occasion as gracious as the gift itself.

An emissary was chosen in the person of Frederic A. Delano, among other things a friend and chairman of the National Capital Park and Planning Commission, which oversaw the capital's public and recreational lands, the Mall in particular. Finley—whether he or Mellon hatched the idea is unclear—recruited him for a special errand late in 1936. Mr. Delano would have Christmas dinner with a celebrated nephew and would be pleased to take along a letter from Mellon to give to the host:

My Dear Mr. President:

Over a period of many years I have been acquiring important and rare paintings and sculpture with the idea that ultimately they would become the property of the people of the United States and be made available to them in a national art gallery to be maintained in the City of Washington for the purpose of encouraging and developing a study of the fine arts . . . .

Straightforward but longwinded, it was as carefully composed a document as any business agreement or government policy statement Mellon ever made. Whatever he had in mind, it was not caprice, nor would the gift be made final until certain conditions were met by the president and Congress to the donor's satisfaction.

He remarked that over a period of years he had given art works to the E&C Trust whose trustees were empowered to deed them "to a national gallery if and when such an institution shall assume and be prepared to carry out the purposes intended." He had also given the trustees "securities ample to erect a gallery building of sufficient size to house these works of art and to permit the indefinite growth of the collection under a conservative policy regulating acquisitions."

The gallery would be for the benefit of the general public. Thus, so that other citizens might eventually "contribute works of art of the highest quality to form a great national collection," Mellon stipulated that the "intended

President Roosevelt works in his upstairs library at the White House, the cluttered and comfortable room where he receives Andrew Mellon.

gift… shall not bear my name." Rather, if all these conditions ever came to pass, it "shall be known as 'The National Art Gallery' or by such other name as may appropriately identify it as a gallery of art of the National Government."

"In order to carry out this purpose, and with the approval of the other [E&C] trustees," he proposed to give the collection to the Smithsonian or to the federal government. Then the trustees (of whom he was one) would "erect or cause to be erected on public land a suitable building…. Mr. John Russell Pope of New York has been employed as architect to study this project and will furnish designs…."

Displaying the care of a judicial writ, the letter plowed on into curious detail. It suggested placing the gallery on the Mall so that it would "not only be readily accessible…but with sufficient surrounding property under control of public authorities, to protect it from undesirable encroachments." Further, Mellon would fund endowments to pay the salaries of the top administrative officers, who would be exempt from civil service, and to buy future acquisitions which "shall be limited to objects of the highest standard of quality." However, the building's upkeep, staff salaries and "other administrative expenses and cost of operation" would be funded by Congress. Of prime importance, Mellon proposed to vest his gallery's governance in "a competent and separate Board of Trustees." He did not want the gift to be controlled by federal bureaucrats or presidential appointees.

Mellon's closing paragraph placed the ball squarely in Roosevelt's court: "If this plan meets with your approval, I will submit a formal offer of gift stating specifically the terms thereof, and the erection of the building may proceed immediately upon the acceptance of such offer and the passage of necessary legislation by Congress. Appropriate instruments of conveyance and gift will then be executed."

The letter is most eloquent in what it overlooked and omitted. For one thing, that Roosevelt already knew about the gallery idea both officially and informally, as did every Wash-

ington resident who had read the newspapers two years earlier. Much of what the Christmas epistle contained was old news, albeit penned on new bond. Why the charade? Perhaps simply for the sake of starting fresh and having everything very clearly understood. As for the omissions, the most spectacular was any reference to the reason that Mellon's gift was already known, the tax case of course, which was still hanging fire. In light of that, Mellon's offer late in 1936 seems the height of noblesse oblige.

In any case, the Christmas letter opened a new chapter in which Mellon and Roosevelt never forgot their stations or their manners. The gentlemen declined to let any ongoing unpleasantness in another venue tarnish the opportunity at hand. They kept their eye on loftier things. Witness the President's reply the day after Christmas:

My Dear Mr. Mellon:

When my uncle handed me your letter of December twenty-second I was not only completely taken by surprise but was delighted by your very wonderful offer to the people of the United States.

This was especially so because for many years I have felt the need for a national gallery of art in the Capitol [sic]. Your proposed gift does more than furnish what you call a "nucleus" because I am confident that the collections you have been making are of the first importance and will place the nation well up in the first rank….

Because the formal offer calls for specific statement of the terms and will have to be worked out before any request is made by me to the Congress for the necessary legislation, may I suggest that you, or whoever you may care to designate, should come to see me some afternoon this week?

Also I think that we should discuss the formal announcement and the terms of it.

With renewed appreciation of your letter, believe me….

Roosevelt and Mellon's second, and last, meeting took place days later, on New Year's Eve. For years the only public record was Finley's

fusty report. On receiving Roosevelt's letter,

Mr. Mellon said: "I would like to talk with the President about it." Knowing the excitement Mr. Mellon's presence at The White House would cause, I [Finley] said: "Let me arrange for you to talk with the President in the Mansion," which I did....

Mr. Mellon and I went to The White House at five o'clock. We found Mr. Roosevelt seated on a sofa in front of the fire [in his library on the second floor]. He motioned Mr. Mellon to sit beside him and I sat near Mr. Cummings [Attorney General]. The President turned on his charm, and he and Mr. Mellon were deep in conversation for some time. At last Mr. Mellon pulled a letter out of his pocket; "Here, Mr. President, is my offer. I hope it can be carried out."...

The President read the letter, apparently with pleasure, then tossed it to the Attorney General, asking whether there was any reason why the govern-

ment could not do what Mr. Mellon had outlined in his letter. The Attorney General read the letter and said that the government could do everything requested in the letter. Then put it through, said Mr. Roosevelt, as Mr. Mellon had outlined in his letter. He added that it was a most generous offer and a wonderful thing for the country.

At that point, Miss LeHand came in to pour tea, with some of the Roosevelt grandchildren to look on. We had a very pleasant time and finally Mr. Mellon arose to go. He thanked President Roosevelt for his help and we returned to Massachusetts Avenue.

If the Hudson Valley squire charmed the baron of American business, had he been enchanted himself? That question arises from one of the few deletions in the typescript of Andrew Mellon's authorized but unpublished biography (finished circa 1943). After Mellon and Finley left the White House, Burton

Hendrick wrote, Mellon said "What a wonderfully attractive man the President is." The next sentence, scratched out in the typescript but still legible, reads "And afterward he added, with a slightly wry expression, 'I came through it much better than I expected to!'"

And how puzzling that Finley's is the most complete account of the event published to date. Because though the politics and deeds of the Roosevelt years continue to attract scholarly and popular attention, the founding of the National Gallery has gotten very little ink. Here was a princely gift offered on Christmas Day, then accepted in principle and announced to the nation before the New Year's holiday was over, then debated by Congress and chartered less than three months later. The result changed the face of Washington, boosted the city's international eminence, and has touched the lives of millions of people each year for half a century. Yet it gets less mention in history books than the First Dog, Fala.

Neither Mellon nor Roosevelt is known to have written about their fireside chat, and so Finley's incomparably sedate version has stood alone for years. Yet another point of view has survived. Homer Cummings' private diary, preserved at the University of Virginia, sheds new and puzzling light—even a wry gleam—on the event. The day after Christmas, a Saturday, he went to his office and prepared to brief the President on the New Deal's most pressing problem: the famously intractable Supreme Court.

[At] 5 P.M. I went to the White House and had a two-hour conference with the President. This was one of the longest and most interesting conferences I have had with him in a long time....

[Roosevelt] said he was going to read me a letter, which he had received the day before, and which he had not yet answered. But, he informed me he was not going to tell me who wrote it. He then started reading the letter. Before he had read three paragraphs I began to laugh and he said "Do you suspect the author now?" I said "You must remember I am a G-man, and I think I know who wrote the letter; it is

AWM." He laughed heartily and said that was correct. [Interestingly, Mellon was high enough in Cummings' thoughts to be identified by his initials.] ...

It was a long, well constructed, and modestly phrased document. I talked to him for a little while about the possible effect of this gift on the pending litigation [i.e. the tax case of which he says no more], and we discussed the form of reply the President was to make.

When the President had finished reading the letter to me, he said "what would you think about it?" I said "I would do some heavy thinking," and he said "I have been doing that." Of course, the acceptance of such a gift involves necessary Congressional action. The letter the President is to write will, I think, result in further discussion of details and the magnificence of the offer. Apparently it is the sort of a gift that could not be rejected. Indeed, it is a magnificent conception and would supply a need which has been felt for a long time by those who have thought about the subject at all.

Roosevelt evidently wrote his reply to Mellon's offer that evening and the topic remained high on his agenda, for at a cabinet meeting on the 29th Cummings recorded: "The President also explained the Mellon proposition with regard to the Art Gallery...." Two days later, on the 31st, Cummings received a "rather mysterious call... asking me to be at the White House at 5 o'clock." He was sufficiently intrigued to arrive a little early.

Shortly thereafter, Mr. Andrew Mellon, accompanied by his Secretary, arrived. We had an amiable discussion and I remained there about an hour. During this period tea was served by Miss LeHand, Mr. James Roosevelt and his wife and little girl coming in and out and the whole thing was rather informal and family like.

The main purpose of the meeting was to enable Mr. Mellon to confer personally with the President with reference to the proposed National Gallery of Art. Mr. Mellon presented a letter, which was more or less in the form of an outline of the project with

VOL. LXXXVI... No. 28,884.

WEATHER.
U. S. Weather Bureau Forecast:
Occasional rain with slowly rising temperature today, fair and colder tonight and tomorrow. Temperature— Highest, 43, at 12:01 a.m. yesterday; lowest, 36, at 11 a.m. yesterday.
Full report on page B-3.
(AP) Means Associated Press.

The Sunday Star

WITH DAILY EVENING EDITION

WASHINGTON, D. C., SUNDAY MORNING, JANUARY 3, 1937—100 P

No. 1,659—No. 33,850. Entered as second class matter post office, Washington, D. C.

MELLON GIVES PRICELESS ART, BUILDING TO U.S.

Offer to President Made in Letters Now Public.

STRUCTURE COST OVER $8,000,000

Site on Mall Specified for National Exhibit of Finest Works.

Andrew W. Mellon, former Secretary of the Treasury, has tendered to the Nation through President Roosevelt, and the Executive will recommend acceptance, the priceless Mellon art collection—ranked among the world's finest—together with a projected $8,000,000-to-$9,000,000 "National Gallery of Art" on the Mall in which to house it.

The gift, destined to make Washington one of the principal art capitals of the world, was disclosed last night when the President made public a series of four letters exchanged between Mellon and himself since December 22.

At the same time, Mellon disclosed here a number of recent acquisitions that add immeasurably to the importance of his remarkable collection of old World masters. In addition to the notable assortment of Raphaels, Rembrandts, Rubens and masterpieces of other great painters, he has secured within recent weeks the famed Dreyfus collection of Italian Renaissance sculptures in Paris. He also bought recently the Clarke collection of historical American portraits.

Actual Work Indefinite.

Connoisseurs and Mellon himself are reluctant to place a monetary value on the entire collection, but it is known that five of the Hermitage collection paintings which Mellon purchased in Russia in 1930 him $3,-... considered by experts a bargain. This became known when ... sought to obtain tax reductions ... amount paid for these paintings.

... collection, prior to the recent ... tions, has been roughly estimated ... worth from $50,000,000 to ... 0. The works are held by ... Educational and Cha...

ANDREW W. MELLON.

LOW-PAID GROUPS IN U. S. SERVICE GET SENATORS' AID

Robinson and Bulow Favor Upward Revision in Lower Brackets.

BY J. A. O'LEARY.

Two more Senators — Majority Leader Robinson of Arkansas and Chairman Bulow of the Civil Service Committee—expressed themselves yesterday in sympathy with the proposal to have the Seventy-fifth Congress, which convenes Tuesday, consider an upward revision of salaries in the lower brackets of the Government service.

Asked to comment on the ... tion adva...

STAY-IN STRIKERS ORDERED TO QUIT FISHER FACTORIES; PICKETING BARRED

Police Carry Court Order to 400 Occupying Plants at Flint—Immediate Action on Injunction Deferred.

30,000 WORKERS IDLE; 135,000 FACE LAY-OFF

Union Officials Complete Plans for Meeting Today of Representatives from 10 Cities—Will Consider Bargaining Contract as Basis for Negotiations.

BACKGROUND—

Occupational strike method, widely used for first time last Summer in European labor disputes, particularly in France, after advent of Popular Front government. Practice quickly adopted by American labor, first major strike of this kind occurring last November at the Bendix plant in South Bend, Ind.

Present wave of stay-in strikes which have hit automobile industry began November 18 when the Fisher body plant at Atlanta was closed. Movement spread, becoming aggravated during past week to the point where 30,000 automobile workers are idle.

Automobile industry opens year curtailed when leaders were expecting a 5,000,000-unit year.

By the Associated Press.

DETROIT, January 2—Strikers in two Fisher body plants of the General Motors Corp. at Flint were ordered to vacate the plants in an injunction signed today by Circuit Judge Edward D. Black Sheriff's officers said that while 7,500 employes of the two plants were affected by the suspension of work, there were only about 200 "stay in" strikers in each building.

Action on the injunction at Flint was deferred and a force of 175 officers who had been held in readiness to eject the strikers was ...
Strike lea...

WAGE-HOUR BILLS EXPECTED TO TOP CONGRESS AGENDA

Robinson Favors Amendment to Constitution as Best Solution.

BY G. GOULD LINCOLN.

The third New Deal Congress—the Seventy-fifth Congress, in the old phraseology—assembles at noon Tuesday.

As a New Deal Congress it is bigger than ever—owing to the sweeping Roosevelt victory in the recent ... and it ma...

Invitation List For Inaugural Includes Hoover

Survivors of Wilson Cabinet Also Are Sent Bids.

Former President Herbert Hoover and Mrs. Hoover and the living widows of all other former Chief Executives are being invited to attend the inauguration ceremonies for President Roosevelt January 20 as distinguished guests of honor, Rear Admiral Cary T. Grayson, Inaugural Committee head, announced yesterday.

Among others invited as special guests will be the members of the Woodrow Wilson cabinet who still alive
The ...

MATTSONS RENEW EFFORT TO REACH KIDNAPER WITH AD

Supposed "Contact" Message Again Is Placed in Seattle Paper.

BACKGROUND—

Last Sunday night a masked, bearded man ... French ...

e New York Times.

Second-Class Matter,
New York, N. Y.

NEW YORK, SUNDAY, JANUARY 3, 1937.

Including Rotogravure Picture, Magazine and Book Review.

P P

TEN CENTS

TWELVE CENTS Beyond 200 Miles Except in 7th and 8th Postal Zones.

LATE CITY EDITION

Rain and warmer today, clearing and colder tonight. Tomorrow generally fair and much colder.
Temperatures yesterday Max. 44, Min. 34

Section 1

---

gn Accord

GUNMEN TERRORIZE STORE, GET $22,000;

EASING TRUST ACT TO SPUR BUSINESS URGED BY DRAPER

on Also Essential fidence, Assistant retary Asserts.

RY ASKED TO AID

deral Body Is Proposed efine Rules, as in the Revenue Bureau.

By FELIX BELAIR JR.
Special to THE NEW YORK TIMES.

WASHINGTON, Jan. 2.—Clarification and revision of anti-trust laws to facilitate voluntary agreements covering interstate business and industry which would eliminate "obviously unfair trade practices" was urged today by Ernest G. Draper, Assistant Secretary of Commerce, in the first concrete proposal from an official source for carrying out President Roosevelt's expressed determination to abolish child labor and sweatshop wages and hours.

Mr. Draper urged business and industrial leaders to come forward and assert their right to know definitely the rules under which they were asked to meet the responsibility of giving employment, creating purchasing power, and supplying the goods and services which keep such purchasing power in motion.

These rules, embodied in the anti-trust laws, now are "often unintelligible, contradictory, and sometimes absurd as the result of changes in economic and social conditions," Mr. Draper said. Only the lack of clarity and the existence of unnecessary prohibitions in such laws stand in the way of an industrial cooperation that could abolish existing abuses, according to Mr. Draper.

In a statement to THE NEW YORK TIMES Mr. Draper declared that "the anti-trust laws should be clarified and modernized," and that, "where necessary to accomplish that result, they should be revised." He recommended that in addition "the methods and agencies for their enforcement should be simplified and strengthened."

Interpreting Body Proposed

As an integral part of his plan for giving effect to the President's ideal, Mr. Draper suggested the creation of a division of industrial economics in the Department of Commerce. Such an agency, he argued, might interpret the clarified laws, but specific regulations

---

Mellon Gives Art to U. S.; $27,000,000, With Gallery

Collection of Notable Works Valued at $19,000,000 to Be Housed in Capital— President 'Happy' at Project.

Special to THE NEW YORK TIMES.

WASHINGTON, Jan. 2.—A project for a National Gallery of Art centering around the great $19,000,000 collection of masterpieces gathered over a period of many years by Andrew W. Mellon of Pittsburgh, former Secretary of the Treasury, which it is hoped may eventually make Washington a rival of Paris as an art capital, was announced today in an exchange of letters between President Roosevelt and Mr. Mellon.

Mr. Mellon offered to give not only his collection for the possession of the people of the United States, as a nucleus for the gallery, but also to erect the building to house them and provide an endowment fund for certain purposes in connection with it. The President tentatively accepted, pending Congressional action.

The building alone would cost from $8,000,000 to $9,000,000. Mr. Mellon suggested that this building, plans for which are already being developed by John Russell Pope, the New York architect, be situated on the north side of the Mall on Constitution Avenue between Fourth and Seventh Streets, N. W., an area now devoted to the Smithsonian Institution and new government buildings.

It would bear the name "National Gallery of Art" or some other suitable designation, but not the name of Mellon, the donor specified.

Referring to the plan as "this fine project," Mr. Roosevelt, after obtaining details of the proposed gift from Mr. Mellon, said he was referring the correspondence to the Attorney General and the appropriate representatives of the Smithsonian Institution and would "be happy to submit the matter, with a favorable recommendation, to the Congress at the first opportunity."

Mr. Mellon has long contemplated giving to the nation his works of art, comprising one of the greatest private collections in the world. His plans were first announced two years ago during the hearings of the Board of Tax Appeals on his charges of overassessment of taxes, a case which is still pending.

At that time some government

Continued on Page Thirty-eight

Correspondence between Mr. Mellon and the President, Page 38.

AMENDMENT RISES AS A SESSION ISSUE

Robinson Says 'Something Must Be Done' to Permit Pay and Hour Regulation.

COURT DECISIONS CITED

Senator Assails 'Exploitation' of Women and Children— Sharp Debate Likely.

By TURNER CATLEDGE
Special to THE NEW YORK TIMES.

WASHINGTON, Jan. 2.—As Senators and Representatives gathered in Washington today for the opening of Congress next week, the question of a Constitutional Amendment granting the Federal or State Governments power to regulate hours, wages and working condi-

---

GUNS KEEP WOMAN IN POST AS MAYOR

Mrs. Armstrong Holds Fort in Daytona, Says Only Court Can Order Her Out.

SHE PROCLAIMS A 'HOLIDAY'

Her Rival, Sholtz Appointee, Shouts 'Fascism' as He Promises Hard Fight.

By The Associated Press.

DAYTONA BEACH, Fla., Jan. 2.—The woman Mayor of Daytona Beach, defiant in the face of a Gubernatorial ouster, stood her ground behind heavily armed guards today while the man designated to replace her hurled charges of "fascism" at her administration.

"I shall hold this office until a competent court orders me out,"

STRIKERS IN FLINT DEFY INJUNCTION TO END SIT-DOWNS

Sheriff Mobilizes Deputies for Forcible Ejection, but No Action Is Taken.

GAS USE WAS PLANNED

Judge Fails to Issue Warrants and Further Steps Wait Until Monday.

KNUDSEN SEES 135,000 IDLE

He Says Lack of Parts Will Virtually Halt Operations Within a Week.

By The Associated Press.

FLINT, Mich., Sunday, Jan. 3.—Striking workmen, occupying two plants of the Fisher Body Company of the General Motors Corporation, were assured early today of holding their positions until Monday when midnight passed without issuance of warrants required for their forcible ejection.

Despite a far-reaching Circuit Court injunction obtained by the company, the "stay-in" strikers remained in the factories, some 300 in plant No. 1 and 200 in plant No. 2. Circuit Judge Edward D. Black granted the injunction, but when he had not issued bench warrants for the strikers at midnight, he became powerless to act in the case until the next legal court day, Monday.

E. J. Parker, resident manager of the Fisher company, after a conference with Roy E. Brownell, company attorney, and local authorities that lasted until after midnight, issued a statement that "it is now squarely up to the men and their advisers as to whether they will obey or defy and continue to defy the order of the court."

One hundred and seventy-five officers, held in readiness for possible action to remove the striking workers, were demobilized soon after 8 o'clock last night.

Parker's statement following the conference related that "certain of our employes and others have taken possession of our two local plants, machines and equipment and have seized control of the gates.

"The company believes that it is entitled to the possession of its own property and the approaches to the

---

FIVE CENTS
IN WASHINGTON AND SUBURBS
TEN CENTS
ELSEWHERE

ENSION GROWS S SPAIN DEFIES AZIS' THREATS

ques Warn Shellfire Will nswer Attempts to Interfere With Shipping.

G ON FREIGHTER SOTON TERMED AN "ACT OF WAR"

y Determined to Get Full Satision in Palos Incident—Paris Sees Threat to Peace.

of Spanish freighter Soton by German cruiser Koenigsure of another merchantman by Admiral Spee in reprisal Reich vessel by Socialists, may be the spark which will ting European war conflagration.

has been growing during recent weeks with Britain and for non-intervention in Spanish civil war. Non- ve was climaxed early in the week with France's rmany to prevent further departure of volunteers for nd demand that Adolf Hitler sign general disarmament reply is expected early this week.

BULLETIN.
January 2 (A.P.).—A Basque government ued here tonight asserted four Spanish wlers had fired 16 shots Friday in an ursuit of the British merchant vessel

was stated to have taken place 7 miles e coast in the vicinity of the town of

unter-threats in the wake of German ure of a German freighter

---

many of the important details sketched in. The net result of the conference was that the President was to write a letter to Mr. Mellon, in answer to this particular letter, thus making a group of four letters in all, which it was proposed to release to the press . . . .

On January 3, the Sunday papers carried long accounts of the gift. At the next cabinet meeting,

When we turned to other subjects there was discussion about a conservation bill, labor matters, immigration control, and the Mellon gift of a National Gallery of Art. When this latter subject was under discussion I brought up the matter of the implications involved from the sixth paragraph of Mr. Mellon's offer, dealing with a self perpetuating Board of Trustees [of which more later].

No official action was taken and I think I rather gathered what the President's impressions were. After I returned to the office I dictated a memorandum to Judge Townsend who has the matter in charge.

Newman A. Townsend had served as a North Carolina legislator, Superior Court judge and counsel to Governor O. Max Gardner who later founded a Washington law firm. (Ironically, in 1946 Gardner became Under Secretary of the Treasury and helped reorganize the Bureau of Internal Revenue. Then President Truman named him Ambassador in London, but he died the day he was to sail for England.) Townsend, an Assistant Solicitor General, performed the work of a legal counsel: drafting position papers, reviewing constitutional questions, writing messages and speeches for FDR.

Two weeks into the new year, Cummings sent the President a formal letter accompanying a draft of the Joint Resolution "embodying the conditions upon which the gift to the United States . . . will be made." Cummings wrote, "We have endeavored to present in language that is clear and unambiguous the conditions which Mr. Mellon and his associates insist must be included in the legislation. It is my opinion that the Congress, if it desires to do so, has full power to enact into law the provisions contained in the proposed draft." In brief, these were the salient points that Cummings raised and that survived review:

• The tract on the Mall bounded by Seventh Street, Constitution Avenue, Fourth Street and North Mall Drive (later Madison Drive) will be dedicated for the Gallery. The area directly eastward across Fourth Street is reserved "for future additions."

• The Gallery, established as a bureau within the Smithsonian, will have its own board of trustees comprising four ex-officio members (the Chief Justice and Secretaries of State, Treasury and the Smithsonian) and five "general" members from outside government. The first slate of general trustees, named with Mellon's approval and serving terms of different lengths, will thereafter fill vacancies in their ranks by electing successors to ten-year terms. Thus, the General Trustees may always be a self-perpetuating majority.

• Mellon will erect an approved building and give a collection of artworks to be exhibited in it. Then "the faith of the United States is pledged" to maintain, protect, curate, administer and operate the Gallery, and "for these purposes" Congress will appropriate "such sums as may be necessary."

• The trustees will appoint well-qualified executive officers and pay their salaries from private endowment funds. Other employees will be governed by civil service rules and paid from federal funds.

• The board's actions "shall not be subject to review by any [federal] officer or agency other than a court of law."

• The Gallery will display no works of art "unless they are of similar high standard of quality" of the ones in Mellon's collection.

• The Smithsonian's national gallery of art will become the National Collection of Fine Arts.

On the same day as his formal letter of

transmittal, Cummings confided quite a different message to FDR in a separate "Personal and Confidential" three-page memorandum. Far less amiable, it details Cummings' (and Townsend's) caveats about the proposal.

First Cummings reveals that Mellon's representatives, certainly his principal lawyer Donald Shepard for one, were "at times rather difficult to deal with. They assumed, and adhered to the position, that as Mr. Mellon was making the gift he was entitled to dictate the terms thereof." The bill does not violate "the general form outlined by Mr. Mellon in his correspondence," Cummings acknowledges. "Nevertheless there was but little give and take in our negotiations."

The Attorney General was most concerned about

the control of the gift. As drafted the bill provides for a Board to be known as "The Trustees of the National Gallery of Art." This Board will be made up of nine members, of whom four hold office ex-officio. The other five are to be private citizens and ... constitute a self-perpetuating body. The net result is that they will control the management of the Gallery, the site, and the contents thereof for all time. Moreover, they are not responsible to any officer or agency other than a court of law. All attempts to secure a modification of this arrangement were unavailing, although half a dozen different devices were suggested. Mr. Mellon and his representatives do not desire that the management of the Gallery should pass out of private hands into governmental control. No doubt there is something to be said for this point of view and from his standpoint it is understandable. On the other hand, the site is appropriated to the Smithsonian Institution and this would carry with it the structure erected thereon. The anomaly is therefore presented of government property being managed by a private group.

Cummings fretted that the "'General Trustees' are, in the first instance to be chosen by the Board of Regents of the Smithsonian Institution, subject to the approval of the donor. It is, therefore, apparent that these five general

trustees must be persons of whom Mr. Mellon approves." Further the five original general trustees will chose their own successors and fill vacancies while "the other four ex-officio trustees will have no power in that regard."

He also noted that the gift's donor, sagely, is deemed to be the E&C Trust, not Mellon himself as inferred from the earlier letters to the President. It troubled the Attorney General (though it should not have surprised him) that "the form used in the bill was insisted upon by Mr. Mellon's attorney who quite likely had pending litigation in mind." Mellon believed he had already given the pictures to the Trust—no matter how vehemently the government argued otherwise in the tax case.

The Gallery would appropriate a Smithsonian bureau's name, Cummings went on, and "my impression is that Dr. Abbott [sic] did not like to surrender this title and suggested various alternatives.... without avail." Next, he points out that the Gallery would be technically part of the Smithsonian but "that institution will have no control over it. The [Gallery] Board of Trustees has full power subject only to judicial regulation" and Cummings predicted that this might become a "source of friction."

Penultimately, "the faith of the United States is pledged," Cummings wrote FDR, quoting the draft bill. "A question of taste and propriety is raised by this phraseology, but it was a form insisted upon by Mr. Mellon's attorney." As Shepard negotiated the gift, the Gallery became an instrumentality of the United States government, albeit an independent institution. Finally, Sixth Street would be closed, because Mellon's architect frowned on building an archway over that artery or tunnelling it beneath the museum—for engineering reasons as well as esthetic ones. As for authorizing the street closing, Delano's National Capital Park and Planning Commission passed that hot potato to the city's appointed Board of Commissioners which gave its consent.

In short, Cummings, Townsend and company identified virtually every particular that outsiders would question, that in time other institutions would covet, and that would in fact give the Gallery unique privileges and a singular character. In particular, no other privately controlled institution is sustained by an abbreviated form of "the full faith and credit" clause, the standard assurance that applies to conventional government organizations. The Gallery is sustained officially by the Republic. Yet at the same time this institution does not answer to Congress or the executive branch with regard to its artistic judgments or how it spends its own trust funds. Certainly it must account for all the federal moneys it receives. But as for the trust funds established by Mellon and augmented by later gifts, and as for the privately endowed publication program which would become diverse and substantial over the years, its Board, a mixture of government and private-sector members, has total authority.

In important ways, the National Gallery of Art is unique—because of the singular charter that emerged from the unusual circumstances of its creation, and the sagacity of its creator in deal making, and the tenacity of the attorneys who represented him.

In the meantime, reaction to the proposal had not been entirely positive. Congressman Wright Patman of Texas, already a vehement critic of Mellon and what he symbolized, was incensed. In a letter to the President he wrote "The precedent is a very bad one. If we allow Mellon this privilege, Hearst and Morgan will come in next with an offer just as attractive." It sounded like John C. Calhoun's charge a century earlier that if James Smithson's bequest were accepted, "every whippersnapper vagabond" would line up to buy respectability at the expense of America's honor. "Mellon's citizenship is nothing to be proud of," Patman railed. "A lasting memorial in his honor should not be constructed at the Nation's capital, even at his own expense."

Patman, who had filed impeachment charges against Mellon, maintained that he had escaped a full investigation only by resigning his cabinet post and becoming an ambassador, "therefore making unnecessary the further prosecution." In his view Mellon remained "an untried criminal" however an influential one. The donor, Patman said, had made (or increased) his fortune with profits from World War I and from "the country's [present] misery." He should not be allowed to "glorify himself" by spending that tainted wealth on a Gallery the government would have to maintain. Finally, if a National Gallery was needed, "the Government should pay for it" and an appropriation should be passed to buy Mellon's paintings "for a reasonable price." The Texan insisted on looking the gift horse in the mouth.

Judge Townsend would later propose to Cummings the creation of an independent advisory committee to fill future vacancies on the board of trustees. The idea, he wrote, "is new, but the principle involved was suggested by Dr. Abbot in our conference with Mr. Sheppard [sic].... The suggestion was not acceptable." All points were not unconditionally surrendered however, the judge suggested, because he had conferred with Congressman Keller, chairman of the Committee on the Library, who would chair hearings on the matter.

By the time those hearings were held, on February 17, witnesses testified that the major outstanding problems had been resolved.

After the House membership voted to accept the gift, on March 16 the Senate debated the proposal for five hours, managing to touch on topics from political spoils to Florida grapefruit. "Suppose that we had before us a bill to appropriate $30 million to buy an art collection comparable to that offered by Mr. Mellon," said Senator Tom Connally of Texas, the bill's champion. "Every Senator who voted for that bill knows he would have candidates on every stump in his state campaigning against him ... [for squandering] hard-earned taxes to buy the works of a foreigner named Leonardo da Cinci," as the *New York Times* garbled. But this proposition would not cost the nation millions, Connally continued. "To my mind it is only a question of whether we will take this bill or leave it. The Government is no pauper. We could build our own gallery, and the Government could run it. Then if a constituent paints a picture and brings it to us we can put it in the gallery. We'll run the gallery like the people want it run.…" But, he concluded, if the nation wanted to accept Mellon's pictures and the gallery he offered, it would have to be run as the donor wanted to run it.

Senator La Follette raised the matter of Mellon's pending tax case, and Connally challenged its relevance: "What does this bill have to do with tax questions? Does the Senator want to kick Mr. Mellon around?" The Wisconsin liberal directly took issue with the composition of the board of trustees and its power to refuse pictures deemed inferior to Mellon's old masters, but his offered amendments died. And so it went, until the bill passed on a voice vote with a few dissents. After a conference committee ironed out differences between the two versions, the bill was enacted as a public resolution on March 24, 1937, Mellon's eighty-second birthday. Barely three months after his formal offer to the President, Mellon had a charter for his museum on the Mall. All that remained was to design, build, staff and open it.

Tangentially, it is worth noting the fate of certain ideas voiced (or implied) in the Senate that day.

Two years later, a museum of popular or current arts was planned for the Mall and assigned the site on the south side opposite the Gallery. This Smithsonian Gallery of Art was also authorized by a joint resolution of Congress, which mandated "a suitable building for properly housing and displaying the national collections of fine arts."

Unlike Mellon's museum, designed to celebrate great art of the past, the new Smithsonian museum would look around and ahead. As the American Federation of Arts argued: "The importance of the new museum will arrive from the potentialities of a unique service in the cause of American art that are inherent in its program of activities rather than from the value of the present Smithsonian collections, important though they are." This gallery would encourage the visual arts "in collaboration with … the Mellon bequest." It would be "a dynamic rather than a static" museum, one designed to influence living American artists—to "stimulate the creation of works of art of distinction and to elevate and sustain the public appreciation of these works throughout the country.… Let the National Gallery cosset its old masters, this museum would inspire America's talent, living and yet unborn."

Given that charge, a distinguished jury was gathered, including the redoubtable Frederic A. Delano, Walter Gropius of the revolutionary

Eliel and Eero Saarinen and J. Robert Swanson's winning design for the Smithsonian's national art gallery calls for a hard-edged and severely plain building, a representative of the new International School of architecture. It is never built.

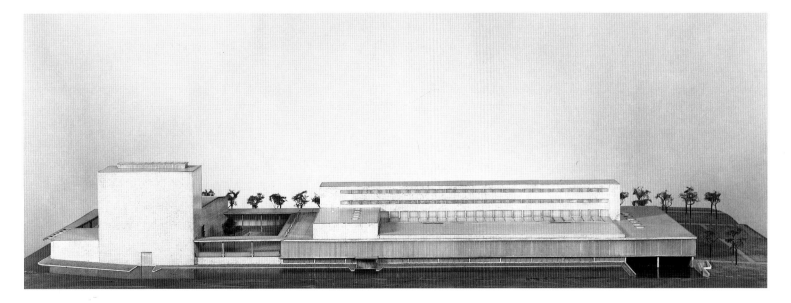

Bauhaus and recently of influential Harvard, and three other architects. From some 408 entries, they selected a daring design by Eliel Saarinen, his son Eero Saarinen and J. Robert Swanson, for the prize of $7,500. Theirs was a very modern design and it was applauded by those who championed the new International architecture. But aside from the prize money, funds were never appropriated to build this monument to living art, and it remained a museum on paper.

While Congress was working its will, Mellon was feeling his age, though he continued to take cogent interest in the Gallery's affairs. Certainly he stepped aside as Shepard and Finley testified at the hearings (where his appearance would have brought endless noise and distraction). He remained closely enough involved to personally review changes in construction cost estimates and the like, though he did not witness the Gallery's groundbreaking. There wasn't one for

reasons that will become clear.

"In the early summer of 1937 the family noticed a change," biographer Hendrick wrote. Appearing weak and tired, Mellon admitted he wasn't feeling well, but shook off attempts to treat him like an invalid. When the changes became more obvious, business held less of his interest; his four-year-old granddaughter, Audrey Bruce, held more. Then "he gave up his walks, his appetite failed him and he even showed an aversion to smoking—neglecting the little 'rat-tails' that had been his constant solace all his life." Alarmed, the Bruces called a specialist who found evidence of a tumor. "The physician assured his patient that it was not malignant, and Mellon himself was not much concerned over his condition. He still refused to acknowledge that he was ill, but would say simply that he 'did not feel quite right.'" His entourage became increasingly alarmed and edgy.

Mellon enjoys a summer's day with Ailsa on Long Island. All he ever sees of his great gift, the National Gallery, is a hole in the ground (shown at left)—as it appeared within a fortnight of his death.

Andrew W. Mellon Long a Dominant Figure in the B

MEMORIAL OF ART LEFT BY FINANCIER

Mellon's Collection of Great Canvases Given by Him for Public Gallery

MELLON DIES AT 82 IN SOUTHAMPTON

Continued From Page One

announcement by Howard M. Johnson, the financier's secretary, through The Associated Press.

Mr. Mellon and his brother, R. B. Mellon, contributed the funds

The New York Times.

"All the News That's Fit to Print."

Copyright, 1937, by The New York Times Company.

VOL. LXXXVI.....No. 26,070.

Entered as Second-Class Matter,
Postoffice, New York, N. Y.

NEW YORK, FRIDAY, AUGUST 27, 1937.

P   TWO C

ANDREW MELLON DIES AT AGE OF 82 IN SOUTHAMPTON

EX-TREASURY HEAD

Financier Served Under 3 Presidents—Later Envoy to London

GAVE ART TO THE NATION

Busy on Plans for National Gallery in Washington at Time of His Death

A PIONEER IN ALUMINUM

Founded Vast Companies in Pittsburgh to Amass One of Nation's Biggest Fortunes

Special to THE NEW YORK TIMES.
SOUTHAMPTON, L. I., Aug. 26.—Andrew W. Mellon, Secretary of the Treasury in the Cabinets of Presidents Harding, Coolidge and Hoover, former Ambassador to Great Britain and one of the nation's leading financiers and industrialists, died here at 8:30 o'clock, Eastern daylight time, tonight. He was 82 years old.

Mr. Mellon, a philanthropist whose benefactions, particularly to art, claimed a large part of his fortune, succumbed at Bonnie Dune, the home of his son-in-law and daughter, Mr. and Mrs. David K. E. Bruce, here.

With him at the end were his

'Crossroads of America Loses Its Shaft of C

Special to THE NE
LINTON, Ind.,
zens of Linton ar
cause of the thef
which marked the
ulation of the Uni
When it was de
this city was the s
ter of population,
organizations erect
on the spot. It was
because this city is
the State's deep
mining area.
Today a visitor ex
sire to see the popu
When a guide acc
to the site of the "
America" it was fo
marker no longer ex
Investigation reve
needy family had use
for fuel last Winter.

BANK RATE I
TO 1% WORI

Federal Reserve R
Charge Here Small
Set by a Central

ANTICIPATES CRED

Action Also Taken as
Prevent Dumping of
Securities by Meml

MELLON'S PUBLIC CAREER NOTABLE

Term as Secretary of Treasury Marked by Post-War Financing.

Characteristic Studies of Andrew W. Mel

Rare Masterpieces in Mellon Art Gift to the

A-4

MELLON WAS ONCE HELD FOR 'RANSOM'

Delighted in Telling Friends How Taxi Driver Refused to Trust Him.

Philip H. Love, a member of the editorial staff of The Star, is the author of "Andrew W. Mellon: The Man and His Work," the first published biography of the former Secretary of the Treasury. In the following article he presents a brief study of the personality, character and career of the famous financier, whose long career has just been ended by death.

BY PHILIP H. LOVE.

On a rainy morning in April, 1921, a taxicab drew up to the curb in front of one of the Fifteenth street entrances to the Treasury and a slight, gray-haired man stepped out.

While the elderly passenger groped in a pocket of his carefully creased gray trousers, the driver slapped the taximeter flag back into the "vacant" position with the announcement, "Two-eighty."

The well-dressed "fare" switched his small black cigar from one side of his gray-mustached mouth to the other and reached into another pocket. His lean face reddened as he exclaimed:

"By jove, I've come out without my wallet!"

"Old stuff," the taximan sneered. "Come across with the jack, Mister, or I'll call a cop."

"Oh, there's no need to do that," the embarrassed passenger answered

"The Madonna ana Child," a Florentine painting on panel by Sandro Botticelli, 1444-1510. The panel is 29 by 22 inches.

"The Madonna and Child With St. John the Baptis art of the late fifteenth century by Giovanni Battista da This painting is on a panel 41 by 57½ inches.

TRIBUTE IS PAID MELLON IN DEATH

D i Hoover Says

Mellon Re Dream

Former Secr
Work Bef

Barber Made Home With Mellon,

When Washington's summer began in earnest, Finley feared the worst and one noon rousted the Gallery's contractors out of the restaurant where they lunched. The reason: Mr. Mellon was suffering from the heat and the apartment had to be air-conditioned immediately. The construction chiefs scared up some window units, then jury-rigged them with lumber and canvas in the full-length casement windows, only to find the electrical wiring was already overloaded with lamps to shine on every painting. Summoned to the study, the men were told by Mr. Mellon that he hadn't expected instant solutions anyway. Nonetheless, crews and subcontractors were brought in from the Gallery job to install new wiring and new insulation during the night. By the next noon the apartment was cool, though it is doubtful that Finley rested any easier.

Mellon was failing. He insisted on staying in Washington until late June when the Fine Arts Commission gave its blessing to Pope's design and he gave his to the choice of Tennessee pink marble for the building's exterior. Only then did he agree to go to Ailsa's summer house. "As he drove to the Union Station he passed the site of the Gallery," Hendrick wrote. "The excavation was fairly advanced, and that was all of the structure that Mellon's eyes ever rested upon." A special railroad car was waiting; he observed that he had never before hired one for his private use. On Long Island, throughout July one subject seemed to hold his interest: the Gallery's progress. In August he was bedridden, then pneumonia set in and he died peacefully on the evening of August 26, 1937. Another private railroad car, this the one President Roosevelt used for a journey the previous day, bore his body back to Pittsburgh.

Newspapers and news magazines throughout the country ran his obituary. Virtually every journal mentioned Mellon's wealth, his success in business and his service as Treasury Secretary. Most mentioned his ambassadorship, some the tax case. All detailed his unprecedented gift to his countrymen, posterity and the world—the National Gallery of Art. ❧

Andrew Mellon's death gets even more attention than the announcement of his gift eight months earlier.

The Master Builder
and His Masterpieces

John Russell Pope, dean of architects and champion of neoclassicism, poses for an official portrait upon his election to the American Academy of Arts and Letters in 1927. Ten years later construction begins on his masterpiece, the National Gallery of Art.

A dyed-in-the-wool modernist might say that John Russell Pope never had an original architectural idea, but post-modernists and others who admire proportion, detailing, and allusions to history in buildings have rediscovered Pope's spectacular appeal.

Call him the Great Synthesist, the architect whose gift was adaptation. By training and dedication Pope believed that the greatest architectural ideals had been formulated long ago. Consequently the wise architect of his time would temper a worthy form with contemporary taste, liberate it with modern materials and methods, bend it to a new environment and noble purpose. While others of his generation, like Frank Lloyd Wright, broke the ancient molds quite intentionally, he ignored the new and severe International School. A designer of grand houses and monuments, Pope was a deft and ubiquitous borrower of antique motifs, which he meant to honor by imitation, at the same

time enhancing his own world and posterity's. An associate said Pope "firmly believed that a monumental piece of architecture must adhere closely to its Greek and Roman roots with a minimum of personal deviation. By this philosophy he substantially raised the quality of public buildings in this country.... He was always guided by an ideal—the perfection of classical architecture adapted to contemporary life."

"When Mr. Mellon asked Mr. Pope to design the building," a contemporary recalled, "everyone knew what kind of building it would be"—grand, indeed very grand. He built one Long Island estate that had as many stalls for the polo ponies in the stable as maids' rooms in the main house and slept more servants than members of the family. He designed a museum space in London that King George called "the world's finest sculpture gallery," and enough granite tombs to house all the immortals left homeless by the burning of Valhalla. He designed the spare Grecian temple of Lincoln's Birthplace Memorial in Kentucky and mixed Greek Revival with American Colonial for Washington's Con-

stitution Hall, a commission he accepted gratis in honor of his mother for the Daughters of the American Revolution. (Partial to gentry, he traced his ancestry to a Massachusetts colonist of the 1630s and married an heiress who traced her Carolina fortune back to colonial days.) Pope drew a Georgian campus for Dartmouth, a Greek revival one for Johns Hopkins and for Yale a Gothic plan (although it was never fully realized). Not just a neoclassicist, Pope was an unexcelled master of eclecticism and adaptation. In praising him, critic Royal Cortissoz declared, "tradition is not the master of the true architect but his servant, leaving him freer to place his own stamp on a given building."

Born in New York in 1874, "Jack" Pope studied at City College and Columbia University, then in 1895 won two awards for foreign study—the McKim Fellowship from the premier architecture firm of the time, McKim, Mead and White, and the Prix de Rome, from what became the American Academy in Rome (which he would later chair). These stipends and those he received as a Schermerhorn Travelling Fellow supported his journeys through Italy, Sicily and Greece, where he made measured drawings of the great buildings of antiquity as he went. Next he settled in Paris for two years to earn a diploma from the Ecole des Beaux-Arts, then the capital of classicism in architecture.

When and where Andrew Mellon first encountered Pope remains an open question. Pope certainly worked with Mellon on the Federal Triangle for which he designed the National Archives, the most distinctly monumental building of the lot. Before that, Pope served on the Fine Arts Commission in Washington and renovated Henry Clay Frick's palatial Manhattan home to serve as a public museum of which Mellon was a trustee. Earlier yet, Pope had designed a Long Island mansion for Ogden Mills, Mellon's deputy secretary at the Treasury Department and his eventual successor. Duveen claimed credit for getting them together first—Pope had designed Duveen's

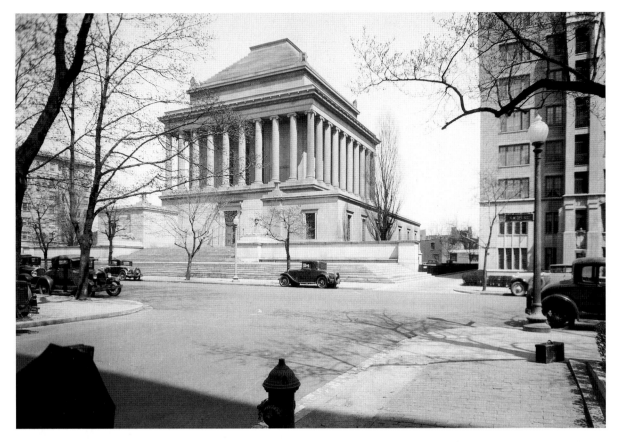

house in Manhattan and his British Museum addition in London—but then the dealer took credit for most of Mellon's artful decisions.

In any case, it is clear that Mellon had picked Pope as his architect quite early; he was identified during the tax trial and stipulated when Mellon offered the gift of the Gallery to the nation in 1936. One other architect had been seriously considered: Cass Gilbert, who designed the Supreme Court building and New York's neo-Gothic Woolworth Building, in its time the paradigm of the skyscraper.

Above all, Pope was, according to the *Dictionary of American Biography,* perhaps the individual most responsible for "that last flowering of the classic ideal which has placed its stamp so firmly" on Washington. He designed public buildings here as well as ceremonial buildings, memorials both major and minor, and a number of grand dwellings. There are the towering National Christian Church on Thomas Circle and the massive Scottish Rite Temple a dozen blocks north of the White House. There are the scattered residences preserved today as the

Textile Museum, a trade association at 1500 Rhode Island Avenue NW, and the Audubon Naturalist Society's "Woodend" in suburban Chevy Chase. Across upper Sixteenth Street from Meridian Hill Park is the stately pair of side-by-side mansions commissioned by neighborly diplomats Henry White and Irwin Laughlin that figure curiously in the Gallery story. (David Bruce's second wife lived there as a girl and Laughlin himself would help decorate the Gallery interiors.) There are the American Pharmaceutical Institute fronting the Mall, and the Second Division Memorial also on Constitution Avenue, and the Jefferson Memorial at a major focal point of the McMillan Plan for Washington.

Pope made many plans for the site beside the Tidal Basin. He once designed for it a monumental quartet of marble artifices around a vast round pool as Theodore Roosevelt's never-built memorial, a vision in white marble as grandiose as Teddy himself. Pope also made an early and somewhat generic design for the National Gallery on the Tidal Basin site, one of more than

a score of surviving plans roughed out for Mellon. Which makes manifest another point: the National Gallery of Art did not spring fullborn from Pope's designing brow.

Edwin B. Olsen, who worked for Pope, then for Eggers & Higgins and still later for McKim, Mead and White, recalls that the great museums of Europe were all considered and compared. "In the beginning we made an album of important large European museum plans for Mr. Mellon"—such as Florence's Uffizi, Pitti and Medici; Paris' Louvre; London's Tate and National Gallery; and Madrid's Prado.

Fully ten preliminary concepts were committed to paper early on—undated, unsited elevations for generic museums with one neoclassical look or another. One possibly intended for the Tidal Basin location has been dubbed "Union Station," it displays such all-purpose neoclassicism. Another shows four square pods around a central square hub, a shape that somehow recalls the Taj Mahal. Dated drawings from Pope's atelier prove that the present site was under serious and perhaps exclusive consideration by January 1936—nearly a year before

Mellon approached President Roosevelt. These drawings were among a selection loaned by Pope's office for a brief exhibition during the Christmas holidays in 1941. This small group is better than nothing, because after Pope's death his associates reorganized as Eggers & Higgins, and Pope's records, drawings included, were eventually lost in an office move.

The surviving cache displays various schemes, all of them for approximately the site the Gallery would actually occupy: the land bounded by Seventh Street, Constitution Avenue, Fourth Street and Madison Drive. A sketch dated February 13, 1936, is the first to

show a dome and all the major elements of the eventual building including Garden Courts. This one is signed by Pope and seems to be in his hand. It has higher attics than were actually built, huge unpartitioned galleries and circular staircases. Later drawings play many variations on this theme, and they in turn lose the Garden Courts, gain three vast galleries in a row down the central spine, get a grand central staircase, grow porticoes at the ends of the building, lose the porticoes, acquire circular stairs at both ends and four double porticoes. There is a plan with stairs where the Garden Courts had been, another with a flat cupola built of square elements. Surviving plans include E11 and E5 dated April 7, and E6 with no dome on June 11, then the dome rises again on the 17th. There is a Sketch 18 and a Scheme X and, by June 2, a Revision A. And these postdate one with the handwritten legend "This drawing was shown Mr. Mellon April 5th when he approved this scheme.... He also instructed me at this time to proceed with the working drawings." As for the numbers, this design anticipated a building contain-

ing 13,398,236 cubic feet, which at 85 cents a foot would cost $11,388,500.60, a figure that proved to be optimistic.

Though Pope himself was an exceptionally skilled draftsman, after about 1910 he did scant work at the drawing board but instead directed his firm in the grand manner, says Pope scholar Steven Bedford. Pope held court in his Manhattan townhouse while two associates, Otto R. Eggers and Daniel Paul Higgins, actually ran the shop downtown. When a major commission was at hand, Eggers would bring conceptual sketches up to 81st Street, receive the master's instructions, and return to the drawing board downtown to renew his labors. Though Pope did not do his own drawing any more, his hand might just as well have held the pencil, said Theodore J. Young, who worked for his firm and its successor, Eggers & Higgins, for fifty years: "He did not in any way delegate the responsibility for the design to anybody else. He always, whether it was [with] a sketch on a squared pad ... indicated what direction" to take. Not incidentally, it was Eggers who did the spectacular presentation

Pope's Jefferson Memorial shines in the sun—despite having almost been scotched more than once. Its construction was the subject of several controversies; critics said its dome aped the Gallery's, for one thing. Nonetheless, it remains one of Pope's most popular designs.

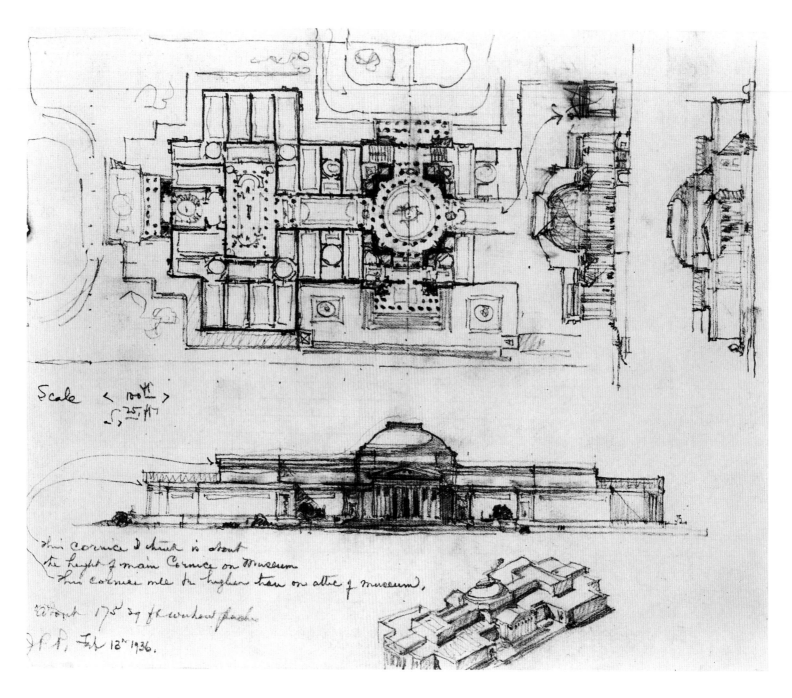

drawings which did much to broaden Pope's reputation. As a critic wrote in the 1930s, Eggers "has exerted more influence on the development of architectural draftsmanship and rendering in this country than any other man of his time."

However grand his manner, an associate said Pope worked without respite, in fact he is said to have worked himself to death. Ted Young, the "Principal in Charge" of the Mellon job (Pope's man on the Mall), said in an interview for the Gallery's oral history program that his mentor "was a man totally dedicated to his profession . . . .

The opportunity to design a great building in the classical style was his reason for living." Advised to have surgery for a treatable malignancy, he postponed it because of his commitment to the Gallery and kept working on his magnum opus. Thus he died prematurely on August 27, 1937, the day after Mellon.

Each serious student of the National Gallery's design has his own candidate for the precedent that inspired it. David Finley saw the inspiration in George Hadfield's "old City Hall," the extant 1820 courthouse a few blocks away.

Gervase Jackson-Stops, architectural advisor to Britain's National Trust, infers that Pope was inspired by Kedleston Hall, an eighteenth-century house in Derbyshire famous for its central dome and skylit central galleries. Sculpture Curator C. Douglas Lewis says the model must have been Berlin's early nineteenth-century Altes-Museum designed by Karl Friedrich Schinkel. Director J. Carter Brown also adduces Schinkel, and suggests that the Prado, with its central dome and two wings, played a part in Pope's thinking. William J. Williams of the Gallery's education department would suggest an indistinct number of traditions afoot here: The building "incorporates elements of the architecture of ancient Rome and the Italian Renaissance as well as the late eighteenth-through early nineteenth-century neoclassical styles of France, Germany, Britain and America."

Even reflecting art deco and modern stream-lining, in sum it combines so much that it is absolutely original.

The National Gallery of Art is unconditionally John Russell Pope's masterpiece. It was also very distinctly, perhaps uniquely, a practical collaboration by architect, client and their respective successors. It began with Pope, who conceived a grandly symmetrical Beaux-Arts plan around the central Rotunda and sketched the Greco-Roman exterior of balanced wings extending from the low dome. This was amended by Mellon who, according to David Finley, wanted a simpler exterior, lower attics and no porticoes at the east and west ends. (Did Mellon champion the "less is more" idea before its time?) Then it was finished by both their heirs, for the principals died when construction was barely underway and few details of the grand

Portico and pediment of the Gallery's Mall entrance mimic Hadrian's Pantheon in many major elements— but not the ornate style of its Corinthian columns. Rather, Mellon and Pope choose the understated elegance of the Ionic order.

The Master Builder and His Masterpieces

The nearly spherical Rotunda is frankly modeled on the Pantheon in Rome—down to (or up to) the coffered ceiling. The glass-vaulted Garden Courts at both ends of the building recall atria in a thousand Mediterranean villas as well as the single garden room Pope designed for Henry Clay Frick's museum in New York.

design were certain. Here is an instance of design-by-committee that in its brilliant synthesis proves all genius need not be ruggedly individual.

In its interior, the Gallery was of the Beaux-Arts tradition, which put great store in the dynamic flow within a building. Thus Pope designed a formal and imposing principal entrance on the Mall. One mounts a broad flight of shallow steps to approach bronze doors thirty feet tall, then enters a relatively narrow vestibule with two pairs of columns that usher the visitor onward. Passing these sentinel columns, one enters the space of the Rotunda, an enormous near-sphere measuring 103 feet up to the glass oculus in the coffered ceiling and 101 feet in diameter, a space modeled on the Pantheon in Rome. In its center, frozen in flight with winged feet, dances brazen Mercury above a raised fountain, his index finger pointing aloft. Here is a place that declares itself the hub, the epicenter. So the visitor, drawn to the middle as if by a magnet, finds himself embraced in the space and, only after entering it, sees halls to the right and left marking the building's grand axis.

While the Rotunda seems dark within its ring of deep green columns supporting the dome, two vast adjoining halls are bright with their arched back-lit ceilings and white limestone walls. Again, the visitor is drawn into a new and contrasting space—114 feet long, 38 feet wide and 49 feet high, though the vertical

dimension seems indefinable as light sifting through the etched-glass ceiling makes that boundary indistinct. At last there are choices now, whether to enter one of the open doors to a picture gallery, a room of more human or even intimate scale, or to seek some implied grail at the end of this expansive interior avenue. If one takes the latter course, it leads to a columned Garden Court, nearly a Tuscan cloister with liv-ing trees and greenery, a fountain from Versailles playing in the center a few steps down, and places to sit. (Pope had first used the garden court device in a museum when he converted Henry Frick's home into the building for the Frick Collection. There he provided the old car-riage court with a glass roof, enclosing it as a place of repose with a long shallow pool, a respite from the visually busy exhibition rooms.

It served its peaceful purpose, and he adapted the idea to the symmetrical, linear plan of Mellon's building, which of course meant two Garden Courts.) If one detours into a picture gallery, another door then leads to another gallery, then another like as not, which opens onto yet another . . . .

It is possible to go through the entire main floor without retracing one's steps, entering a central hall only at the start, then to cross it and to exit. But in this serene maze Pope had another trick up his sleeve. Pope had anticipated the arrangement of the picture galleries in concentric rings so to speak, a layout designed after his death. One dilemma the Gallery staff faced at first was a shortage of art; the building comprises 500,000 square feet—eleven acres—more than half of it exhibition space. Larger than London's National Gallery, it is a titanic building in plan and said to have been the largest marble building in the world when it opened. Yet Andrew Mellon bequeathed hardly more pictures than decorated his apartment. (A wag said when the museum opened that guards were there to steer visitors to the next picture, they were so few and far between.) Pope's plan for gallery spaces allowed great flexibility in the number of rooms that might be open; at first, pictures hung only in the rooms nearest the central halls, and visitors had no way of knowing they might be two or three empty rooms away from the outside wall.

All this was the main floor, the one reached from the Mall by that monumental stair of forty-four shallow steps set in three ranges. The ground floor was entered directly through three doors opening onto Constitution Avenue at the foot of Sixth Street. (The huge bronze portals at the ends of the building were rarely opened in the early decades—the west only for the president and visiting heads of state, the east hardly ever used until the East Building opened.) The ground floor held the public cafeteria, private dining rooms, storage ranges, utilities, work rooms, laboratories served by corridors with mustard-colored tile wainscotting—the "yellow brick road"—and an elegant warren of offices,

called "Peacock Alley." Basement levels contained shops and more utilities. The undercroft also housed pumps to hold back the meandering waters of the swamp that once soaked this site. The lowest floor was a reinforced concrete slab several feet thick (the better to keep the building from floating), which in turn rested upon 6,800 cement-filled steel casings that had been driven some forty feet down "to refusal," the point where they would sink no lower.

However classical the details—and no detail down to bronze grills and doors on electrical panels was beneath the architect's notice—the building employed devices that classical builders never dreamed of, witness the Gallery's frame, made of steel beams. This skeleton allowed great flexibility in arranging individual gallery rooms. Also reflecting the very latest technology was the air conditioning and humidity control system, supplied by the young Carrier Corporation of Texas. Pope's West Building was probably among the first structures of its size to have been air-conditioned from its inception.

As for the exterior, Pope modeled that on the Roman tradition, after a fashion. There is the low dome, suggesting a ceremonial building, flanked by the varied masses of the long symmetrical wings. At the ends of the building, Pope called for pediments and colonnades, but Mellon had misgivings and with Finley he often visited Judiciary Square to study Hadfield's old Courthouse there, a model of simplicity. (Might they have been given pause by Pope's Archives Building with its forest of Corinthian columns and a myriad of decorative devices?) In any case, Finley's memoirs politely confirm what surviving drawings suggest: That Pope originally planned porticoes at the east and west ends, but these were removed at the client's request or insistence. Mellon's aide gently led Pope to understand that the building would be better off without them. "Mr. Mellon was not happy about the multitude of columns," Finley wrote.

I suggested that we talk with Mr. Pope about it. "Mr. Pope is a very high-powered man," said Mr. Mellon,

"I would not want to hurt his feelings." "I know Mr. Pope very well," I said. "Let me talk with him." "Go ahead," said Mr. Mellon, "and see what you can do." Mr. Pope was always amenable to suggestions, if he thought they had merit. I explained that, in Mr. Mellon's mind and my opinion as laymen, it was enough to have a pediment and columns in the center of the north and south sides of the building but that a pediment and columns on the east and west ends would distract the eye from the central motif and make for restlessness.

The amenable architect studied the suggestions, which included minimizing the number of wall niches and lowering the attics so that the skylights would not be seen glittering from the ground. In due course Pope altered the design. Finley concluded: Pope "was delighted with the change and so was Mr. Mellon."

As for the niches, the few that remained invited statuary, as did the north and south pediments—like as not sculptures of historical figures, gods or allegorical heroes. By the time those details had to be settled, Mellon and Pope were dead; the client was the E&C Trust, chaired by David Bruce, and the architect was now the firm of Eggers & Higgins led by Pope's long-time associates. Given the traditions of corporate architecture, these men were keepers of the flame dedicated to building a more Pope-ish edifice than Pope himself could have made. It was a tenet in those days that a Great Architect's heirs carried on *his* work. Thus Eggers and Higgins advocated more of the exterior decoration so dear to Pope's heart. Had they gotten their way, there might have been a pantheon of gods and heroes in high relief and chasing the Virtues across pediments that peak 106 feet above the ground atop the 49-foot columns. Bruce, Finley and associates, mindful of *their* dead principal's principles, asked whether such sculpture could measure up to the great art inside. David Bruce and Paul Mellon in particular opposed this extraneous decoration. But the debate joined by the client's heirs and the architect's successors went on to such lengths that

trial sculptures were commissioned—and finally seen to be wanting. And that was finally that.

The shortage of windows created special design problems for Pope himself, for fenestration breaks up the monotony of blank walls—especially in a building nearly eight hundred feet long. Unable to use that traditional device for creating light and shade, Pope had to find other means of punctuating his long walls, and in the end conceived a rhythmic series of masses and recessed planes, which presented an imposing look of admirable grace.

In choosing the exterior material, Mellon believed limestone would be very bright, hard on the eyes in sunny Washington, and white marble would be worse. He liked the look of the Morgan Library in New York, which was built of Tennessee pink marble. This would add millions to the building's cost, but as he told Finley with regard to other elements, "I don't care if they are expensive, if they don't look expensive."

Pink marble could be had in Tennessee, but something on the order of eight hundred railroad cars of stone for the project had to be mined, and only one block out of three would be judged good enough for the exterior. Yet the first fact to be faced was temporal: quarrying some 310,000 cubic feet of uniformly colored marble would ordinarily take about a decade. The second, closely related problem was chromatic, because pink marble of a consistent color does not just lie in the ground in huge amounts waiting to be quarried. Found in Tennessee in several small quarries, the stone occurs in a range of colors, and simply to ship it north as it came out of the ground would give the masons a batch of light pink stones and then a batch of dark as they erected the walls course by course. "And what then?" asked Malcolm Rice, Pope's man in the quarries, "Would it be Jacob's coat?"

Avoiding that would require a unique effort: In order to supply in reasonable time enough marble within a reasonable range of color, a joint venture was formed by three small quarry companies, Tennessee, Gray Knox and Candora. (Not that they weren't glad for the work. Busi-

Designers focus on every detail that may catch a visitor's eye. Pope's successors take special care in working out harmonious detailing down to the legs of carved marble benches (opposite), or a stairwell's stone cornice with Greek key and egg-and-dart motifs.

ness had been so slow in the 1930s that "pecker-woods were eating the wooden derricks down.") Samples representing the range of colors found in a dozen quarries were gathered at one plant and laid on the ground. While bosses from Pope's team and the Mellon office looked down from a scaffold, the samples were hosed down with water to bring out the color, and workmen were instructed to move sample after sample until they arrived at a balanced color-coded arrangement. Based on that, a trial wall was erected at the building site to confirm the result before quarrying began in earnest. Then true samples of seven hues of pink marble were distributed among the quarries. As stones were taken out of the ground at each quarry, they were graded—matched against seven stone swatches as it were—then stacked accordingly.

Some 35,000 finished stones were shipped to Washington in roughly the order they would be set in the walls, generally the darker stones at the bottom and lighter ones higher up. Indeed, today the color variation remains visible: the darker stones run as high as the first string-course molding, then—though there is considerable cogent mixing—lighter ones reach up to the next horizontal break in the wall, and above that the lightest stones find their place.

The dark green columns for the Rotunda came from Italy, out of a quarry not far from one where Michelangelo found some of the large blocks of white marble for his sculpture. It was hoped that the columns of Verte Imperial stone could be mined there, each in one piece, then lathed and finished in Italy, then shipped direct to Washington. But it seemed risky—to trust monoliths more than five feet in diameter and thirty-six-feet long to shipment over the high seas. They were simply too tall and too far away from the building site, and so after being quarried as blocks in Italy, they were shipped to Vermont where they were lathed into "drums" that would stack up five to the column. The Vermont Marble Company in Proctor received the blocks and turned them into cylinders, which were then examined and compared, turned on dollies and matched for both color and pattern. Again men from the Pope and Mellon offices climbed scaffolds to eyeball the stone elements, while workmen shifted them about until the best juxtapositions were found.

When 120 of the six-foot drums were chosen, and their positions all determined, they received final finishing and polish; only then were they shipped down to Washington and erected in situ: trucked to the Mall, then rolled up a ramp under the Rotunda and hoisted through the hole where the fountain would be. There could be very little hit or miss in this, for the columns' dimensions were dictated by rules laid down by the ancient Ionic formula that mandates an exact entasis, the swelling of a column as it rises. In spite of such care, after they

had all been positioned and the lintel installed atop them, two columns were found to be wrong! The lintel was removed and the errant columns rotated in place 180 degrees.

Beautiful, practical and impressive though it is, the National Gallery is not a perfect building: Pope may have put the main entrance in the wrong place! As Ted Young put it, "This arises from the dilemma that sometimes occurs when there is a conflict between a classical concept … and popular usage." Pope placed the grand entry on the Mall to invite pedestrians approaching along the greensward between the Capitol and Washington Monument. But in equal numbers over the years people have come to the Gallery from the north where there is public transpor-

Far from the clutter of a marble quarry in Tennessee (opposite), flatcars in Italy hold squared blocks of dark green marble from local stone yards (below), raw material for the Rotunda's solemn columns (left). In all, eight states and three foreign countries supply stone for the Gallery. From Alabama, for example, comes limestone for the sculpture halls adjoining the Rotunda. For the exterior, Tennessee produces some 35,000 finished stones in seven shades of pink, enough to fill eight hundred railroad cars.

Polished to a mirror finish, the new Rotunda dwarfs a human figure. This photograph comes from a series of interior portraits taken just before the West Building's opening in 1941.

tation. This Sixth Street entrance admitted them through rather ordinary doors into a lower-ceilinged lobby that seemed more like the entrance to a well-endowed hospital. (In 1984 this lobby would be altered with an oculus in the ceiling above so that visitors entering the ground floor room could look up to glimpse the Rotunda above.)

When the principal building contractor, Vermylia-Brown, was ready to begin construction on the dignified enterprise, practical men decided that a little street-sense might be in order, especially since there was strong opposition to the closing of Sixth Street among merchants and residents of the southeast part of town for which it was a major artery. Alexander Reed, who was clerk of the works for Mellon's E&C Trust, explained in his cocky memoir why there was no ceremonial groundbreaking for the original National Gallery: because ground was broken in the dark of night. The local citizens' association had withdrawn its formal opposition, but the builders feared that commuters might object to the street closing. So Reed conferred with one of the presidentially appointed officials who ran the city and asked for police to be on hand to direct traffic when it was torn up. Then one midnight, work crews and two steamshovels began breaking up the street, curbs and sidewalks. By the time rush hour began—with the police rerouting confused commuters—the offending portion of Sixth Street had been torn up and was gone. "Everyone, including members of Congress on their way to work," Reed wrote, "could see that the Mellon Gallery had been started. This created a mild furor."

And nearly four years later when the building opened, it was not to unanimous praise. While periodicals that addressed themselves to everyday folk lauded the edifice in oval tones, critics in tonier magazines looked down their finely chiseled noses. They were, after all, the sort likely to be on the cutting edge of taste and, as a little hindsight now proves beyond contradiction, America was then on the cusp of a new architecture. The authoritative *Magazine of Art* sedately

applauded the contents of Mellon's building, but carped at its package. Another journal disparaged it as "the last of the Romans." *New Yorker* critic Robert M. Coates was ambivalent:

Nothing quite like the new National Gallery of Art, in Washington, ever happened before. No other great museum I know of started with so rich an endowment, so nearly complete a plant, so costly an aggregation of art. The Louvre began with the private collection of François I, called the Cabinet du Roi; other rulers added to it, notably Louis XIV, but as late as the end of the seventeenth century it contained only about five hundred paintings…. It had to wait until Napoleon had ransacked Egypt and Italy before its collection really attained impressive size. The Metropolitan was incorporated in 1870, but at first it was housed in an old brownstone on Fifth Avenue, and ten years passed before it settled in a permanent home. The National Gallery of London began with only thirty-eight pictures, and was fourteen years getting properly located.

John Russell Pope enjoys the garden of his summer home, The Waves, in Newport.

"By contrast the National Gallery of Washington springs into existence almost full-grown," Coates acknowledged, hastening on to bash it. Its dimensions were "almost frightening," the Rotunda "huge" and the exterior "rather forbidding." Yet, he found

the interior is surprisingly intimate in feeling; indeed, homelike is almost the word, for each of the fifty-odd exhibition galleries in use is about the size of an average living room and the disposition of the pictures is as uncrowded as it would be in the ordinary home. In such circumstances, even the *"Alba Madonna"*—large and flowing in style, blue in its tonality—has a cozy air, as if it had been bought for that spot, and hung lovingly, and no other place for it would do.

In time, it would appear, as collections grew and the Gallery's staff more skillfully displayed them, this building would come to be fittingly the permanent home of many, many more exceptional works of art whose donors decided no other place would do. ⁊

Construction and Dedication

Rising amid brick and rubble, the Rotunda proves the artifice of Pope's neoclassicism: Modern tools and materials create the ancient form and graceful polish of this space. Here a derrick dominates the site, awaiting more green marble "drums" to stack into stately columns, while the brick of the circular wall awaits its veneer.

Construction of the Gallery, its front longer than the Capitol looming above it, took nearly four years. It inevitably involved occasional delays and problems that the Mellon team resolved from offices in a townhouse on Lafayette Square. When the city claimed that a five-foot water main from the Tidal Basin could not possibly serve the museum, consulting engineers working at the Gallery's expense found the pipe blocked with debris left over from the main's construction. When a strike brought virtually all painting to a halt in eastern cities, clerk-of-the-works Alexander Reed claimed his crew stayed busily at work behind a guard force that at least once stared down a carload of thugs. Perhaps the construction phase was more notable for the problems that did not arise. For one, the massive fountain in the Rotunda, a wonder in itself, was carved from a single piece of Tennessee marble. When it arrived at the construction site,

An aerial view of John Russell Pope's Gallery, drawn by master draftsman Otto Eggers and embellished by landscape architect Alfred Geiffert, shows a fountain and landscaped plaza on the future site of the East Building.

Otto Eggers' 1937 sketch (right) proposes a design for a wood-panelled gallery. Early proposals, with many changes, are not made final for two years.

it looked too broad to fit through the bronze portal already in place. Only then did someone take the trouble to measure—and find it would clear the jambs with three-eighths of an inch to spare on either side. As for the painstakingly polished green marble columns, when finally in place, two of them were discovered to be facing the wrong direction. Then the lintel above was removed and the two columns were rotated 180 degrees.

In surprisingly short order, as Mellon had hoped, the notion of a national museum per se captured the imaginations of other collectors. Before the building opened several collections appeared: an incomparable selection of Italian paintings given by dime store king Samuel H. Kress; some early American paintings loaned by investment baron Chester Dale, a swashbuckling buyer of French art; a spectacular variety of objects and images amassed by P.A.B. Widener, the late Philadelphia streetcar magnate, and his son Joseph E. Widener. This gift would be delayed while the early donation of some prints—duplicates in the donor's collection— proved to be a bellwether of riches to come from Lessing Rosenwald who was still building the most comprehensive prints and drawings holdings in the land.

Meanwhile, the Smithsonian's Board of

NATIONAL GALLERY OF ART
WASHINGTON D.C.
SHOWING THE PROPOSED DEVELOPMENT OF
THE ADJOINING PLOT BETWEEN 4TH & 3RD STREETS
OFFICE OF JOHN RUSSELL POPE ARCHITECT
OFFICE OF ALFRED E. GEIFFERT JR. LANDSCAPE ARCHITECTS
MARCH 9, 1938

of Americana, art, antiques and history," wrote to the White House seeking a seat on the Gallery board. Roosevelt's personal secretary fielded the request, passed it to the President who sent it along to his aide Stephen T. Early who sought an official opinion before replying to FDR. With admirable concision Early reviewed the relevant facts and concluded in his memo; "There is no vacancy at the present time and as stated above, the President has no power of appointment under the Act of Congress."

There had already been, in fact, two vacancies during the first year of the Gallery's official life, when Mellon died in August and Gilbert the following March. The three survivors elected successors without federal oversight or presidential interference: retired diplomat Ferdinand Lammot Belin, and Paul Mellon, who was elected president of the Gallery—but then served only the briefest of terms before the war. David Bruce, who had been named vice president, succeeded to the presidency, though in all the to-do the board skirted the charter's declaration that no federal officer or employee "shall be eligible to be chosen as a general trustee." Bruce had left

Regents had duly appointed five general trustees to serve on the Gallery's board—a slate that had the founder's blessing. They were: Mellon himself; his personal lawyer Donald D. Shepard; son-in-law David K. E. Bruce; Duncan Phillips who had founded the admired Phillips Collection; and S. Parker Gilbert, a former Treasury hand and international negotiator turned investment banker. The following year the matter of succession was tested, however gently. A New Yorker named Fred J. Peters, of the self-proclaimed "House of Peters, publishers

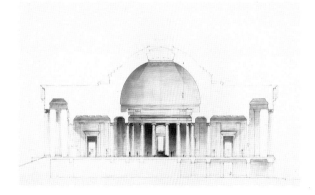

A transverse view shows the building with its dome. The Commission of Fine Arts requests drawings without one but in the end the dome wins out. The intricate drawing (below) shows the full length of the Gallery interior, complete with works of art and visitors.

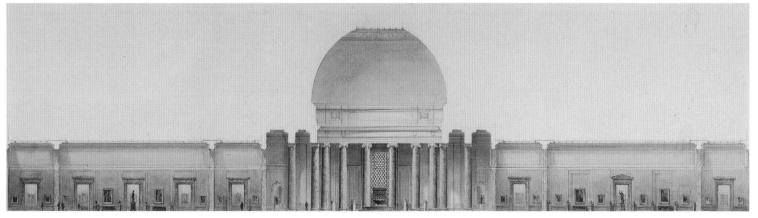

Construction and Dedication   147

the foreign service a decade earlier, but by the time of the Gallery's opening he was helping organize the OSS in London. Still a Gallery trustee, nay its president in absentia, he became OSS's chief of European operations with the rank of an Air Force colonel, a federal officer by any standard. He had been a mainstay during the years of planning, and though he remained deeply interested in the Gallery's well-being, after 1940 he was both too busy and too far away to play a particularly active role in Gallery affairs.

Paul Mellon's departure left a board vacancy, and Joseph Widener was named to fill it. The vice presidential slot was filled by Mott Belin, who in Bruce's perpetual absence became de facto trustee-in-charge for the duration. Given the uncertainty of life around it, the Gallery was developing a kind of corporate stability.

To no one's surprise, David Finley was named director by the original board. He was Andrew Mellon's choice and, after his death, doubtless the man who best knew what the founder had in mind. He was also certainly the one who would most devotedly dedicate his next years to carrying out his late mentor's wishes. After a very discreet survey of wages paid at other art museums around the country, Finley's salary was set at $18,000, compensation second only to one other museum director and a sub-

Construction of the Gallery proceeds serially as a bull's-eye foundation marks the spot of the eventual Rotunda, and concrete forms rise to shape the building's west wing (left). Adjacent plots boast slender saplings (lower left) and tennis courts (lower right) will one day make room for the museum's expansion. The richly columned National Archives building and three-sided Federal Trade Commission mark the eastern tip of the Federal Triangle.

A skeleton of steel I-beams (top left) bares a secret of the building's eventual success: Exterior walls (middle and lower left) bear the weight of roofs, thus precluding the need for many interior bearing walls. This allows designers to place interior partitions wherever they wish to create individual picture galleries. Once the marble facade is in place (right), passersby cannot guess that the building resembles boxes within boxes.

stantial stipend in any profession at the time.

One secret weapon the Gallery had throughout this period was David Finley's deft diplomacy, which would win friends for the museum during all his years as director. Always deferential and considerate, he had the gift of offering something and making it seem as if the person he was honoring (or courting) would do him a favor by accepting. Early in 1940, for example, he offered the President a private viewing of the

Gallery's growing collections, then safely stashed in the secure basement of the Corcoran Gallery. "The rooms can always be opened on a few hours' notice at any time that may suit your convenience," he told Roosevelt in a letter. "It would give me the greatest pleasure to show you the Collection and tell you about the progress of the new building and plans which are now being made for the Gallery." Because the rooms were unheated and uncomfortable in winter, a presi-

A central hall's glass roof
(above) lets in natural light
during construction—as it
will in the finished building. Later, false ceilings of
horizontal lay lights
(opposite) conceal from
visitors the electric lamps
that illuminate the galleries
on dark days and at night.

dential aide suggested that the visit might wait
until spring when "a julep or old fashioned
would not hurt the retinas." FDR fired back to
the aide one of the shortest of his eloquently
terse memos: "O.K. for May and Juleps,"
though it never happened.

Construction proceeded apace; the work
schedule was even accelerated in an effort to finish up and dedicate the building before the
nation became consumed by the war effort. As
for the wealth of interior detailing, Finley, his
wife and John Walker, who was coming aboard
as chief curator, worked out many of the details
together because they deemed the architects'
designs too busy. (Margaret Finley, Walker said,

might have been a distinguished architect.)

They settled on dividing the interior into a
larger number of relatively small galleries, which
would accommodate suites of pictures and
sculpture in roughly chronological order as visitors moved from room to room. To augment the
intimacy of the galleries, the whole sweep and
flow of the interior was carefully manipulated:
doors were placed so that one could usually see
only into adjoining rooms, not through a room
and into the next. This rule was broken intentionally when an axis was to be emphasized, for
example in the galleries opening onto the
Garden Courts and across the Court into galleries beyond. The planning process was so

meticulous that maquettes were made of different galleries; in these models, to-scale photographs of the artworks were "hung" on the miniature walls to see how they would look. Such lavish care would prove crucial when securing the gift of Joseph Widener's art, for it illustrated to the still-undecided collector how his collections would be installed if he gave them to the Gallery.

John Walker would remember,

We also felt strongly that works of art should be given becoming backgrounds, that they are more than documents of culture, that they exist to stimulate and please the human eye. Just as acoustics affect the enjoyment of music, so do the size and shape of galleries and their backgrounds affect the delight we receive from works of art. Such pleasure is enhanced if the spectator is able to contemplate each painting or sculpture as a separate entity. We spaced the collection more generously than any other museum I have ever seen, and to gain greater isolation for each

picture and statue we used panels in many rooms. These provide a second frame, so to speak, but their disadvantage is that they do limit flexibility. Perhaps that is why they have been so little used. But then

A compressor (above) chills water for the air-conditioning system. Engineers marvel at the built-in triple redundancy: While one machine is being stripped and cleaned during routine maintenance, a second runs the operation, and the third stands by in good running condition to take over should the second one break down.

Brass and bronze details take quality to great lengths and small ends, much to the frustration and pride of the bronze foundries. Clockwise from top left: a ventilator grill; door knocker at the Constitution Avenue entrance; window in an office hallway's leather-covered door; stairway handrail; circular pull on a marble panel; and, in the center, a purely decorative boss.

what sacrifices have modern museums made to gain flexibility!

The architects' designs for the marble floors also seemed wrong to Finley's eye, and he called in Irwin Laughlin, the man of taste who had commissioned Pope to design one of the houses on Meridian Hill. Finley recalled, "He climbed a ladder in his library, got down some books on design of French garden parterres; and worked out with me the floor designs that can now be seen in the rotunda and the two sculpture halls." In his home (which, with its sibling Pope house, survives as the foreign exchange organization Meridian House International) Laughlin had used an antique French technique to achieve especially rich and subtle wall colors. It starts with a base coat of orange or vermillion, say, then six coats of white or green paint; in the process different shades are applied to moldings and panels for gentle contrast in the final result.

Finley ordered the same technique for the

picture galleries that would be painted. Others among these rooms got damask wall coverings if they were to receive baroque pictures, stone trim for the display of quattrocento Italian art, or plaster—whatever was in keeping with the pictures that would hang there.

Details like handrails, radiator grills and other hardware were also attended to with great care, as was the stonework in the stairways and sculpture halls. An axiom has it that genius is the capacity to take infinite pains, so, the finishing of the interior involved genius. And just to make sure they got it right, David Bruce persuaded a neoclassical architect nearly of Pope's caliber to serve as a confidential consultant on interior design matters. William Delano accepted the task, for an honorarium of $5,000, a sum that Bruce negotiated personally and advised Finley should be kept secret.

By June 1940, completion of the building was in sight, and the staff had grown to the munificent number of a dozen—most of whom were involved in ordering furniture, planning staff organization and preparing catalogues. The E&C Trust had advanced the trustees a sum of money, which was to be repaid from earnings, to start a publications program. The idea was to provide "the highest quality" catalogues, handbooks, reproductions of pictures, postcards and the like at modest cost to the public. This would prove to be one of the Gallery's most successful long-term programs, and it saw the distribution of high quality art reproductions to a very wide audience.

The trustees were also still receiving art and objects from the E&C trust. Notably, two of Andrew Mellon's last acquisitions were the fountains made by Pierre Legros and Jean-Baptiste Tubi in 1674 on orders from Louis XIV for the Théâtre d'Eau at Versailles and installed in the Gallery's East and West Garden Courts. At about the same time, the board approved the return of a terra-cotta bust that Mellon had bought as a Verrocchio. An art critic attending a preview had praised the Mellon Collection highly—but singled out this bust as a modern

While the building rises, the collection grows. This small devotional panel for private worship, a gem of the Sienese Gothic style, is promised to the Gallery in 1939 by Samuel H. Kress, who becomes the first to heed Andrew Mellon's call for donors.

Sassetta, *Madonna and Child*, c. 1435
Samuel H. Kress Collection

Images of the ideal and the actual greet the Gallery's first visitors: Mellon's bequest includes a clement inland-seascape by Aelbert Cuyp, a seventeenth-century Dutch master who painted portraits of the ships that sustained Holland's wealth. Kress' original gift includes a painting of the Virgin Mary meeting her cousin, Elizabeth, in a Florentine settting complete with scholarly saints and vignettes of the Nativity.

Aelbert Cuyp, *The Maas at Dordrecht*, c. 1660
Andrew W. Mellon Collection

Piero di Cosimo, *The Visitation with Saint Nicholas and Saint Anthony Abbot*, c. 1490
Samuel H. Kress Collection

Majesty in portraiture has many faces (clockwise from top left): An unknown artist's Byzantine madonna glows with other-wordly warmth, the result of painting on gold in very thin layers of pigment. Rogier van der Weyden's ethereal lady owes her tranlsucent flesh and transparent veil to the Flemish method of priming a wood panel with gesso and building a figure out of many thin glazes of color. Hans Holbein's baby seems regal, thanks to the infant's gesture and princely garb—elements chosen by the artist who painted little Prince Edward's picture for his father, King Henry VIII. Lorenzo Lotto's Saint Catherine denotes her royal birth with a crown of gold and her martyrdom with a palm frond (symbols that contemporary viewers recognized instantly). The third-century Alexandria princess was beheaded by Roman Emperor Maxentius after she beat philosophers in a debate and miracu-loulsy broke her torturer's iron-toothed wheel.

Anonymous Byzantine,
*Madonna and Child on a
Curved Throne,* 13th century
Andrew W. Mellon Collection

Lorenzo Lotto, *Saint
Catherine,* 1522
Samuel H. Kress Collection

Rogier van der Weyden,
Portrait of a Lady, c. 1460
Andrew W. Mellon Collection

Hans Holbein, the Younger,
Edward VI as a Child,
probably 1538
Andrew W. Mellon Collection

Construction and Dedication

counterfeit. It had been returned to Duveen who was so infuriated, the story goes, that he smashed it with his cane. In return he offered two monumental marble vases signed by Clodion and dated 1782 and also made for Versailles, along with Aelbert Cuyp's masterpiece harbor scene, *The Maas at Dordrecht*. In this the Gallery clearly got the better side of the bargain.

Late in November 1940, the small staff moved into the building, and began expanding almost immediately so that by the end of the fis-

cal year civil service employees numbered 229. On December 1 the trustees received certification from Eggers & Higgins that the Gallery project was indeed complete, and it was theirs after three-and-a-half years of construction—not bad for what was reportedly the largest marble building in the world. The approved budget had been $15 million and, needless to say, the job cost more than expected—by all of $35,597.50!—a difference that seems minute today. Right after the New Year, the Mellon art was installed, then

Raphael ... is to assert the belief of the people of this democratic nation in a human spirit which is now everywhere endangered.... To accept this work today is to assert the purpose of the people of America that the freedom of the human spirit and human mind—which has produced the world's great art and all its science—shall not be utterly destroyed."

He recalled that during the Civil War, despite the press of immediate business (or perhaps in light of it!) President Lincoln insisted that the Capital dome be completed. "It had been an expensive, a laborious business, diverting money and labor from the prosecution of the war," Roosevelt said. "Certain critics—for there were critics in 1863 ... found much to criticize. There were new marble pillars in the Senate wing of the Capitol, there was a bronze door for the central portal; and other such expenditures and embellishments. But the President ... answered 'If the people see the Capitol is going on, it is a sign that we intend this Union to go on.'" Roosevelt borrowed Lincoln's example and found in Mellon's gift a national symbol. "The dedication of this gallery to a living past and a greater and more richly living future is the measure of the earnestness of our intention that the freedom of the human spirit shall go on too." ❧

November 1940: The museum appears finished save for landscaping, yet remains as empty as the nearby Capitol dome. Days later, staffers begin installing the permanent collection prior to the ceremonial opening in March when President Roosevelt (above) accepts the gift for the American people. Sitting in the front row at his right are: Bearded Chief Justice Charles Evans Hughes and Paul Mellon who presented the gift in his late father's stead.

later in the month the Kress Collection began arriving—in good time for the dedication, on March 17, 1941.

As recalled earlier, the opening was a grand event that featured vintage presidential oratory with a peroration that both summed up the universality of art and offered a rallying cry for the years ahead. As the *New York Times* recorded President Roosevelt's words: "To accept today, the work of German painters such as Holbein and Dürer, and of Italians like Botticelli and

The First Director

A formal portrait of the Gallery's founding director, David E. Finley projects his legendary old school manner, if not his famous charm.

David Edward Finley, who would have more influence on the Gallery in its early years than anyone including Andrew Mellon, was a small man of immense capacities: for handling detail, for personal politics and diplomacy, for pure work among other things. Around the Gallery he is remembered still, decades after his retirement, with a blend of affection and admiration, not only for his service but for his dignity and mannerly consideration. "He was Christian," said a staffer who knew him at work and at church for thirty years. "He believed in doing the right thing." Born a Southern gentleman, he became in turn a Philadelphia lawyer and Washington bureaucrat, and then did nothing so well as serve Andrew Mellon—at the Treasury Department, in London, then in private life, then posthumously as his Gallery's founding director. While Mellon lived, Finley was his amanuensis, his Boswell, his Chauvin and his Tonto. He ghosted almost everything Mellon wrote, escorted him everywhere, supervised his household (even

161

seeing to his children's social lives) and superintended his art collection. But to hear modest Finley tell it, he hardly made so much as a telephone call except on instructions from Mr. Mellon. Alter ego or clone, Finley was a complex and successful individual.

Born in South Carolina in 1890, he came to Washington as the eight-year-old son of a dyed-in-Dixie Congressman, then returned home to attend the University of South Carolina (where he ran the hundred-yard dash), and came back to Washington for law school. He served a brief stint in a Philadelphia law office before enlisting in the army for World War I, mustering out as a Signal Corps lieutenant and hanging out his shingle in Washington. He found tax law "a terrible bore" and joined the War Finance Corporation, a part of Harding's Treasury Department, where he caught the eye of dollar-a-year man Eugene Meyer and that of Under Secretary S. Parker Gilbert, one of the smart incumbents whom Mellon asked to remain in harness.

Finley settled in as an executive secretary to the inner circle. Among other duties, he handled correspondence for Gilbert and Mellon. Finding much of it repetitive—taxpayers often wrote in asking the same questions—he proposed that the Secretary write a book. The idea was approved and Finley ghosted it in a matter of weeks: *Taxation, The People's Business.* In short order Mellon named him his "special assistant," reportedly the first to bear this title in official Washington.

(Meyer, incidentally, was named to the Federal Reserve Board by Hoover, became a close friend of Mellon's, and lived in one of Pope's houses on Meridian Hill. He bought the struggling *Washington Post* and subsidized it for several hard years during which time Mellon offered to buy it for the cost of his investment plus a round profit of $1 million. Meyer declined the offer, bought out the paper's chief competitor and started the *Post* on its way to star status. When the Gallery was firmly established he and his wife, Agnes E. Meyer, gave several French

U.S.C.S. Hudson— New York Harbor. August 20. 1928

pictures to the permanent collection.)

Was it odd that Finley, a Southern Democrat, would serve a series of Republican administrations? Perhaps, but he honored more allegiances than he had names, and they were several. He was "Edward" to kin including a brother called "States" (as in States Rights Gist Finley, named for a grandfather killed in the Civil War). He was "David" to friends and peers. He was "Mr. Finley" to virtually everyone at the Gallery, including senior associates who held him in high respect. Only soldiers ever called him "Dave"—men like Eisenhower, and OSS's Wild Bill Donovan when they found common cause in proposing C. V. (Sonny) Whitney for membership in New York's Century Association, one of several exclusive clubs to which Finley belonged.

Finley's politics seem poly-partisan; he cultivated those in power. He wrote letters of congeniality and praise to every president from Roosevelt onward; he arranged to have at least one congressman's children admitted to a private Washington school. Nor were his attentions ignored; he had the gift for getting close to power. Traveling in Italy in 1927, he wrote "I have been everywhere and seen everyone, including both Mussolini and the Pope." As for Il Duce, then a white knight in America's eyes since Italy had been our World War I ally, "I was delighted, of course, to have an opportunity of talking with someone I admire so much," he told Mellon in a letter. "He asked particularly about you and sent you his regards. He gave me a signed photograph! which I told him I would put between yours and President Coolidge's."

In society Finley flew very high. FDR press aide Jonathan Daniels later wrote "Nothing indicated [Finley's] social place better than his marriage to a Eustis" in 1931. The wedding at Oatlands, the Eustis family's antebellum Virginia manor, got better play in Washington papers than the Japanese Ambassador's dinner for Charles A. Lindbergh and the presentation at court of Wallis Simpson, the Baltimore divorcee who became the Duchess of Windsor. Finley's bride, née Margaret Eustis, belonged to the Old Washington elite. Her mother, a New York socialite and friend of Franklin Roosevelt since Hyde Park childhood, became one of those who winked at his liaison with Lucy Mercer Rutherfurd. Daniels wrote that Mrs. Eustis arranged clandestine meetings at Oatlands for Lucy and the President. Perhaps she was just helping kin; Lucy was the widow of an old gentleman whose first wife had been Mrs. Eustis' sister, Alice.

Possessing influence and wealth, the Eustises were aristocrats of the Gilded Age. Margaret's mother, Edith, was one of five celebrated sisters who were both beautiful and intriguing enough to have inspired artist Charles Dana Gibson. Their Manhattan house had a ballroom that novelist Edith Wharton wrote about. Margaret's grandfather, Levi P. Morton, had been on his way to riches when the Civil War alienated his Southern creditors and ruined him. Yet he recovered and founded the bank that became

No less charming than husband David, Margaret Eustis Finley gets a grin from swashbuckler Douglas Fairbanks, Jr. on a movie set during a trip the Finleys take to Hollywood in the 1940s.

Guaranty Trust, then went into politics, serving as minister to France, as Benjamin Harrison's vice president, and as governor of New York. He was a likely GOP presidential nominee in 1896 before things were wrapped up for McKinley. Edith married William Corcoran Eustis, whose mother was the daughter of banker W. W. Corcoran, the federal city's "first philanthropist," a Southern sympathizer, and founder of the Corcoran Gallery in what is now the Renwick Gallery. Corcoran's grand residence at 1607 H Street overlooking Lafayette Square was one of Washington's celebrated homes, which had been occupied in turn by Daniel Webster and Henry Adams. That house was eventually razed to make way for the U.S. Chamber of Commerce; while Oatlands was given to the National Trust, which Finley chaired, and is now a National Historic Landmark.

So by marriage as well as by work and talent, Finley was well connected. Possessed of elegant manners and a tenor voice that sounded more Windsor than Carolina, he was enthusiastic,

ingratiating and famously persuasive. A decade after the National Gallery opened, the *Saturday Evening Post* wrote that he "has a very high opinion of millionaires.... Sometimes, when they don't have what Finley wants, they go out and buy it, just for the pleasure of handing it over to him." Lessing Rosenwald (for one) gave his incomparable collection of prints and drawings to the National Gallery "because of David Finley and only because of Finley," says a senior curator.

Designer, diplomat and orchestrator, Finley treated donors very well in many ways. When the first major post-Mellon gift was promised to the Gallery, he saw to it that the donor, Samuel H. Kress, got public thanks from the President—and a blizzard of publicity second only to the acclaim that Mellon had received. In offering his Italian collection, Kress explained:

I have followed with interest the establishment of the National Gallery of Art in Washington and the construction of the great edifice there.... I have also noted with pleasure the Nation-wide interest exhibited in this Gallery [which is] dedicated to the encouragement and development of the study of the fine arts.... Realizing what it would mean to the Gallery at its opening, I decided some months ago that if the arrangements of the gift were satisfactory I would

Finley's personal charm, diplomacy, and contacts win many early gifts for the Gallery, including these French pictures, given by his former boss, Federal Reserve Governor Eugene Meyer and his wife Agnes E. Meyer. Le Château Noir *came in 1958, seventeen years after the Gallery opened, as the first painting by Paul Cézanne to enter the collection.*

Paul Cézanne, *Still Life with Apples and Peaches,* c. 1905
Gift of Eugene and Agnes E. Meyer

Paul Cézanne, *Le Château Noir,* 1900/1904
Gift of Eugene and Agnes E. Meyer

give up the pleasure of having possession of the collection in my home, and arrange to consummate the gift so that rooms may be prepared for the placing of the objects of art for the opening of the Gallery.

The ever-hospitable director shows H. M. Queen Elizabeth The Queeen Mother through the Gallery in 1954.

Roosevelt replied in a fashion that flattered the donor and encouraged others:

Not only are the treasures you plan to bestow on the Nation incalculable in value and in interest, but in their bestowal you are giving an example which may well be followed by others of our countrymen.... I feel that your proposed donation is a decided step in the realization of the true purpose of the National Gallery.

This paved the way for the Trustees to boast of the implication of receiving the greatest collection of Italian art in private hands:

With Mr. Kress' collection and the paintings and sculpture donated by Mr. Mellon, the National Gallery will immediately become a center for the study of art in the United States, and one of the great galleries in the world.

Some in a position to know say Finley's influence upon the conception and development of the National Gallery of Art cannot be overstated. He was there at the creation as Andrew Mellon's aide, counsellor and companion. Then as his spiritual executor, Finley saw the unfinished Gallery building fully designed, deciding many details himself (with his wife's and friends' help) and opened to the public. As the museum's first director, he most faithfully perpetuated the founder's vision. He also set a number of precedents by taking a very active role in the affairs of official Washington, thus making it appear almost inevitable that he who runs the Gallery has a hand on the helm of culture in the Capital, for instance by chairing the Commission of Fine Arts. Finley himself also became the willing advisor of presidents (and First Ladies) in matters ranging from the provenance of a painting in the State Dining Room to preservation of the archi-

tecture around Lafayette Square.

As its director for eighteen years, Finley shaped the National Gallery though he was too modest to admit it. In his memoir of the Gallery, *A Standard of Excellence*, and in his personal papers, he almost always attributed every opinion or act to a superior, be it Mellon or, later, a trustee. Finley suggested that he was always simply carrying out a master's bidding. He was an avid churchman who served on the vestries of the little Virginia parish near Oatlands and Washington's St. John's, the "Church of the Presidents" on Lafayette Square. He was also a pillar of the National Cathedral, seat of the Episcopal diocese where Ailsa Mellon was married. Perhaps inevitably he was an elitist. Yet he limited the reach of his biases. In spite of his growing up in the segregated South, his National Gallery posted no color bars; in the 1940s its dining room was known as the one decent eating place in town where all people were welcome to partake of the homey fare.

On one occasion, an important dealer learned of Finley's "personal interest" in two important American paintings and wrote that his firm would "be happy to treat these as though they were a consideration by the Museum and favor you with a discount accordingly." Finley declined, pleading "so many other commitments of a more practical and pressing nature that I don't indulge myself in buying pictures just now." Perhaps that was true, or perhaps he didn't want those paintings, though this letter seems the gracious evasion of an insider's favor without giving offense. Two days after the 1968 election he wrote to Richard M. Nixon, "I cannot tell you how delighted my wife and I are that you are to be our next President.... I have retired as Director of the National Gallery, but am particularly interested in the newly established National Portrait Gallery.... It will have an added interest for me and for many people when your own portrait is there in the room of Presidential portraits." The commission that established the Portrait Gallery was one of the many boards on which Finley served. In addition to his career at the Gallery, he was a member of the Commission of Fine Arts for eight years and its chairman for an additional fourteen; chairman of the National Trust for Historic Preservation (which had its first meeting, on Finley's initiative, in the board room of the National Gallery, and which took as its headquarters the McCormick apartment house); chairman of the White House Historical Association; and a trustee of the Corcoran Gallery.

Letters that Finley received also reveal the measure of the man: "You have given me a surprise, in that most welcome and unexpected—unexpected, I mean, from anybody!—box of eggs.... I cannot remember when I last saw so many eggs at once." This from T. S. Eliot when food shortages still plagued post-war England. Then, after the Queen Mother came to Washington, Mamie Eisenhower thanked Finley "for coming in to assist me. It is wonderful to know that I may call on you again."

Finally, Finley made a faithful friend in Jacqueline Kennedy, helping her save Lafayette Square from architectural destruction and start-

ing the effort to make the White House a showcase of antique decor. Thus on hearing that he had resigned as chairman of the Commission of Fine Arts, Mrs. Kennedy wrote:

You have been such a marvelous and unselfish helper and your fantastic backing and loyalty are what gave me the courage to do all the things people said we were mad to attempt. The President told me you were the only person who stood by President Truman on his balcony problem. [When Truman wanted to build the balcony overlooking the South Lawn, architectural purists opposed it but Finley championed William A. Delano's unobtrusive solution.] This letter is really outside the realm of protocol or whatever governs official life—but I told Jack I was going to write you and he said yes, you must.... One thing you must *never* do is resign from the White House Historical Association! Please promise that.

In the summer of 1964 Mrs. Kennedy wrote to Finley again, this time to explain the symbolic gift she was sending:

This little gold box comes with a long story attached to it. President Kennedy was going to give you the Citation of Merit this last July 4. He had created it the year before—for people who had given great service to their country. All your years on the Fine Arts Commission ... all the wonderful things you did, and then your time ended during his term, which was sad for him. Because he so deeply appreciated all you had done to make his dream of what the White House should be come true—and all that you had done before. Your loyalty, your approval of his vision—all your help in those shining years—to ensure that the President's House would be forever what it should be.... When I finally collected my thoughts this winter—I felt so terribly that you would never receive the Citation from him—I thought of giving you the document, but it wouldn't have had his signature. So I had this little box made.... It comes with my devotion—and my great sadness that we could not have all been there together in the Rose Garden—his beloved Garden—to see you receive the Citation of Merit from President Kennedy. So please accept this poor substitute.

With love from Jacqueline Kennedy.

If Finley's appointment as the founding director was foreordained, so too were the kinds of choices he made in selecting blue-ribbon associates to organize and run the Gallery at the beginning. Building the staff of a new museum is like recruiting a cadre for a revolution: Start with people you know and let the word go forth. That seems to have been Mellon's approach when he approved the original slate of nominees for the Gallery's Board of Trustees. And it was certainly the approach that Finley followed. The executive officers, remember, were hired and paid from a private endowment by the trustees without federal oversight. As his immediate successor, John Walker, wrote, Mellon had

felt the selection of the most responsible officers should not be hampered by any mechanical standards established by the government. Certain qualities—charm, sophistication, savoir-faire—all of them important in carrying out our major objective, to snare collectors, he realized were not recognized by the bureaucrats who drafted the Civil Service regulations. This point of view helped to make possible the success of the National Gallery of Art, but it is also true that we were quite ignorant about museum management.

The only original executive with museum experience was Macgill James, who came aboard in 1940 as assistant director. He had been one of David Bruce's ushers, but more important he was director of the Peale Museum, formally the Municipal Museum of the City of Baltimore, and a product of the legendary museum training course at Harvard under Paul J. Sachs. Very social and a genuinely congenial man, he served as facilitator without portfolio. A star reporter for the *New York Times* showed up one day during the war and declared "I'm tired. I've just come from overseas. I need a drink." As a Gallery hand with a long memory remembers it,

"Macgill had been told, ordered like all of us, that there will be no alcohol in the National Gallery!" But putting things in perspective, he thereafter kept a bottle in his desk drawer so that "he could service … [journalists and] other people who felt the need of bolstering."

Also a gentle mediator, James was the sort who could persuade his superiors not to be hogtied by principle if it reflected past errors. For example, he came across a unique portrait of John James Audubon and recommended its purchase as a painting of rare historical value. The Board had reserved unto itself certain prerogatives, among them approval of all acquisitions whether by gift or purchase and changes in attributions. The trustees decided such matters after receiving staff recommendations, of course, but in fact they exercised these powers absolutely. When the Acquisitions Committee saw the Audubon likeness, Paul Mellon revealed that he had owned it. In fact it had hung over the mantel of his New York townhouse, until he tired of it and returned it to the dealer. By the time Macgill James came upon it, the portrait had changed hands untold times and its price had risen accordingly. He persuaded the Board to swallow hard and buy it back for "many times" what Mellon had cashed it in for. (In addition to a National Gallery of Art, Andrew Mellon believed that America should also have its own portrait gallery. Among the paintings in the Andrew W. Mellon collection given to the National Gallery were twenty portraits of important Americans. These were held for a future portrait gallery. In 1962 the Audubon and other works were transferred to the then newly-established National Portrait Gallery.)

Donald Shepard, at first Andrew Mellon's lawyer, had shared the Jackson Place office with Finley. He was an E&C trustee and an original Gallery trustee, then an executive employee as secretary, treasurer and general counsel. It was he who had written the draft charter, then negotiated it without giving an inch to the Justice Department so that the bill was presented to Congress virtually intact. His hand seems visible in the prose of the first annual report, published by the Smithsonian, which recorded solemnly that after the trustees elected officers and adopted bylaws on March 9, 1938, their first order of business was: "To cause to be established an appropriate accounting system, including provisions for the keeping of the necessary books and records, so that the works of art... and all funds, securities, and... other properties of whatsoever character belonging to or under the control of the Board and of such additions and receipts thereto and disposition, withdrawals and disbursements therefrom, may be properly recorded." (Such records soon revealed that the Gallery's initial artistic assets had cost "the last person to acquire the works of art by purchase" the aggregate sum of $31,303,162.31.)

Shepard's office in the new building was the most imposing corner suite, complete with a walk-in vault and a desk of such mighty dimensions as to make an emperor blush, an associate muttered. As one of Mellon's close aides, Shepard was more than a keeper of the flame; he was perhaps the most fierce protector of Gallery interests. As late as 1942, for example, he would write to David Bruce "One of the principal things to be guarded against, in my opinion is... as far as possible, the spending of Trust Funds when public funds are available." Mellon's endowment fund, eventually $10 million, was to buy art and pay executives; the government could honor its part of the bargain and fund the rest.

Shepard was also custodian of the Publications Fund, which was ordered to make avail-

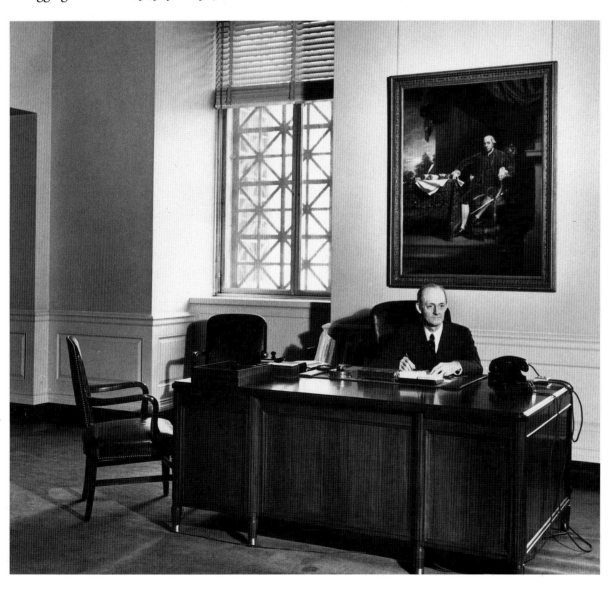

A man of few esthetic pretensions before he worked for Mellon, Finley runs the Gallery from a room that has all the charm of a passport office—save for a Copley portrait. That picture is part of a large selection of historically important American likenesses that the A. W. Mellon Educational and Charitable Trust transfers to the National Portrait Gallery which Congress finally establishes in 1962.

able at modest prices "catalogs, handbooks, color reproductions, postcards and similar material, of the highest quality... to the public for education and study purposes." Launched with an initial $40,000, the program would repay the loan with profits earned on sales in the "Card Room" and become a revolving fund that extended the Gallery's reach as visitors packed home first-class reproductions. The prints arguably improved decor around America and introduced millions to world-class art.

Finley's first administrator was Harry A. McBride, a former Foreign Service officer and bureaucrat who had been Assistant to the Secretary of State. Like many, his Gallery career would be interrupted by the war; he was tapped for a mission as President Roosevelt's "special representative" to Liberia. His first object, FDR ordered, was to secure the use "for belligerent purposes" of an essential air field as a way station for planes bound for "the battle front in various parts of the world." Familiar with the African nation, McBride was instructed to report also on "the presence of German agents on Liberian soil; the development and export of Liberian resources, including materials needed in the defense of the United States... road construction; and health conditions." He succeeded in his mission, evidently a competent agent provocateur.

Other early staff included Charles Seymour, an art historian at Yale, who became curator of sculpture. George T. Heckert was named assistant administrator. The chief engineer and building superintendent, Sterling P. Eagleton, had been the Carrier Corporation's unsung hero who installed the museum's cellar-to-attic air-conditioning system. The recruit of most lasting influence was John Walker. Lured to Washington from the American Academy in Rome, he would remain with the Gallery for the rest of his career and have only one promotion—from his original executive post as Chief Curator to the office of Director as Finley's successor. Thus his importance to the Gallery's life in its first three decades would be immense.

Walker was a Pittsburgh boy—"excessively affluent, but in other respects I was excessively normal," as he would write in his autobiography, *Self-Portrait with Donors*. A year older than Paul Mellon, he had grown up in the same circles though they had never been particularly close friends. Indeed their association might have proved more of a hindrance than a help to Walker after he let one of Andrew Mellon's cats out of a confidential bag: Paul was at Cambridge and John Walker in Florence working as a sort of secretary to Bernard Berenson, then the grayest eminence in the field of European art. Walker had written to Paul asking for a list of his father's Italian pictures to include in Berenson's newest book. Through some slip of the tongue or the pen, the final list that Berenson sent to the printer included Raphael's *Alba Madonna*, one of Andrew's Hermitage paintings—a secret purchase that was meant to remain secret. This earned Paul Mellon a stern caution from Finley about Walker's indiscretion along with explicit instructions about how to handle the matter. Then all was forgiven, and when it was time to find a chief curator, Walker got the nod—because he was a known quantity and admirably suited to the job.

Walker was born on Christmas Eve 1906, the son of a socially ambitious Christian Scientist who gambled and an amiable cynic who "preferred a sedentary life with a whiskey and soda close at hand." It was Mother who

gambled; this was her only vice. For the rest she believed in the finer things of life, which Father laughed at. These values she wished to pass on to me. My exaggerated compliance with her wishes proved a bitter disappointment. For example, she wanted me to marry into the local aristocracy; I chose instead the daughter of a British peer. She wanted me to be religious; I became a Catholic. She wanted me to like art; I devoted my life to it. She would have been so happy, she often said, if I had only settled down as a Pittsburgh lawyer and married the daughter of one of her friends. Cosmopolitanism, religion and culture were good things in their way, but Mother thought they could be overdone.

Father had gone to Princeton—but was expelled for leading a cow up to the roof of the president's house. Going home to Pittsburgh, he went to work for a family firm that sold fire brick for blast furnaces, branched out on his own, made a lot of money, which he spent, drove an Army ambulance "rather like Ernest Hemingway," and retired to his club leaving his wife a clubman's widow. "They ultimately divorced, which was unusual at the time. But he remained my hero. When he died I was seventeen. He left me all he had: a Patek Phillipe watch with my mother's picture in it and a silver cocktail shaker."

By then the lad (evidently enriched by other legacies) was a confirmed esthete and devoted to museums. Five years earlier he had contracted polio and recuperating in New York discovered the delights of the Metropolitan in his wheelchair.

It was not the beauty of the works of art I found exhilarating; it was the endless corridors where I could wheel myself about and enjoy the illusion of mobility. Those were the days before museum directors boosted their attendance by bringing in thousands of school children. On weekdays I would be there more or less alone, and there was nothing to tarnish the excitement of discovery. My curiosity about the works of art became increasingly intense, and the only way I could satisfy it was to read serious handbooks …. All my tedium and loneliness vanished. I had found my profession. I wanted to be a curator.

He found his first love there, "a blond girl in an empire dress; attributed to Jacques-Louis David, now to the infinitely lesser Constance Marie Charpentier." His adolescent experience proved that "the ideal way to visit a museum is in a wheel chair," he decided. "I insisted when the National Gallery opened that we purchase a large supply, and I tried to persuade our visitors to use them regardless of physical incapacity. My success was minimal … it takes moral fortitude to get into one."

Walker went to Harvard, and thrived. He

John Walker, the first chief curator and Finley's heir apparent, provides much of the Gallery's art expertise in the early years.

worked with Lincoln Kirstein on a journal that they modeled on T. S. Eliot's *Criterion.* "My contributions to the *Hound and Horn* were a number of book reviews written in a glutinous prose, but they were enough to gain me membership in the outer circle at least of the intellectual life of Harvard, which centered around Lincoln and his magazine." Then he joined up with Kirstein's Society for Contemporary Art, which opened a gallery on Harvard Square. Their dedication to the new vernacular was all the stronger because the lion of Harvard's art faculty "was as determined as Hitler to prevent the dissemination of what he considered decadent art." The Contemporary Art group received help from Chester and Maud Dale, also from Duncan Phillips, and thus introduced Walker to the world of great American collectors.

"My idea of the purpose of museums was unconsciously formulated in those early days at Harvard," Walker remembered.

I believed then and I still believe that they should be places of enjoyment and enlightenment. I am indifferent to their function in community relations, in solving racial problems, in propaganda for any cause.

In retirement with his wife at her family's heirloom estate, Oatlands plantation, David Finley carries on as Chairman of the National Trust for Historic Preservation. He has served the Gallery as director for eighteen years.

My beliefs were later reinforced when, after I graduated from Harvard, the faculty of the Department of Fine Arts sent me to Florence to work with Bernard Berenson, the great critic of Italian painting. The most passionate viewer of works of art I have ever known, he felt that museums existed primarily for the satisfaction of people like himself. I adopted the same philosophy: I was, and still am, an elitist, knowing full well that this is now an unfashionable attitude. It was my hope that through education … I might increase the minority I served; but I constantly preached an understanding and a respect for quality in works of art. I have been unchanging in my passionately held opinion that the success or failure of a museum is not to be measured by attendance but by the beauty of its collections and the harmony of their display.

Walker's time at Berenson's villa was a sojourn in paradise:

I soon had my desk in the library, and a little later the occupancy of a wisteria-covered *villino* in an adjacent olive grove. The happiness of those years is impossible to convey. Daily life had a routine. After a leisurely breakfast before a fire in winter, or on the terrace of my *villino* in other seasons, I would walk the few hundred yards to I Tatti [Berenson's house]. Then would follow two hours of solid work, writing one's own articles or helping B.B. with his catalogue of Florentine drawings. At eleven he would appear in the library, ready for a walk in the garden …. It is difficult to say what my role in the household was. I was certainly a pupil, though I received no formal instruction; I was something of a research assistant, though my undergraduate education had given me very little preparation for the high level of scholarship required; and I was undoubtedly a disciple, eagerly absorbing some of the most brilliant conversation of our time.

After three years at I Tatti, Walker moved on to the American Academy in Rome where he taught (and studied) the fine arts, continued to write essays in order to build a scholarly reputation, and kept in close touch with Berenson. It

was there that he married Margaret Drummond, the titled eldest daughter of the British Ambassador, and from there that he wrote Paul Mellon to inquire about working for his father's museum in Washington. Having spent four years in Rome, he was confirmed by the trustees as Chief Curator in the summer of 1938. The timing was fortuitous, as a major gift of Italian art was then hanging in the balance.

John Walker returned to Italy at about the time that the Gallery trustees and Samuel Kress were having second thoughts about the likely gift of Kress' great collection of Italian art (of which more anon). Finishing out his term at the American Academy and wrapping up his affairs, Walker inevitably went to I Tatti. Berenson had just received a thousand photographs of Kress possessions and was assigning attributions to them. Walker spent days studying the objects, Berenson's opinions of them, and the opinions of other respected scholars. "Never in my life have I worked so hard as I did those few days," Walker said. "I memorized the attribution given by each expert to every painting and sculpture. Before I left for America I was letter-perfect."

Landing in New York he visited Kress, who was wavering as to whether to give his art to the Gallery or the Metropolitan or to found a museum of his own. He led Walker and Finley a merry chase through his collection, asking their opinion of every work in the apartment and his offices downtown. Fresh from his I Tatti tutorial Walker could say, "I believe, Mr. Kress, Berenson would attribute it to so-and-so. However I don't doubt that Van Marle would disagree and ascribe it to such-and-such. Probably Longhi and Perkins would go along with Van Marle." By the time this virtuoso performance was done, "Sam Kress had become less dubious about the collection going to Washington, though as we left David Finley whispered to me that he had the look of a man who had just married off his daughters" to men of uncertain reputations. "Perhaps he suspected I was cheating in some way he couldn't quite understand." ❧

Aging director David Finley still uses a steel-nibbed pen to sign gracious epistles and such.

The Brothers Kress:
Following the Leader

Samuel H. Kress was the first to heed Andrew Mellon's call for men of means (and great collections) to augment his gift with pictures worthy of a truly national gallery. Though they may have never met, these two had much in common, as both sprang from the same soil, harnessed the same kind of drive and rode the same laissez-faire economy to rich success. If Kress never amassed Mellon's enormous fortune, he improved his personal lot by a like factor since he started out nearer the bottom of the heap. Nor was he a financial genius like Mellon who bestrode several industrial realms. Sam Kress was not a banker, he was a merchant and not even a dealer in great goods. Rather, Kress made a fortune literally in nickels and dimes, the profits of five-, ten-cent and twenty-five-cent stores—a chain that grew from a single shop in

Pennsylvania until it spanned the continent and even leapt to Hawaii. His career might have been inspired by Horatio Alger.

Sam Kress was born of old Pennsylvania Dutch stock in the tiny town of Cherryville in eastern Pennsylvania in 1863 and named for an uncle killed at Gettysburg three weeks earlier. The oldest of a large brood, he tried all kinds of work—clerking, hawking newspapers, quarrying slate—before passing a teacher's exam and starting to teach school at the age of seventeen for the living wage of $25 a month. In seven years he saved enough to buy a notions shop forty miles up the road in Nanticoke and three years after that a wholesale stationery store in bustling Wilkes-Barre. By 1890 he saw the future in small-scale retailing in the South and opened a five-and-dime in Memphis. Genius lay in the new-found idea of finding out what simple items people wanted and offering a variety under one roof rather than settling for what manufacturers happened to supply. As a journalist explained decades later, "Kress's fortune was made, not from exploitation of the poor, but by selling to everyone of us those small things that made life easier: can openers, razor blades, pencils, flower pots, kitchenware—infinite numbers of gadgets found all in one place for our convenience."

Within four years S. H. Kress & Company had stores in a dozen southern cities, and the founder's brothers, Claude and Rush (who studied business in college), had joined the enterprise. In short order, they abandoned Pennsylvania and moved to New York, whence they would direct coast-to-coast operations of around 250 stores and employ 20,000 people from headquarters downtown on Fifth Avenue. Sam, a bachelor, took up residence in a triplex penthouse farther up Fifth across from the Metropolitan Museum and there led the life of an urbane gentleman. Descended through both parents from patriots who served in the Revolution, he joined the Sons of the American Revolution, the Military Order of the Loyal Legion, and the Masons. A lifelong member of

the Lutheran Church and the Republican Party, he did what all tycoons were doing: traveled abroad, but entering his fifties found exotic European vacations boring. John Walker, who came to know him well, later wrote that "a very clever and attractive lady" who accompanied him on these trips "soon recognized that she would have to find an antidote for his ennui or be poisoned with it herself."

The lady won Kress an introduction to Count Alessandro Contini-Bonacossi, an elegant, intelligent and well-connected Florentine connoisseur. Kress thought him the epitome of continental aristocracy and always addressed him by his title, which had been recently conferred by the King; he was also a senator, an art collector and a dealer. The Count introduced Kress to art, and as he found a new purpose in his de rigueur holidays, the ever energetic retailer began collecting with the determination that had brought such success in the notions business. "To his credit," Kenneth Clark wrote decades later, Contini-Bonacossi "did not sell him forged or repainted 'masterpieces' but a great many quite decent small pictures by minor Italian painters of the quattrocento." He also introduced him to Berenson, to the literature of Italian art, and to the mysteries of provenance in Renaissance painting, or at least to the scholarly debates among experts that influenced prices. Once there were dollars at stake, Kress was hooked.

By the late 1920s he was an Italophile. He supported architectural restoration by funding the rebuilding of several buildings: the ducal palace in Mantua, the Church of St. John the Evangelist in Ravenna, the Basilica of Santa Eufemia at Spoleto and the surviving remnant of the Temple of Hera on the toe of the Italian boot. Receiving solemn thanks from Mussolini, Kress scotched the rumor that he'd given $1 million: "I don't want so much more credit than I deserve," he said with the kind of book-balancing precision that was one key element in his character. The King made him a Grand Officer of the Order of the Crown when he gave

another gift, this one barely in five figures.

Kress concentrated on neglected Italian painters, realizing that the cream of more popular French and old master schools had been skimmed by established collectors, including Mellon. He had, initially, no intention of joining the herd, and thus bought principally from dealers abroad. Pointedly, it was not until after Andrew Mellon's

death that he became Joseph Duveen's most important customer, often buying art as he bought combs and safety pins and bars of soap: in large lots. The dealer, who usually let a client consider only one picture at a time found it profitable to show Kress many at once. Duveen's biographer, S. N. Behrman, wrote that Kress "got more pleasure out of haggling over a picture's price than he did out of owning it. He

While he intends to establish his own museum, Kress enjoys his art—the Titians et al., in his otherworldly Fifth Avenue apartment— a residence done up in what John Walker calls "New York Renaissance."

A sitting room boasts leaded windows, overstuffed chairs and Madonnas by Gentile da Fabriano and Pietro Perugino. The hall features a large Coronation of the Virgin *by Agnolo Gaddi beside the stair.*

bought art on such a scale that when someone asked where a certain picture was, all he could say was that he thought it was in 'that third lot that came from Duveen.'"

Kress furnished his palatial apartment in what John Walker dismissed as "New York Renaissance," crowding the walls with pictures. Dealers visiting the penthouse learned to have the cab driver (or chauffeur) drop them a block away so that Sam—who watched eagle-eyed from his window—would think them frugal. He had not amassed a fortune out of small change by encouraging extravagance among his suppliers. But when it came to sharing his wealth, he was extravagant, establishing in 1929 a foundation that would give some $100 million to a variety of museums, colleges and medical causes. "The money came from the public and this is being done for the public," as Rush Kress said in his brother's name when distributing one huge gift in particular—a wealth of art to twenty-one regional museums in cities where S. H. Kress stores had prospered.

For decades Sam Kress the collector cosseted his passion for precious "items" as he called them—paintings, altarpieces, Renaissance bronzes. Kress the shopkeeper gave front-window treatment to one of them, the so-called

Allendale Nativity, or *Adoration of the Shepherds.* Variously attributed to Giorgione, Titian and Bellini, this was the painting that brought about the split between Duveen and his august consultant Bernard Berenson, to whom he had paid a substantial retainer for decades. Duveen told Berenson he had paid $300,000 for the *Adoration,* and he wanted the connoisseur to endorse its attribution to Giorgione, the Venetian master who revolutionized Renaissance painting and died young, leaving a very small and very precious *oeuvre.* But Berenson at the time believed it to be the work of Giorgione's pupil, Titian,

Giorgione, *The Adoration of the Shepherds,* c. 1505/1510

who lived to a ripe old age and with the help of a busy workshop left so many works that they commanded lesser prices. B.B. wouldn't budge in his opinion then—though years later he changed his mind to say that Giorgione started the work and Titian finished it. Kress, accepting the opinion of other experts, bought it as a Giorgione and weeks later he hung the new work in the window of his flagship Fifth Avenue store for the enjoyment of Christmas passersby. It became a shoppers' icon, as much a seasonal attraction as the lighted evergreen towering over Prometheus' gilded statue at nearby Rockefeller Center—until Kress surprised even himself and bestowed the painting on the National Gallery.

He had long intended to house his collection in a museum he would build along the lines of the Frick Collection. He had amassed his collection with so little fanfare (save in the *Adoration*'s display) that David Finley heard about the wealth of his holdings almost by happenstance. Two Washington friends, who had a passion for visiting private collections, saw the apartment and urged Finley to meet Kress in order to tell him about the nascent National Gallery. John Walker later ascribed to Finley the coup in getting Kress to abandon his plans for a New York museum:

Mr. Kress and Mr. Finley had met once on shipboard, though with characteristic modesty Samuel Kress had scarcely mentioned his collection. When [Finley] . . . saw what his steamship companion had brought together, he realized the collection must be procured for Washington. He had arrived at three in the afternoon; he left at ten in the evening. During those seven hours, with his inimitable powers of persuasion, he induced Samuel Kress to give up his plan for a private museum, for which property was already under option and architectural drawings prepared, and send the works of art instead to the National Gallery. Had David Finley not arrived when he did, the Kress Collection would have remained on Fifth Avenue in its own building.

So wrote Walker nearly forty years after the fact in a tome describing the Gallery's collections. But evidently there was more to it. For one thing there was Walker's bravura performance on returning from I Tatti. Secondly, there was Kenneth Clark's experience which he recalled in a review of Walker's massive book on the Gallery's collections.

Clark, then director of London's National Gallery, on a New York trip had gone to Kress' apartment to see his Italian paintings:

After I had praised them quite sincerely, because I found them historically interesting, Mr. Kress led me into his bathroom and locked the door, What should he do with them? Make a private museum or give them to the National Gallery? I had no hesitation in saying that he should give them to the National Gallery. Very few private collections of old masters, perhaps only the Wallace Collection and the Frick, stand on their own feet. Mr. Kress was pleased with

182

my advice, but when he put the proposition to John Walker it caused serious embarrassment.

The problem arose because the charter that Mellon's associates had composed, and that Congress had granted with slight amendments, ultimately contained an important caveat: "No work of art shall be included in the Permanent Collection of the National Gallery of Art unless it be of similar high standard of quality to those in the Collection acquired from the donor," that is, Mellon via the E&C Trust. Yet in his collecting that amassed something on the order of 1,300 canvases and panels, Kress had inevitably acquired a number of images of distinctly lesser quality—along with landmark works by Giotto, Duccio, Sassetta, Fra Angelico, Bellini, Giorgione, Titian, Tintoretto and others, to say nothing of sculpture by Desiderio da Settignano, Luca and Andrea della Robbia, Verrocchio and others. Indeed, thanks to Contini-Bonacossi's initial influence, Kress' collection comprised a definitive survey of Italian art from the fourteenth century to the eighteenth. Along with dross, it had choice examples of every important artist, every turning point and new influence. Beyond being so comprehensive, it was regarded as the most important collection of Italian art in private hands. But what to do about the lesser works?

This was the first offer of a major collection that the Gallery had received and its acceptance (or refusal) would set precedents for years to come. In a number of items—the *Allendale Nativity* for example—Kress' gift was the perfect response to Mellon's challenge to great American collectors. Among his vast holdings were paintings absolutely worthy of joining Mellon's to enhance the building (which was still under construction) and to establish the Gallery's reputation as the national showcase of European art. Nor would it do to ask Kress to keep some of the works; he had made clear to David Finley that his offer was a package deal, all or nothing. As the staff struggled with the dilemma, it fell to John Walker, the young chief curator, to declare

Rush Kress (opposite), the founder's younger brother and long-time business associate, succeeds Sam— both as head of the family's charitable foundation and as a Gallery trustee. The manifold Kress gifts to the Gallery eventually include nine pictures by Giovanni Bellini, the great Venetian *portrait painter and innovator. Early to use the new oil paints introduced from Northern Europe, he also adapts the three-quarter pose which allows more characterization than a profile. Witness this signed likeness in the new style.*

Leopold Seyffert, *Rush Harrison Kress,* 1953
Samuel H. Kress Collection

Giovanni Bellini, *Portrait of a Venetian Gentleman,* c. 1500
Samuel H. Kress Collection

Sam Kress buys pictures
of every Italian period and
school, especially those that
seem to mark new direc-
tions, such as a lush nude by
a sixteenth-century Vene-
tian whose work anticipates
the baroque style.

Jacopo Tintoretto and
Studio, *Susanna*, c. 1575
Samuel H. Kress Collection

in an affidavit to Congress that Kress' works were up to Mellon's standard. To say he had second thoughts is to mince words. As Walker wrote in his memoirs, "I had no choice. I had to lie." In order to get the gold, he certified the pinchbeck as twenty-four-karat. In *Self-Portrait with Donors—Confessions of an Art Collector,* Walker wrote,

Andrew Mellon had acquired two or three weak paintings, which were as undistinguished as anything in the Kress Collection. Couldn't one argue, bearing these Mellon duds in mind, that the Kress works of art were of a similar high standard of quality to (*some of*) "those in the collection acquired from the donor"? With this rationalization, which still makes me shudder, I signed the affidavit and put myself on record that the Kress gift met Andrew Mellon's stipulations.

However duplicitous the deed, it was fortuitous, because a policy evolved that honored Mellon's intent: Sam Kress, who became president of the Gallery, continued buying important works and donating them. As he did so, better examples of the Italian masters entered the collections to replace lesser ones, which were then sold or consigned to study collections. In any case, when the Gallery opened it possessed 375 paintings and eighteen pieces of sculpture given by Samuel H. Kress.

Sad to say, in 1946 he suffered a paralytic stroke that left him a speechless invalid for the last nine years of his life. At that point his brother Rush, some fifteen years his junior, succeeded him in the retail company and as president of the Samuel H. Kress Foundation, which he spurred on to even greater activity in buying art and serving philanthropy. Rush, who was later elected to the Gallery's board of trustees, was a family man and one of wider interests. Reflecting this (and the suggestions of John Walker) under his guidance the Foundation abandoned its concentration on Italian art and bought widely in other schools as well. It also made gifts to a number of regional and university museums, notably in cities where Kress stores

had prospered. But the Gallery got first pick of their superb collection.

Thus it was thanks to the brothers Kress and their foundation that the Gallery ultimately received 1,401 Renaissance bronzes and works of sculpture and some 379 pictures including the *Allendale Nativity,* El Greco's *Laocoön, Mary, Queen of Heaven* by the Flemish Master of the Saint Lucy Legend, David's portrait of Napoleon, *Adoration of the Magi* by Fra Angelico and Fra Filippo Lippi, Giotto's *Madonna and Child,* Grünewald's *Small Crucifixion,* the only painting in America by this German Renaissance master, and many, many others. The Kress Foundation has continued to benefit the Gallery in intangible ways as well by having established fellowships for scholars, given funds for book and photograph purchases for the library, and having introduced its own guiding light, physician and businessman Dr. Franklin Murphy, into the Gallery circle. Eventually he became Board Chairman.

Summing up the importance of the broad distribution of pictures, a writer mused:

During the past half-century capitalistic America has heard many hard things said about it. It has been

Challenged in Rome by the Vatican's famed statuary group Laocoön, *could El Greco have painted the mythological scene in order to prove the superiority of paint over marble? So suggests John Walker of this unique picture in the Kress Collection—the only surviving pagan subject painted during the Spanish Inquisition.*

El Greco (Domenikos Theotokopoulos), *Laocoön,* c. 1610/1614
Samuel H. Kress Collection

Under Rush's direction, Kress Collection paintings range far beyond Italy: the Flemish altarpiece of Mary amid celestial musicians comes from a Spanish convent; the Crucifixion is one of only a dozen paintings ascribed to the provocative German, Mathis Grüne- wald, and his only work in America; Jacques-Louis David's flattery of Napo- leon approaches mercenary unction; and Dürer paints his Madonna in the style of

Giovanni Bellini after the German master makes a visit to Venice.

Master of the Saint Lucy Legend, *Mary, Queen of Heaven,* c. 1485/1500
Samuel H. Kress Collection

Jacques-Louis David, *Napoleon in His Study,* 1812
Samuel H. Kress Collection

Mathis Grünewald, *The Small Crucifixion,* c. 1511/1520
Samuel H. Kress Collection

Albrecht Dürer, *Madonna and Child,* c. 1496/1499
Samuel H. Kress Collection

Giotto's tender icon reveals a new humanity in medieval thought as the Christ Child trustingly grasps his mother's index finger to steady himself.

Giotto, *Madonna and Child,* probably c. 1320/1330

This lavish collaboration by two monks, inspires a generation of Florentine artists to imitate its vitality. A Medici inventory lists a tondo of this dimension and subject as the most expensive of Lorenzo the Magnificent's paintings.

Fra Angelico and Filippo Lippi, *The Adoration of the Magi*, c. 1445
Samuel H. Kress Collection

fashionable in some quarters to abuse the American man of wealth as an uncultivated materialist given to throwing both his money and his weight around. We need to remember that never before in history have so many men of wealth devoted such vast sums to the public interest. America offered poor men opportunities, and many of them, having accumulated fortunes, returned some or all of their accumulations to the Nation. Samuel H. Kress is a typical example of this tradition of success and generosity....

It was Kenneth Clark, however, who put

Sam Kress' beneficent pursuits in cultural perspective: "There can be no doubt that this is one of the most remarkable collections of fourteenth- and fifteenth-century Italian art ever formed. It is very comprehensive, containing masters hardly represented in any other American collection; and Mr. Kress has managed to assemble a number of real masterpieces of a kind one had supposed no longer available." And having amassed such visual riches by serving as masterful merchant to the American people, he repaid the people in the coin of art. ❧

The Wideners'
Most Manifold Gift

ere the Wideners the first to meet Mellon's

challenge of supporting a national museum? Samuel Kress' gift arrived three years earlier, but

President Roosevelt gave the Wideners equal billing when accepting the National Gallery for the

nation. Call it a photo finish, the kind of victory favored by Joseph Widener who was better known

John Singer Sargent's mas-   by the general public for owning Hialeah racetrack than for his superb connoisseurship and
terful brush captures Peter
A. B. Widener, a butcher   patronage of art.
boy who made good. He
switched from selling mut-   His late father, Philadelphia multi-millionaire Peter A. B. Widener, had held the idea of a
ton to running streetcars
and amassed the largest   national museum close to his heart. Joseph, first, last and always the keeper of his father's flame, was a
fortune Philadelphia had
ever seen. This in turn   Mellon friend and the two evidently discussed a national museum to the point of debating its artistic
sustained an art collection
worthy of complementing   ken. Mellon meant the nation's art gallery to contain only masterpiece paintings, like its London
Andrew Mellon's in the
new National Gallery.   model, while Widener insisted on including the decorative arts, which his father and he collected as

well. Apparently they debated back and forth, and one source hints at plans for a final meeting to work out an agreement in 1937. But Joseph Widener went straight home to Philadelphia after the Florida racing season that spring without stopping en route to see Mellon, who died before summer's end. His heirs then took a different tack, and four years later FDR honored both Widener and Kress as "those other collectors... who have already joined, or who propose to join, their works of art to Mr. Mellon's." But the Widener art remained in Pennsylvania, tethered by a legal argument, and when it finally came to Washington, the end of an era was at hand.

Peter A. B. Widener started out as a butcher's

boy, and by the time of the Civil War had a sound enough business—and strong enough political friends—to win the contract to supply all the mutton to Union troops within ten miles of Philadelphia. In tune with his times, "Grandfather must have been very unscrupulous in many of his business methods," opined Joseph's son P. A. B. Widener (called by his second name Arrell) three score years later. Anticipating the city's growth after the war, Peter switched from meat to horse cars and made an enormous fortune in "traction" (public transportation). Like Mellon he began collecting art in the 1880s, buying lavishly if not always with perfect discrimination. As critic Aline Saarinen has written, he was one of a generation of ambitious rivals bent on pursuing "... High Art. They

John Singer Sargent, *Peter A. B. Widener,* 1902

Built by Peter Widener on a three-hundred-acre estate, Lynnewood Hall transplants the ideal of the English country seat and bests most of them in its furnishings and art. Completed in 1900, it is altered frequently, for example with the addition of statuary in the pediment as a memorial to two Wideners who went down with the Titanic *in 1912.*

sought Great Names and paid Great Prices, but undeniably they acquired Great Pictures" along with some less than great. And they nursed Great Grudges. When Joseph, a director of the Philadelphia Museum of Art, was entrusted with a certain sum to buy the best picture he could find for the money, he bought one of Cézanne's *Bathers.* Another Philadelphia art collector, the eccentric Dr. Albert Barnes, roared his contempt at the choice in the press. Later, crossing the Atlantic on the *Normandie,* the two men found themselves assigned to adjacent deckchairs. They sat in them daily—and did not speak on the entire voyage.

Snubbed by Philadelphia society, Peter had

come to lord it over more gentle-born folk. By 1900 he finished building Lynnewood Hall, which "can, I suppose, be called the last of the American Versailles" Arrell mused in his memoir, *Without Drums.* Set on three-hundred acres in suburban Elkins Park, the house

stood there, solid and aloof, a vast pile of limestone, shaped like a split cross. It resembled pictures of museums and Greek temples I had seen in Father's art books. Tall, Corinthian columns arose two stories high before the entrance. Two long wings jutted out on each side from the columned entrance. In the west wing were the apartments of my grandfather and of my parents and myself…. In the east wing

At Lynnewood Hall son Joseph Widener creates this series of intimate galleries out of the single vast exhibition space that his father, Peter, modeled on European examples. The handsome doorway itself, with its half-round pediment, is then copied in the National Gallery for some of the rooms designed to receive Widener's Italian sculpture.

were the rooms of my aunt and uncle and [cousins] Dimple and George.

(As a man, Arrell could look back in candor: "I supposed every little boy had a pony, a French governess, an English nurse, red satin quilts on his bed, a house as big as a palace with servants more numerous than the whole family, third and fourth generations thrown in." But of course not every little boy's grandfather died leaving the biggest estate in the history of the City of Brotherly Love.)

A third wing extending "directly behind the flank of columns" contained art galleries "where every guest was led… on a sort of glorified

Lynnewood Hall has this vestibule with its Raphaelesque ceiling as well as a special room for Bellini's Feast of the Gods. *Such amenities are created by Joseph Widener (right), a famous horseman yet even more distinguished as a discriminating collector.*

Cook's tour before final departure." Lynnewood Hall was a museum, open to the public daily from October to June for twenty-five years. Year-round it was open to visiting royalty and people with proper introductions from cognoscenti like Duveen, who sent down clients to see what money had bought. (More often Duveen sent trucks of objects so that Widener money could buy even more.) In Lynnewood Hall were the chalice made for Abbot Suger of St. Denis, the peerless Mazarin tapestry, a singular array of Chinese porcelains and rooms full of antique European furniture as well as pictures and sculpture. There were two John Singer Sargent portraits, one of Peter in his patriarchal prime, the other of Joseph's wife, née Ella Pancoast, the socialite who married into a family that had once been *not* invited to the major society ball, a snub that some say the Wideners never forgot.

At one time Lynnewood Hall had fourteen

Rembrandts including the 1650 *Self-Portrait* and *The Mill* which a mad visitor attacked with a hatpin. It also had: Van Dyck's *Marchesa Elena Grimaldi* which had been smuggled out of Italy; two marble sculptures attributed to Donatello that the Italian government allowed the Wideners to export in return for the gift of another Donatello to a Florentine museum. There were Vermeer's *Woman Holding a Balance,* Titian's *Venus and Adonis,* and Raphael's *Small Cowper Madonna.* There were walls of English pictures, including a pair of Turners that Joseph bought at a price his father thought outlandish, though cabling him to "use your own judgement" which proved sound indeed. And there was Bellini's *Feast of the Gods* displayed in a circular stone room that Joseph built especially for

it, a chamber with "hidden jewel cases...which are never opened until after the visitor has had time to inspect the Bellini," the grandson confided. "Then, as he is about to leave, the jewel cabinets are opened. There against white velvet backgrounds hang fabulous jewels wrought by Benvenuto Cellini, fitting companions for the great Italian picture."

The two elder Wideners had been, in Arrell's eyes "modern Marco Polos, journeying together to the ends of the earth in search of aesthetic pleasure." Even the central wing of Lynnewood Hall proved it:

Crystal chandeliers patterned after those at Versailles spilled light down the red plush carpeting of the marble staircase, which led from the gallery where we

The raucous humor in Jan Steen's genre scene of merry-making peasants disguises an allegory of the five senses: the taste of food, aroma of tobacco, sight of soap bubbles, sound of flute and violin, and the dancing couple's touch.

Jan Steen, *The Dancing Couple,* 1663
Widener Collection

At the Gallery, the Wideners' select grouping of eighteenth-century French furniture is installed in a suite of rooms especially designed to complement the quality of the pieces, twelve of which are signed by court cabinetmakers.

One of the rarest objets d'art surviving from the Middle Ages, this chalice celebrated the Mass for centuries at Saint-Denis, the royal abbey where French princes are educated and French kings are buried. In the Gallery, it dominates an installation of the Wideners' liturgical arts, a room the staff affectionately dubs the "Treasury."

French, *Chalice of the Abbot Suger of Saint-Denis*, c. 1140
Widener Collection

hid [as children watching great gentlemen and ladies arrive in evening dress for grand repasts]. Red velvet draperies embroidered in gold hung at the many exits from the hall. Fat Chinese lamps stood about on numerous tabourets. Porcelain urns as tall as a man were ornate sentinels stationed here and there. Oriental and animal skin rugs were scattered across the marble floor. There was one gem, at least, concealed within the clutter of the hall. This was a white hawthorne vase from China. It stood upon an ornate carved animal pedestal, a lonely vestal in a Victorian shrine... the only one in the world to have been royally feted.... When it originally left the Orient great men of China attended a farewell dinner held in its honor.

This for Arrell and his generation was "the most untouchable of all the untouchables in the house."

Joseph hoped the country palace might be deemed an American Wallace Collection. He refined and improved P.A.B.'s collections, weeding out the lesser of his father's five hundred pictures while making notable purchases of his own—*The Mill* was one—thus reducing the lot to about a hundred first-class pictures and raising the collection to a new level of grandeur. Edith Standen, who tended the collection for the last dozen years of Joseph's life, remembers his criterion when culling the collection: "'If the

painter had only done this one picture would he be as famous as he is?' If the answer was no, then the picture would go.... Mr. Joseph Widener really loved and enjoyed his works of art," Ms. Standen asserted to a Gallery oral history interviewer. "When he was at home he did a great deal of taking his own visitors through the gallery and he loved talking about his works of art.... He had a real understanding...for the things that he had."

"He was perfectly convinced that there was no good painting after Renoir," says Standen. He had Degas' *The Races* and *Before the Ballet*, and Manet's *Dead Toreador* and kings' ransoms in old masters. Further, he insisted that every

treasure be fastidiously displayed. "Everything was to the last quarter of an inch the way he wanted it." Widener was an elegant and scrupulous man, and his household reflected his demeanor, a palace transplanted from somewhere between Albion and Elysium. Masden, a butler so proud that he insisted on the title of steward, found himself above speaking to the housekeeper; thus he sent her messages via footmen and she replied by way of the housemaids. Even the French chef was grand, a collector of antique firearms. Lynnewood Hall was so exalted that it was hardly touched by the De-

pression, and when it did feel the pinch, the company of twenty-some gardeners was reduced by half a dozen.

David Finley coveted the exalted Widener Collection for the Gallery and with the trustees' approval went great lengths to secure it, while Joseph Widener stood firm in supporting his father's vision: The cream of Widener art in every medium and genre would go to one museum. As in Kress' case, it was all or nothing. To get *The Mill* and *The Feast of the Gods,* they'd have to take the china, and the refectory table,

and the Savonarola chairs. In the winter of 1937 Finley and David Bruce presented themselves at Lynnewood Hall. The following year it was Finley and Paul Mellon who came away from a luncheon with a proposal for the trustees: Temper the founder's exclusion of decorative arts by installing the Widener porcelains, furniture et al in the segregated glory of galleries on the ground floor apart from the permanent collection. The trustees agreed, and Finley could almost taste success as he augmented his considerable persuasive skills with Otto Eggers' artifice.

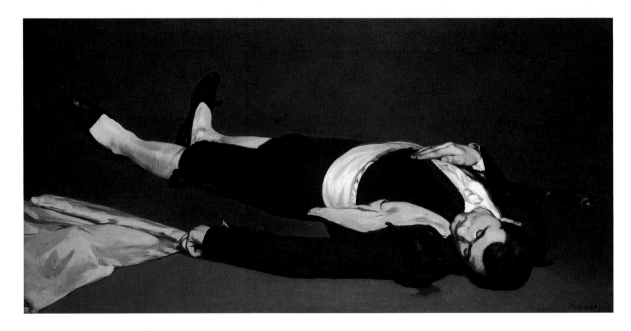

The Wideners' catholic taste encompasses a stormy British seascape and Dutch portraits as well as this Spanish genre scene of uncertain content. While some scholars think it portrays Galician doxies, Joseph Widener prefers the title A Girl and Her Duenna.

Joseph Mallord William Turner, *The Junction of the Thames and the Medway,* c. 1805/1808
Widener Collection

Bartolomé Esteban Murillo, *Two Women at a Window,* c. 1670
Widener Collection

Rembrandt van Rijn, *Portrait of a Lady with an Ostrich-Feather Fan,* c. 1660
Widener Collection

The Triumph of Christ, *woven at the incredibly detailed density of twenty-two warps per inch, is acknowledged as the finest medieval tapestry still extant. It acquires the name "Mazarin Tapestry" from a former owner, Cardinal Mazarin, who considered it his prize possession, as do the Wideners. In the Gallery, the thirteen-foot-long textile hangs in a hall of medieval and Renaissance decorative arts.*

The director instructed John Russell Pope's peerless draftsman to draw color renderings of the ground floor rooms finished to resemble the Lynnewood Hall galleries with Widener's favorite pieces ensconced: the Suger chalice, the Mazarin tapestry, the furniture, the bronzes, the perfect Chinese ceramics. When Widener saw the drawings, Finley reported, "his eyes filled with tears. 'If you will do this for my porcelains,' he said, 'you can have everything else and I will ask no questions.'"

Now that might be too good to be true, but Finley thought he had himself a deal in the making even though he knew that more diplomacy would be required. When Paul Mellon's departure in 1939 left a vacancy on the board, the trustees elected Joseph to fill it. Peter Widener's will called for even his paintings collection to

remain of a piece; but now it was Joseph's turn to concede a small point. Finley told him honestly that he had declined Sam Kress' similar request to segregate his collection because it violated the founder's vision and the trustee's considered policy. A compromise had been reached by planning the layout of the galleries in chronological order room by room if not picture by picture. Kress' Venetian art would be displayed in rooms adjacent to rooms of other people's Titians and Bellinis. So, too, Widener agreed to let his Rembrandts hang in rooms next to other Dutch masters, and his British peers next to rooms of Mellon's Raeburns and Romneys.

At about that time, Finley wrote, a number of interior design matters were being ironed out: the height of gallery ceilings at twenty-one feet, the choices of wall treatments to harmonize with

the art in each gallery—oak paneling for the northern baroque, travertine marble detailing for the quattrocento, complex cornices with egg-and-dart moldings for the Georgian suites, and so on. Widener, on a visit to Washington, came to inspect the rooms his pictures would fill, and seemed to agree to the arrangements. But next morning he phoned from his horse farm in Kentucky: "I have been thinking about things since I left you and I have changed my mind," he told Finley, who suddenly felt himself aging years in as many seconds. "I thought those cor-

nices ought to be a little deeper—say six inches." "You couldn't be more right," the director replied. "Would you like them to be twelve inches deeper?"

The rooms, so much like Lynnewood Hall's, were finished to Widener's satisfaction—especially a round, vaulted gallery off the West Garden Court designed for a presumed Donatello marble, *The David of the Casa Martelli,* of which Widener was exceptionally proud. But the state of Pennsylvania threw the entire matter of the Widener gift into legal limbo. Perhaps still chafing at the loss of

Netherlandish, *The Mazarin Tapestry with The Triumph of Christ,* c. 1500
Widener Collection

The Wideners' Most Manifold Gift   201

Mellon's art (or simply once bitten, twice shy), the Commonwealth meant to keep its magnates' collections at home, or get a pound of fiscal flesh. This despite the fact that President Roosevelt had publicly identified Widener as a major donor when the Gallery opened.

Peter, who died in 1915, had left control of the collection (but not legal title) to his son with binding and cogent restrictions: First, he could sell the art to enrich the estate if he chose, or he could give the art to any museum "now or here-after established" in Philadelphia, New York or Washington. But the entire manifold gift must be kept intact, and the estate could pay no inheritance taxes.

In January 1939 Joseph agreed to give the collection to the nascent Gallery; in May he became a Gallery trustee; in June Pennsylvania passed legislation exempting cultural institutions within the state from a five-percent levy on bequests. Tax law was never made in heaven: If Peter's estate sold the art for whatever the market would bear, Pennsylvania collected no tax; ditto if Joseph gave the collection, as the will allowed, to Pennsylvania's Philadelphia Museum of Art, which had lobbied for the new legislation. The Commonwealth got the duty only if the collection went to New York or Washington. On this point state legislators were adamant—despite blandishments from allies of Widener and Mellon alike—even to the point of refusing to estimate what the tax might be.

Roosevelt, perhaps the most culturally aware president since Jefferson and the Gallery's proven friend, came to the rescue with a proposal: Whereas Peter Widener's estate was forbidden by his will from paying any tax, and whereas Pennsylvania insisted on levying a tax if it lost the art, and whereas the nation would benefit from the art's consignment to the Gallery, therefore let the nation pay. A bill was introduced, expert witnesses testified, and in an unguarded moment Congress signed what amounted to a blank check, because the art had not been appraised and no-one knew what five-percent of its value might amount to. The three interested

parties—Pennsylvania, the United States and the Gallery—each had the collection appraised by authorities who judged its worth at between $3.8 and $7.1 million (the highest figure being the state's appraisal, of course). In the end Congress got a real bargain when it paid Pennsylvania a paltry $307,630.50 and secured the Widener Collection for the National Gallery in Washington.

And here was an instance in which the cloud of the Depression, hanging like a pall over the nation, had a silver lining: Along with everything else, the price of great art had plummeted (notwithstanding Duveen's testimony at Mellon's tax trial) and even the highest appraisal reflected the diminished value. Joseph Widener had long since ordered Edith Standen to destroy bills of sale, but having learned museology from Paul Sachs at Harvard, she had faithfully copied every bill before she burned it, knowing how important all sorts of documents and data could be to art historians. Her records showed that the Wideners had spent upwards of $20 million on their treasures during the first quarter of the century when the dollar was worth considerably more than during the Depression. Even Pennsylvania's $7-million appraisal fell far short.

In the fall of 1942 John Walker went to Lynnewood Hall to supervise the packing and found Joseph Widener

old and paralyzed. His trained nurse would help him into the long gallery where the paintings were being removed, and as he watched this desolate scene of crates and packing materials his eyes would fill with tears. He wanted to see the treasures he and his father had brought together installed in their new setting, but at the same time their removal broke his heart. Fortunately he was strong enough to pay one last visit to the Gallery, and from a wheel-chair he saw every work of art placed exactly as he wished.

Edith Standen, who would become a textiles curator at the Metropolitan Museum in New York, remembers that seeing the installation

finally gave him "intense pleasure."

Joseph Widener's death soon thereafter meant the end of Lynnewood Hall, which was sold to a charitable institution. As Arrell wrote, "the days of America's privately owned treasure houses are over." Years later, the patrician John Walker expressed it even more forcefully: "The dismantling of the Widener house signified the end of an epoch. The brevity of the way of life represented by Lynnewood Hall has its own historical significance. Whereas the nobility of Europe enjoyed their collections for centuries, the Widener family is remarkable in America for having possessed their works of art for two generations. How often in the United States the museum director follows the hearse!" Ah, but Finley, Walker's mentor, had been furlongs ahead. 🙗

Giovanni Bellini and Titian,
The Feast of the Gods, 1514
Widener Collection

The Fourth Pennsylvanian

Perhaps an astrologer could find some alignment of celestial bodies at work, but whatever the stars' syzygy, the next founding benefactor shared a curious set of traits with his predecessors. Here was yet another Pennsylvania millionaire with a consuming passion for art who had built a spectacular collection for his own pleasure and gave it to the National Gallery during its formative years. The donor to have these elements in common with Andrew Mellon, Samuel Kress and Joseph Widener was retailer and philanthropist Lessing J. Rosenwald. His special distinction lay in the finely focused nature of his interests: he collected books, drawings and prints of every era. While the unique cabinets of rare books went to the Library of Congress, the Gallery got the rest which, according to Andrew Robison, senior curator and curator of

205

graphic arts, amounted to "the most extensive and finest single collection of graphic arts ever formed by one man in America."

What Rosenwald formally gave to the Gallery in 1943 was his entire collection under an agreement that let the museum use anything it pleased but left everything in the donor's hands for his lifetime. In the end this simply made a grander gift. The Gallery was encouraged to bring to Washington whatever works it needed for study under the supervision of Rosenwald's curator, who became a Gallery employee. But so long as the donor lived, the bulk of the collection remained in the state-of-the-art print rooms and library in his home, Alverthorpe, outside Philadelphia. Meanwhile, Rosenwald continued to enhance the gift for four decades after he gave it: buying new prints to fill gaps and especially upgrading the whole by replacing lesser impressions with better ones or by adding other impressions so they could be compared. When he died in 1979 the gift comprised some 22,000 images, a huge aggregation by any standard, and one that comprehensively displayed the history of graphic arts in the Western world. There are, to suggest the gamut,

everything from an anonymous medieval image of Christ printed on linen to Jasper Johns' 1960 *Coat Hanger*. Thus Rosenwald established the Gallery's eminence as a repository of graphic arts. As another collector who had prints wrote to Rosenwald, "At one stroke you have given them more than they could otherwise have obtained in a generation."

In 1895 (when Lessing was four) his father Julius Rosenwald bought an interest in the Sears, Roebuck and Company for $37,500. The haberdasher and retailer became the Chicago firm's president and proceeded to turn Sears into the paradigm of a mail order house and a giant of American retailing. Having made his name in sales, this son of German-Jewish immigrants also made his mark as a philanthropist. Establishing a fund to promote "the well-being of mankind," he helped establish more than 5,000 public schools for blacks in the rural South. Julius was quintessentially democratic, especially where his children were concerned. When the United States geared up for World War I, he served on Woodrow Wilson's War Industries board, while young Lessing served in the Navy as a seaman second class. By the same token, when Lessing left Cornell University without graduating in 1911, he went to work at Sears as a shipping clerk. He got no special favors beyond the expectation that he would learn all aspects of the company's operations and make his own way.

During the post-war business boom that Secretary of the Treasury Mellon oversaw, Sears, Roebuck prepared to open its first plant on the east coast, and Lessing, then twenty-nine, went to Philadelphia to set up the new operation as its general manager in 1920. Not long after his move, he began to take an interest in prints, perhaps inspired by his mother's quiet collecting of turn-of-the-century etchings. Passing a book and print shop in downtown Philadelphia about 1925, he spotted an etching of the Royal Scottish Academy by D. Y. Cameron and bought it on an apparent lark. That was the start. As Sears thrived, Rosenwald nursed a growing interest in

graphic arts in a kind of counterpoint to reading sales catalogues and such. Soon it became a serious hobby which he pursued systematically: buying and studying standard reference works; commissioning agents to attend estate sales to make purchases for him. Meanwhile, he was scaling the ladder of the family corporation, becoming Sears' executive vice-president in 1928, then board chairman after his father's death four years later.

Clearly he was his father's son. Julius sat on President Wilson's War Industries Board; Lessing directed the Bureau of Industrial Conservation within Roosevelt's War Production Board. At various times he served as well on the Selective Service appeals board and Philadelphia's Labor Mediation Tribunal. Directing the foundation that Julius endowed, Lessing was also active on his own behalf in a wide range of philanthropies and institutions. The organizations he advised or directed included Community Chest, Thomas Jefferson University and Hospital, the University of Pennsylvania's Friends of Pennsylvania Libraries, the Philadelphia Museum of Art, Philadelphia Orchestra Association, Princeton's Institute for Advanced Studies, Amherst College's Folger Shakespeare Library in Washington, Harvard's Fogg Museum, the American Council for Judaism and refugee organizations (after World War II).

Meanwhile he ran Chicago-based Sears from Philadelphia while living in suburban Jenkin-

town where he and his wife Edith raised five children. As for his collecting, once nipped by the
bug he bought largely through two local dealers,
J. Leonard Sessler and the brothers A.S.W. and
Philip Rosenbach, at first concentrating on
artists who had been active in the revival of etching in England, France and the United States
during the late nineteenth and early twentieth
centuries. By 1927 he had a solid representative
collection of modern prints. The following year
he turned tentatively to the old masters, starting
with Dürer's *Melancholia I* and Rembrandt's
Self-Portrait at a Sill; "A passion for old master
prints took hold immediately," according to the
definitive monograph on his collection by Ruth
E. Fine, Alverthorpe's curator at the time of
Rosenwald's death.

In the late 1920s many important private
collections came up at auction in Europe, and
Rosenwald commissioned a Philadelphia print
dealer to act as his agent. Under their arrangement, Sessler bought on his own behalf and
offered Rosenwald first choice at a ten-percent
mark-up. Should Sessler ever fail to cover his

MELENCOLIA I

Melancholia I, *a mysterious allegory of knowledge, is the first of some three hundred Dürer graphics to enter the collection, and one of the best to exemplify the significance of an engraving's "state." This very rare first state displays a reversed numeral; in the more common second state the artist corrected the error in the magic square on the wall behind the angel.*

Albrecht Dürer,
Melancholia I, 1514
Rosenwald Collection

expenses, Rosenwald would make up the difference in cash—but, due to Rosenwald's extensive purchases, it never came to that.

Distractions of settling his father's estate (and paying for previous purchases) brought a slow-down in the early thirties; then in the middle of that decade he resumed buying and he realized that the collection was becoming more than he could handle. He wrote in *Recollections of a Collector,* "After my purchases of prints and

Rembrandt van Rijn, *Christ Healing the Sick*, c. 1649
Rosenwald Collection

books in some of the great European sales, I suddenly realized I had acquired a responsibility I was unable to fulfill because of my business duties." His home, called Alverthorpe, built on a fifty-four-acre tract of land, came to include a specially constructed wing for his rare book library and print rooms.

In 1937, he hired Elizabeth Mongan as his curator, and she would make the care of the collection—at Alverthorpe and at the National Gallery—her life's work. The following year Rosenwald retired from Sears at the relatively young age of forty-eight, thereafter making his book and graphics collections prime concerns (along with continued public service). Rosenwald met Mongan through his childhood friend Paul Sachs, who had followed his father to Wall

Street, risen to a partnership at Goldman, Sachs and Company, then retired to become co-director of Harvard's Fogg Museum and a legendary teacher. (Elizabeth's sister, Agnes Mongan, also gained fame as a graphics curator—at the Fogg.) When Sachs decided to concentrate his personal collection on drawings, he offered Rosenwald the prints, which augmented an already sterling collection.

Rosenwald's work with the War Production Board brought him to Washington soon after the Gallery's opening and he became a frequent visitor. In 1941 he donated thirty prints—duplicates from his collection. While working weekdays in Washington during the war, he frequented the Gallery and the Library of Congress. Early in 1943, Rosenwald invited the

Gallery's director David Finley and Librarian of Congress Archibald MacLeish to visit his private gallery in Jenkintown. The donor had nothing less in mind than giving all his holdings—of books and of graphic arts—to the people of the United States. It was an act of patriotism, a beau geste in time of war, and the public applauded it as such. The Library of Congress took title to his books, the illustrations intended for books, the volumes about books, and the like. The Gallery got the rest.

Rosenwald was almost uniquely busy and generous as a lender. Just as anyone with a serious interest or genuine curiosity about his collection could visit Alverthorpe, any museum or gallery could borrow from its collections for their exhibitions. Characteristically Rosenwald wrote to one borrower, "Please rest assured that I will try to cooperate with you in any way that I may be able and that I am delighted with the opportunity of displaying to the public some of the prints and books from which I have derived

Rosenwald pays special attention to works by the English mystic William Blake and American expatriate Mary Cassatt. *Yellow Iris,* by the German expressionist Karl Schmidt-Rottluff, reflects Edith Rosenwald's love of flowers. Mrs. Rosenwald was to make major donations herself to the Gallery's growing collection of graphic arts.

William Blake, *Christ Appearing to His Disciples after the Resurrection,* c. 1795
Rosenwald Collection

Karl Schmidt-Rottluff, *Yellow Iris,* c. 1935
Rosenwald Collection

Mary Cassatt, *In the Omnibus,* c. 1891
Rosenwald Collection

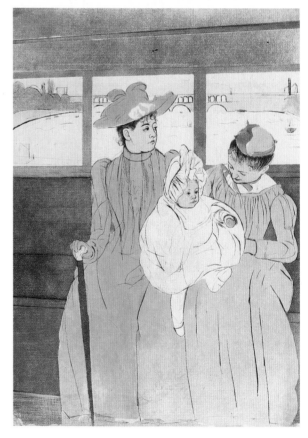

a tremendous amount of pleasure personally." Typically, when he loaned prints or drawings he paid the bills for shipping, printing checklists and catalogues, even for rematting. The Alverthorpe Gallery had such a busy lending program that a Philadelphia journalist wrote, "It is almost impossible to find the entire Rosenwald collection at home. While the little masters are being shown in one city, a general survey of six centuries may be on view in another with various one-man exhibitions of Dürer, Rembrandt, Blake or Whistler to be found in some other museum or gallery."

During the near-four decades of his retirement, Rosenwald kept regular business hours in the museum wing which was open to all comers by appointment. Scholars visited regularly and pored over his matchless collections of William

Blake's oeuvre. Art students came to examine his woodcuts, metalcuts, etchings, engravings. School children came by the busload from around the neighborhood. And most all were greeted warmly by Rosenwald himself. One college instructor remembers that his students found a unique handtinted copy of Blake's poems lying on the coffee table, as casually as a magazine. When the host handed genuine Dürer woodcuts over for the students to examine, the teacher cautioned them, and Rosenwald assured him "They won't hurt them." They didn't; indeed the visiting undergraduates represented less of a risk than the host's ever-present cigarette. Rosenwald not only chainsmoked—even his portrait in the Gallery's Founders' Lounge shows him with a cigarette—but he had the alarming habit of letting the ash grow so long it must certainly fall onto a priceless print.

Lessing Rosenwald thrived on showing his priceless papers: the anonymous Tirolian linen altarpiece which hung above the unused fireplace; works by the Master E. S., a Swiss or South German of the mid-fifteenth century known only by his monogram; the intricate Dürers and moody Rembrandts; the choice images by artists better known for their paintings: Renoir, Mary Cassatt, Whistler, Gauguin and Van Gogh, the Barbizon artists Millet and Corot; the duplicates and counterproofs....

Early examples of graphic arts in the Gallery had come from other sources: some old master prints from Ellen Bullard, Philip Hofer, and Paul Sachs. The first great drawings, by Rodin, came from Mrs. John W. Simpson who had them from the artist himself. In the fall of 1941 Joseph Widener gave a select collection of graphic art especially strong in eighteenth-century French books. But choice as they were, these were eclipsed by the comprehensive holdings that Rosenwald bestowed.

Is it fair to say that the Rosenwald gift could have spoiled the Gallery vis-à-vis works on paper? Thing of it was, the master of Alverthorpe could be counted on to purchase the best prints and drawings that came on the market and add them to his collection, which of course was destined to come to the Gallery. Thus for a significant period the museum was relatively inactive in terms of acquiring prints and drawings. If that habit had its own small price, the Gallery would learn to compensate for it decades later.

When Rosenwald died in 1979, his priceless paper treasures were distributed to the Library of Congress and to the Gallery. As for Alverthorpe, Lessing and Edith Rosenwald used to make improvements and additions to the property as presents to each other—a bike trail for a birthday, for instance, a pond or added parcel for an anniversary. The entire estate, enlarged to over one hundred acres, was then deeded to the local township as a recreational park and cultural center. ❦

As graphics seem infinite in their numbers and variety, so is Lessing Rosenwald's interest—here focused on one of the many exhibitions of works from his collection.

Wages of War

The distant war that soon engulfed the world buffeted the newly opened Gallery in several ways—some of them resonating still.

In proving its patriotism, during the war years the infant Gallery arranged for a series of temporary exhibitions of contemporary art—the more jingoistic the better it appears in retrospect. No matter the then-standing policy (observed by many national museums) that barred works of living artists from the permanent collections; the Gallery became rampantly patriotic in its passing shows.

The temporary exhibition program opened with a three-week show (which had been conceived before the war) of "Two Hundred American Water Colors" in May 1941. The pictures were gleaned from a competition held by a Depression relief agency, the Fine Arts Section of the Public Buildings Administration, and the winning artists got thirty dollars apiece for their paintings, which were destined to decorate a Federal hospital for lepers in Louisiana. David Finley went to great rhetorical

Fearing enemy attack on Washington during World War II, the Gallery sends its most precious of precious masterpieces to a previously prepared sanctuary in a North Carolina mansion. Those objects remain out of harm's way, but the war means a constellation of unanticipated opportunities and problems for the Gallery.

lengths to account for the show in a brochure:

The Government has thus become the most important patron of contemporary painting and ... has succeeded in bringing about a better understanding of art and has encouraged its development in every corner of the United States. To promote such a development of art is one of the fundamental purposes of the National Gallery also. Great art has always had an important influence on artists and their work. By giving the artist and the public an opportunity to study and enjoy works of art which have stood the test of time ... the National Gallery is helping to build up a wider understanding and appreciation of art, so that the public will be better prepared to recognize and enjoy the work of our own creative artists .... It is very fitting, therefore, that the first loan exhibition ... should be the work of contemporary American artists. It is a cause for additional satisfaction that these paintings should be ... selected as a result of a national competition conducted by an agency of the Federal Government....

Mounted on partitions in the ground-floor central gallery, the temporary exhibitions marked the Gallery's enlistment in the war effort. For a time, propaganda in the national interest eclipsed artistic standards in a series of bully shows. With titles like "War Art" and "Art

During the war temporary exhibits stress patriotic themes, and First Lady Eleanor Roosevelt comes to view the work of living artists.

for Bonds," they glorified soldier, sailor and Rosie the Riveter. There was "American Artists' Record of War and Defense"—pictures submitted to the Fine Arts Section for a competition aimed at informing the public about war and defense work. There were: a mixed media show displaying "Activities of the Red Cross" in peace and war; the touring display of three-hundred war posters illustrating themes like "Loose Talk Sinks Ships" and "Victory Starts Here"; and "Soldiers of Production," watercolors and drawings by artists who had been given special permission to visit factories making the tools of war. There was "The Great Fire of London, 1940," a show of pictures by twenty-two Britons serving in the London Auxiliary Fire Service and chosen by a jury headed by Kenneth Clark. (Three firemen accompanied the show to Washington and answered visitors' questions.) In a display of hemispheric solidarity, the Gallery exhibited the distinguished sculptor Jo Davidson's busts of eleven South American presidents plus FDR and Vice President Henry Wallace.

Whatever the relative merits of these shows—doubtless servicemen's art appealed to many, and doubtless some of the art was good if not great—the public loved the Gallery at first sight. People flocked to see the pictures all week long, and hear concerts on Sunday nights, and at mealtime crowded the cafeteria where a steak could be had for sixty cents. Each to his own taste and appetite, some 1,762,016 visitors were counted in nine months of 1941. The number dipped by half a million the following year but rebounded to more than two million in 1943, climbed higher in 1944 and reached a peak of 2,134,089 in 1945. Attendance started a long slow slide thereafter, save in 1948 when an exhibit of art from Berlin museums spiked the figures to nearly the 1945 level, which would stand as a record for thirty-two years. (Not until 1977 did attendance go higher—to 2,678,797 visitors, then to more than twice that number the next year, when the Gallery doubled in size with the opening of the East Building.)

In the early 1940s orchestral music in museums was still rare, but it found a permanent home at the Gallery very early on. The original inspiration was familiar: London's National Gallery. The institution that had given Andrew Mellon so much refreshment was now bereft of its great pictures, which had been spirited out of harm's way for safekeeping in Welsh coal mines. The grand building stood empty when pianist Myra Hess organized a series of daily recitals there in order to put the place to some good use and to boost Londoners' morale. David Bruce reported how inspiring the concerts seemed, and Chester Dale (of whom more later) put up funds for a similar series of events to augment activities designed to serve Washington's exploding population of war workers and military personnel. The Gallery was held open late on Sundays; a bevy of ladies helped Mrs. Finley organize Sunday night suppers for groups of servicemen invited on the spot.

The most enduring institution to arise out of this activity was the National Gallery Orchestra, and one of the Gallery's most lasting personalities, Richard Bales, would be its conductor. A man of multiple gifts, he was composer, conductor, impresario, booking agent and bureaucrat wise to the ways of Washington. He took over a barely established ensemble at the Gallery, raised it to a position of enduring eminence and led its performances in one Garden Court or the other as Assistant to the Director for Music for forty-five years.

Bales, a Virginian, had gone north for his musical education—to the Eastman School of Music—and like many musicians during the Depression soon found himself in an entirely different line of work. About the time the Gallery opened, Bales was aiding England's war effort, laboring in offices on K Street—called "U.K. Street" for all the British missions there—where he wrote cables for His Majesty's quartermasters about supplies being shipped hither and yon.

In his off-hours Bales wrote choral arrangements of works by an amateur composer, a matron who introduced him to the concerts at the Gallery that were being performed by musicians from the fledgling National Symphony under its assistant conductor. Indeed Bales' composing friend was a hostess who helped tap servicemen and women for the Sunday suppers that had become one of the Gallery's wartime hallmarks. Inevitably she invited him to supper one Sunday in 1942. There Bales met David Finley and Macgill James—but smartly didn't press his case as a musician looking for work. Soon thereafter Lamont Moore, head of the Education Division, came to him in search of an original score for a forthcoming film, *Your National Gallery*. Having composed very little, and surely nothing as exacting as movie music, Bales took a quick course in the techniques from a friend and began the task—blocking out measures and tempos—and wrote a score that pleased David Finley mightily.

Bales went back to writing cables on K Street but during the 1943 summer season the Gallery's orchestral podium became vacant, and Bales was invited to conduct the concerts in a Garden Court. His first was on June 6, 1943. During a performance soon after that, David Finley turned to Bales' wife and remarked that the music program was requiring too much of his attention, so "'I want Dick to come and take over the whole thing.' And that was it," as Bales recalls.

In those days the Gallery ran like a benevolent empire in a Victorian novel, an establishment of gentlemen ordered in a clearly understood hierarchy supported by a company of polite female secretaries. If "gentlemen did not read other people's mail" here they initialled it. This is to say that even the Assistant to the Director for Music passed his correspondence on to a superior to be vetted before it left the building.

Popular from the start, the Sunday night concerts put the Gallery on the musical map and augmented the city's reputation as a music town. In addition they established the National Gallery Orchestra as a respected ensemble whose playing was heard widely via radio syndication and record. In a manner of speaking, Bales' Orchestra

220

led the Gallery in becoming a sanctuary for all the arts. It also helped the Gallery take its place as a socially progressive institution.

The Gallery's music program helped desegregate classical music events in a city whose Jim Crow habits had been made especially notorious by the Daughters of the American Revolution. The DAR barred the spectacularly gifted black soprano Marian Anderson from singing in Constitution Hall, John Russell Pope's creation and the biggest hall in town. Representative Adam Clayton Powell, the young Harlem Democrat then known as an effective crusader for minority causes, quickly came forward and nominated two black musicians to perform at the Gallery. Bales says he told David Finley: "I want you to authorize me to engage black artists." Finley agreed and Bales booked a recital by a Washington singer who had made a name for herself on the Chicago opera stage. Thus he was able politely to decline Powell's nominees, writing back to the Congressman "I think you will be pleased to learn that Madame Lillian Evanti is already engaged to sing with the National Gallery Orchestra." Roland Hayes, who had been the first American black to earn an international reputation, soon sang at the Gallery too, as did Shirley Verrett, and the matter of a performer's race became a non-issue.

Making its mark in several ways, the Gallery Orchestra offered a stage on which young professionals could develop. Also, through Bales' brainchild, the American Music Festival, it annually provided a concert stage for living composers. Bales took special pride in championing the neglected composer Charles Ives, who might otherwise have simply been remembered, if at all, as an eccentric musical amateur. With a partner he had founded an insurance company in New York, made a small fortune, and in his spare time wrote distinctly original orchestral music well into the 1920s. Bales heard his Third Symphony on the radio in 1949 and conducted its Washington premiere the same year. When Bales asked his permission to make recordings, Ives hardly lived up to his reputation as a cur-

Trustees declare that the museum has an even greater responsibility in wartime to educate and divert the public—military personnel in particular. Thus David Finley launches Sunday evening concerts and hires young Richard Bales to lead the National Gallery Orchestra, which becomes an ensemble of enviable distinction and longevity.

(following page): Bales' successor George Manos conducts the Orchestra and directs a music program comprising diverse concerts. Other special events include receptions sponsored by corporate underwriters and the biennial Andrew W. Mellon dinner, a full-dress banquet in the Rotunda that is traditionally addressed by the President of the United States.

mudgeon. Instead the composer sent him sheafs of his music with permission to play all of it as he pleased. Bales made the first recording of Ives' Second Symphony—fifty years after its composition—in the Gallery's board room; it called for a high F-sharp chime, which was made to order in the carpenter's shop by cutting a brass tube down to size and thus to pitch.

Bales raised his profile and the Gallery's with his own new works as well, notably in 1953 with the composition and recording of a celebratory cantata, *The Confederacy*, based on well-researched songs and motifs from the antebellum South. Its most widely heard spin-off was Mitch Miller's bowdlerized *The Yellow Rose of Texas*, which made the pop charts. The sing-along version had altered words which glossed over the fact that the song, dating back to 1857, celebrated the charms of a famous mulatto woman of pleasure in what he genteelly calls a "sporting house."

Ultimately Bales booked or conducted nearly 1,700 concerts between 1943 and August 3, 1985, when he passed the baton to George Manos who has carried on since.

The war was less than a month old when it changed the face of the Gallery, because authorities feared an enemy attack on Washington. At an emergency meeting, the trustees voted to send the Gallery's "most fragile and irreplaceable [objects]... to the place of safety which had been determined upon [in advance] and adapted for the purpose." Thus a little motorcade of ordinary trucks headed south under an extraordinary and conspicuous police escort. They fetched up at Biltmore House, the Vanderbilt mansion in Asheville, North Carolina, said to be the largest private home in Dixie. Here guards and members of the curatorial staff chaperoned the objects until 1944. Of greater importance than the brief removal of masterpieces was what happened back in Washington because the trustees believed "that the Gallery has a duty to the public... an obligation as a source of recreation and education to continue its activities, and even increase them, as far as practicable, in wartime...."

As for the walls left vacant by masterpieces sent to Biltmore House, the spaces left by the old master paintings that had made the Gallery famous were filled by other pictures that had themselves been displaced by the war. A goodwill show of late eighteenth- and nineteenth-century French masterpieces, organized by the Louvre for a tour of South America and stranded there, made its way to the Gallery for the duration. So did part of a collection of important Flemish works from Belgium, which were interspersed with the permanent collection.

With its opening, the Gallery assumed special roles as arbiter of national artistic taste and the proper national repository for great art. During the war it performed an especially national duty that launched a uniquely praisewor-

thy policy on the part of the eventual victors; yet this effort would lead to international controversy and an internecine argument that hasn't quite ended yet.

Amidst all the discussion and planning for contingencies that war brings, some interested souls anticipated the need to protect or rescue cultural treasures. Thus was born the American Commission for the Protection and Salvage of Artistic and Historic Monuments in Europe. (It was called the Roberts Commission for short, after its chairman, Supreme Court Justice Owen J. Roberts.) It had been suggested to President Roosevelt by Chief Justice and Gallery Chairman Harlan F. Stone at the behest of the chief executives of the Archaeological Institute of America, the College Art Association, the

The wartime hideaway for Gallery treasures is Biltmore House. A mansion in North Carolina built by the Vanderbilts, Biltmore House is deemed "a place of greater safety" than Washington in 1942.

Metropolitan Museum of Art and the National Gallery. In due course the Commission's short masthead was a distinguished list that included Justice Roberts, Paul J. Sachs, former New York Governor Al Smith, and the Metropolitan's Francis Henry Taylor. It was also heavy with Gallery officers: David Finley as its vice chairman, the newly arrived Huntington Cairns as secretary, and special advisor John Walker. The Commission's task, eventually joined by similar boards in London and Moscow, was to be a sort of ombudsman for art, buildings and cultural artifacts.

At first the Commission fed information to military planners, identifying churches with spires tall enough to threaten unwary bombers and nominating targets that should, if possible, be spared artillery attacks because of their cultural importance. It also recommended specially qualified people—curators, art historians and the like—to serve in a special army unit, the Monuments, Fine Arts and Archives Branch. This outfit did the actual work of rescuing works of art from the chaos of liberation and securing them to be returned to rightful owners. MFA&A's specially qualified officers followed front-line troops into war zones barely before the noise of battle echoed away. Among them were the Gallery's own former registrar and eventual

assistant director Naval Reserve Lt. (j.g.) Charles P. Parkhurst, Jr., and WAC Captain Edith Standen, secretary of the Widener Collection who had supervised the bringing of the collection to the Gallery from Lynnewood Hall.

This unit's successes were legion, and sometimes heroic, as it restored thousands of cultural objects to rightful owners. Standen literally dug up an antique bronze cannon decorated with "figures of all the virtues except Charity." Napoleon had captured it in Vienna in the early nineteenth century and taken it to Paris whence it had been stolen by Nazis, who buried it near Stuttgart shortly before the Allies arrived. Some museum people there asked Standen to let them keep it because it had been made in Stuttgart in the late sixteenth century. "Of course that was rubbish," she said. "It had been taken from the Musée de l'Armée. It went back to the Musée de l'Armée.... Anyway I was delighted to be able to give the cannon back. I have seen it since"— in Paris.

Parkhurst would tell an oral history interviewer forty-five years later: "The finding was either easy or accidental. Usually we had clues; from shippers, from local residents who said, 'well, there's something funny about that castle' or whatever." Tracking down such a rumor one day in Baden, Parkhurst remembers:

Art handlers unpack "the most fragile and irreplaceable works of art in the national collection" at Biltmore House.

I came through a woods, and I had to leave my jeep—I was alone—because there was no bridge and the stream wasn't fordable, and I started walking through the woods toward this castle which none of us had checked before.... I suddenly came into an opening in the woods, and there were seven or eight men standing around. I thought "Well, they're woodchoppers." It seemed like minutes before I realized that they weren't moving... they were absolutely motionless. Just standing with their axes down, or their hands to their heads, or something like that. It was fully a century before it came to me that I was looking at a full-sized cast of the *Burghers of Calais* by Rodin. [The Germans had not been able to get it up the mountain to the castle.] They just left it in the woods. And they looked to me like woodchoppers in that context! So I went up to the castle and sure enough, there was all the stuff from Cologne that we'd been looking for.... The owner of the castle gave me a cup of tea, and he gave me a list of the objects. Said "I've been wondering how long it would take you guys to get here!" Or words to that effect.

However, all was not Nazi loot. For example, partisan Hungarian officers made off with the nation's crown jewels, including the sacred crown of St. Stephen, and went west out of their own country ahead of advancing Russian troops, then hid the jewels where they could. These sacred treasures of considerable profane value were placed "in this iron chest with three locks," Parkhurst remembered. "Each Hungarian colonel—there were three Hungarian colonels—had a key, and no one could open it without the other two, and so on. It was one of those nice little Hungarian puzzles."

After cleverly hiding the trunk, the Hungarian officers didn't know what to do next. The Red Army was notorious for seizing any and all valuables officially or covertly; whether for private gain or national pride didn't matter to people who had lost their cultural patrimony. On the other hand, the colonels didn't immediately trust GIs either—but they had heard about an art restoration unit, and Captain James J. Rorimer found them. A medievalist who had directed the Cloisters Museum as he would the Metropolitan, Rorimer, Parkhurst said, "knew all about this crown."

He persuaded them [the colonels] that he was the man they should talk to. So they took him secretly one night—and Jimmy loves secrecy—and they yanked this chest which they had dropped into a lake. They yanked it out of the lake. And here was this soggy chest full of muddy water, I presume muddy, and they took the chest to where they were staying, and they washed off the crown jewels in the bathtub!...

Then they wrapped the things up and dried the chest... and it was taken, with the three Hungarian officers, to Wiesbaden and locked into the vault

there at the Landesmuseum which was our repository. I saw the crown there. I even tried it on. It was too small. So I figured I'd never be a saint or a king. It was the famous crown with the bent cross where somebody had tried to whack him with this sword one time. But this was a real treasure.... But it was so valuable that it was taken to Fort Knox,

via the National Gallery whose experts conserved the cases and cleaned the jewels first—crown, scepter and orb. Decades later, during President Carter's administration, this trove was returned to Budapest, and one of the National Gallery restorers who accompanied it reported in awe: "I didn't have any idea how sacred that object was. The people knelt in the street when it passed.... It was as though the thing had a light around it. It was incredible. It glowed to these people. Silence prevailed. It was carried like a baby. Like Jesus Christ going into the temple with doves and his mother.... "

In 1945, Standen, and Parkhurst in particular, would find themselves in a brouhaha over whether to rescue some art by removing it from the war zone entirely and stashing it at the Gallery. The fight would change their careers. In the heat of the argument, the Gallery-based Roberts Commission—and Chief Curator John Walker in particular—were accused by their peers of plotting to take away German-owned artworks in order to keep them forever. At the same time, Parkhurst, Standen and company were besmirched for refusing to take the officially sanctioned (if unpopular) step of shipping the art to safety until order was restored in Europe.

Before it was over, the row involved many concerns: not only diplomacy, international law and art history, but such practical matters as whether scarce coal should warm hospitals or art warehouses, and nebulous concerns like sentiment and national pride. Example: Before repatriation began, the Army's cultural advisor Col. John Nicholas Brown said that the first work to be returned to rightful owners should be Van Eyck's unique *Ghent Altarpiece,* called by H.W. Janson "the greatest monument of early Flemish painting." A triptych with two hinged wings, it had been broken up in the course of five hundred years and parts that found their way to Germany were returned to the Church of St. Bavo in Belgium after World War I. When Hitler threatened the low countries, the painting had been sent to France for safekeeping in the Pyrenees. After France fell, Hitler seized the masterpiece over the objections of French authorities. Now, Colonel Brown informed his commanding general, the Allies' return of this work to Belgium would serve as "the symbol of all those things of the spirit which have been crushed and perverted by the Nazis." However, he advised, "due regard must be given to the fact that restitution must be through the French authorities, since it was from France that this work of art came to Germany."

Symbolic repatriation and all good intentions aside, military authorities had practical problems to solve during the summer of 1945—even as literally thousands of objects were successfully located and returned to pre-war owners or their heirs. Thus various proposals were made as to how best to deal with art objects whose legitimate owners could not be identified or those that had been in German museums and were thus presumed to belong to the Reich. The commander of the military government, General Lucius Clay, wanted to safeguard the treasures, but he would have little manpower and resources to spare for the cause. He had to keep the new peace and mete out scarce supplies during the coming winter.

The issues became more confused as coded messages flew back and forth variously between civilian boards, government agencies, alien armies, and jealous nations. Might not unspeakably valuable masterpieces be appraised like cannons or ships and declared spoils or written off as reparations? Were there enough secure collecting centers to store the art that was surfacing from literally hundreds of caches? At first it was widely agreed there were not, though by August MFA&A officers said there were. Then it was suggested that recovered artworks should be doled out to American museums under a trusteeship arrangement that would restore German-owned works when Germany "re-earned its right to be considered as a nation." This "scheme," Colonel Brown reported was "not only dangerous to the whole US policy but hypocritical as well." In this he was joining an argument that was gathering steam.

In the spring of 1945, the three Gallery officers with the most clout on the Roberts Commission had taken an interesting initiative. According to a confidential memo for the record, Finley, Cairns and Walker met with Assistant Secretary of War John J. McCloy. The reason: "We asked if it were possible when the Army withdraws from certain territory… [for troops to remove] the works of art in various repositories of which the American Army has heretofore had custody." If at first blush that sounds today like preparation to snatch booty, Finley clearly had a fiduciary trust in mind. He warned McCloy, "in our opinion, the American Army is at present in the position of Trustees who might be held accountable afterwards if it abandons the works of art now in its possession." Thus the Army should sequester everything of value, and keep the treasures safe at least until the dust settled.

It bears emphasis that this entire effort was laudable and original—the determination by victors to help heal the wounds of war by restoring what might otherwise be taken as spoils. In this, MFA&A officers in Europe were moving ahead—locating and identifying artworks and restoring many of them to rightful owners. There were special problems, of course, such as art looted by Nazis in eastern Europe. Should this be repatriated to new dictatorial governments? And should art that had belonged to exterminated Jewish families be turned over to antisemitic national authorities? These questions aside, the controversy that embroiled the Gallery came to center on one special case: a cache of paintings found in a German salt mine (along with thousands of pounds of gold bullion). These pictures belonged to Berlin's Kaiser Friedrich Museum, but to return them would be an act of dubious wisdom since the museum had holes in the roof and several feet of water in the cellar. Besides, it was located in what had become the Russian Zone of East Berlin, and the Soviets were seizing valuables of every sort as their due.

This cache would get special treatment, which made MFA&A officers especially and almost uniformly disturbed. One wrote to Finley:

Work at the restitution of these things proceeds apace. However, ugly rumors persist to the effect that America will take German art to the States as a token of the victory, or perhaps as "reparations." This travesty certainly would not go through, but the rumor is so persistent that I wish to go on record with you and others of the Commission to the effect that *I will* oppose [such a] suggestion, should it come through. Nor am I alone in this; others have said they will accept courts-martial treatment, sabotage the effort, or ask for transfer. Perhaps these rumors have no foundation. At any rate, you will know and we are hoping that someone in Washington will speak with . . . the President, if necessary. Certainly you are eminently fitted to do so.

Concern was not limited to American esthetes-in-uniform. The director of OSS's Art Looting Investigation Unit warned Huntington Cairns about the hostile opinion of one Lt. Col. Sir Leonard Woolley at the War Office in London. He spoke out after the American Secretary of State told Britain's Foreign Secretary that the Americans intended to ship *all* art owned by Germany before the war—possibly thousands of objects—"to the continental United States for safe keeping." In reply, "Woolley made abundantly clear that the British Government would in no way become a party to [this]," the OSS man warned Cairns, "and that he deplored the implications of such handling" by the Americans. At the end of August, members of the Roberts Commission met at New York's Century Association to discuss proposals to consider artworks grist for reparations. The group was

split, with Metropolitan Museum Director Francis Henry Taylor saying he would not object "to whatever decision the Government might make regarding the use of cultural objects for reparations purposes." But Charles H. Sawyer of the Worcester Art Museum argued that the Commission should uphold a doctrine of "clean hands." On September 1, 1945, President Truman endorsed General Clay's plan to rid himself of the problems of tending all the art. But the official order was unclear on a key point. It stipulated that the objects would come to America "only for the care and safekeeping and

GIs find the Gallery a photogenic backdrop. Inside, special efforts make military personnel welcome during the war. Conveniently, the capital's largest USO center is right across the street.

[but?] that their eventual disposition would be subject to future Allied decisions."

Where would the art be safely kept in America? That had been decided long since: in the National Gallery. The War Department asked the Gallery to accept its custody and David Finley took an overnight train to New England to confer with the Gallery's vacationing chairman in person. Chief Justice Stone approved: "If the Government asks us to take care of these paintings, we must do it. It is a duty which we could not escape if we wanted to, and certainly we do not want to."

And still the matter stewed. Objections were raised to subjecting the pictures to the risks of a sea voyage, which prompted John Walker to reply that every old master painting then in America had come by sea. Of greater substance, opponents of the decision argued a moral question: that Americans had seized art from a defeated enemy and were now confiscating it under the transparent excuse of saving it from harm. As an OSS officer argued, "Unfortunately it so happens that the German Government cloaked its vast depredations of World War II in the occupied countries under the pretext of protecting valuable cultural properties against the hazards of war and vandalism." John Walker dismissed all this: "I am not concerned with the moral question of taking these works of art temporarily from Germany, because I believe that this moral question does not exist.... I am concerned with the safety of the objects.... The policy of a wise custodian would be to bring at least part of this irreplaceable treasure to the safest haven available."

Meanwhile, the Commission sent the Gallery's administrator—now an Army officer—to Germany to set the machinery in motion. Colonel Harry McBride summoned Lt. Parkhurst to his hotel and ordered him to oversee the packing of the art for shipment. More than forty years later Parkhust still vividly remembers refusing the order and walking out, though he says McBride threatened him with court martial or worse. In any case, another officer who had

worked at the Gallery agreed to pack up the pictures.

When the decision was announced to ship the Kaiser Friedrich art to Washington, Sumner Crosby of Yale quit the Roberts Commission in protest, and Edith Standen wrote Parkhurst that the policy is "neither morally tenable nor trustworthy." By November, nearly all the art professionals in the MFA&A signed a petition protesting the shipment of German art to America. This "Wiesbaden Manifesto" declared:

No historical grievance will rankle so long, or be the cause of so much justified bitterness as the removal for any reason of part of the heritage of any nation, even if that... be interpreted as a prize of war. And though this removal may be done with every intention of altruism, we are none the less convinced that it is our duty, individually and collectively, to protest against it, and that though our obligations are to the nation to which we owe allegiance, we have yet further obligation to common justice, decency and the establishment of the power of right, not of expediency or might, among civilized nations.

What troubled Parkhurst and his allies particularly—and rings in his memory—was this: "It was common knowledge, or common comment among the officers of the MFA&A" that of all the art being held by the Army only objects that "fitted nicely into the National Gallery" had been picked to be sent to Washington. The Manifesto signers believed the plan was to fill gaps in the Gallery's collections. Otherwise, they asked, how does one explain this odd lot of 202 paintings chosen from many thousands? The Commission explained that these were the most important works from a group that should not be returned to East Berlin.

Despite the row, the Army prepared to ship to America a consignment of pictures that included works by Rembrandt, Rubens, Tintoretto, El Greco, Daumier, Brueghel, Botticelli, Giorgione, Dürer, Masaccio, and more. General Clay wanted a public announcement assuring the German people that the art would be returned eventually. The President agreed, but the Assistant Secretary of State involved in reparations discussions said the disposition of the art would "be subject to future Allied discussions."

In-transit care of the Kaiser Friedrich art got all the attention it deserved. The journey began November 12, 1945, under armed guard by truck from Wiesbaden to Frankfurt, thence by rail in hospital cars on to Paris and Le Havre where the precious cargo was placed on the troopship *James Parker*. Here new round-the-clock armed guards were pressed into service—or bribed, really, for those who volunteered for guard duty got to eat with the ship's crew instead of with the rest of the troops. After the nine-day voyage, the ship reached New York where the art was loaded

into three trucks and driven to Washington—under guard all the way as one police force after another provided escorts from the Hudson River to the Potomac.

Meanwhile the war of words continued in the press. A Washington *Times Herald* correspondent wrote from Berlin that the case proved "The preservation of German art treasures is considered more important than the fate of German women and children and the repatriation of war-weary GIs." A home-front columnist predicted that "most of the art works in the Hitler and Goering collections will remain in this country permanently, enriching the exhibitions of the National Gallery of Art . . . to a very considerable degree." Noting that Andrew Mellon had not been able to buy one Vermeer in the lot for $1

The Gallery is the likely custodian of art objects removed from Germany for safekeeping near the end of the war and later returned. Chief Curator John Walker, Director David Finley, and Administrator Harry A. McBride (left to right) oversee the transfer.

million, the columnist said these spoils of war resembled cannons and ships as grist for reparations since they were bought and paid for by Hitler and Goering out of their ill-gotten gains.

In Washington Cairns soon got an unofficial but very confidential letter for his burn file. It said that New York cultural lion Lincoln Kirstein, Walker's friend at Harvard, "has been busily spreading around that J.W. marked these pictures and others for eventual shipment to the US (with red tags) at the time of his trip to Europe on the Commission's behalf. Francis [Henry Taylor] himself gives no credence to this story, [but believes that to clear the air] John should make a complete disavowal to the members of the Commission and proceed to pin said Kirstein's ears back—and plenty." Walker's denial in a memo to Cairns was unequivocal:

In connection with the report you mentioned to me that I had selected paintings from German Museums to be sent to America last summer, and discussed with the Arts and Monuments officers which pictures should be shipped to America, I should like you to know that these statements are completely incorrect. I saw none of the pictures subsequently delivered by the War Department to the National Gallery, nor did I know when I was in Germany that the State Department or the War Department had any plans for removing works of art to this country.

Finley would publish equally unconditional statements, noting that "Chief Justice Stone was outraged at statements challenging, as he considered it, the good faith of the American Government and also the integrity of the President and the Chief Justice of the United States." At the time, Finley claimed the high ground for the Gallery. In January he memoed Cairns about the "unduly long delay in carrying out the President's directive to collect and bring to this country for safekeeping" art which the Army held in Germany. "This delay is not due to any laxity or indifference on the part of the [Roberts] Commission or the National Gallery, and I feel that both the Commission and the Gallery should be protected against being held responsible for any losses of works of art" in Germany "through fire, theft, or riot."

However much fire might threaten art in Germany, there was plenty of smoke in America. The president of the College Art Association criticized the sequestering of the art, which prompted a prominent member of the Association to quit in protest. Members of Congress got into the act, filling pages of the Congressional Record with charges and countercharges. By then, the *Washington Post* observed wryly, "It is sometimes rather wonderful to see the alacrity with which Americans accuse fellow Americans of the worst Nazi practices and motives" though the latest "looting" (as some called it) "was not undertaken for profit or even for pleasure." A *New York Times* editorial summed up with a comparison to Caesar's wife, saying the Gallery's integrity was not in question, only its good judgment.

Perhaps more in sorrow than anger, Parkhurst soon wrote Finley that he would not return to the Gallery after his discharge. He likened the rescue of the German art to so much Nazi skullduggery, "work which the MFA&A was sent over here to undo." The decision was also a breach of faith with the MFA&A officers, Parkhurst argued; it besmirched their on-site appraisal of conditions and professional recommendations. Finley replied that the Gallery "had no part in the decision to bring these works of art" to its fold.

A few months later Edith Standen followed Parkhurst. Standen did return—however briefly, at least twice—to view the 202 pictures quite privately in the storage range where they were kept. Lincoln Kirstein came too, with a friend, and assured Finley in his thank-you note "You may be sure that neither [Christopher] Isherwood nor myself will write anything about having seen the pictures." And still it wasn't over. In 1948, the occupation forces prepared to leave Germany and turn the government over to civilian authorities. Before going, General Clay felt a personal obligation to return the art he had salvaged, and so a new argument arose. About then

Senator J. William Fulbright wrote a bill that would keep the Kaiser Friedrich collection in the U.S. in perpetuity!

That idea got lost in the shuffle as people on every side of the initial argument became diverted in a new debate. At issue now was whether the art might tour America before its return to Germany, or whether it was too fragile for a U.S. tour, or whether it should go back to Germany with no further ado or delay. The delayers won this round, and the pictures were hung for display at the National Gallery prior to a national tour. Finley wrote to a friend, "We decided not to have an official preview late Tuesday after-

noon, as we had first planned. We should probably offend more people than we would please...." With that the show opened with no fanfare whatsoever.

"Without a ceremony, the National Gallery of Art here put on public view today the 202 paintings from two German museums which have been in custody of the Gallery at the request of the Army for more than two years," wrote *New York Times* art critic Howard Devree. "As simply as that begins the next to the last chapter in the story of events which, at first, gave rise to as bitter dissension and criticism as anything in the whole art history of our country. The removal and stor-

A guard keeps watch over some of the 202 pictures from Germany stored in a Gallery vault.

When the Berlin paintings go on display without ceremony, visitors swarm to the Gallery in unprecedented numbers: nearly one million people in forty days. The so-called "202" exhibit is the first "blockbuster" show (though the sorry term, first coined in wartime to describe a large bomb, is not applied to museum events until decades later).

ing of these European masterpieces of six countries—'202' as the collection has been familiarly called...has been watched in all quarters of the world." Now it was Washington's turn to watch, and to see. Word spread like wildfire. Within hours people lined up outside the Gallery to get in. In the course of forty days the line often stretched around the building. The event was remarked on everywhere, and 964,970 people came to see the pictures—an unprecedented

number. On one Sunday, the guards counted 67,490 people entering the Gallery, another record. President Truman dropped in during a morning stroll one day, then returned after hours with Margaret and Bess. Among others who got VIP treatment were Mrs. Henry Ford, the Duke of Windsor, John D. Rockefeller, Jr., and Lady Astor.

The pictures—save the most fragile—then toured a dozen cities and John Walker got a last

The Gallery's guard force is increased to handle the crush of visitors and the Army sends a detachment of Military Police to help assure security for the "202." The painting at left is Peter Paul Rubens' Saint Cecelia.

word, complaining that the very people who lobbied hard for this tour had been among the opponents of the art coming to America in the first place because of its fragility. In any case, all the art was finally returned and the paintings came to form the core of the Prussian State Collection in Berlin.

When the pictures left Washington, John Nicholas Brown, by then Assistant Secretary of the Navy for Air, wrote Parkhurst, "The German

picture racket seems to have reached an all-time high in confusion. The local boys here have done their best to prevent other people from seeing the pictures, using the argument that they should be returned to their proper owners. It

seems strange to remember back to the days when you and I and many others felt that argument so strongly that we protested their original removal [from Germany]. However, I suppose it is better in this life not to have too long a memory."

That wisdom notwithstanding, the final result of all this bears out a nameless editorial writer who offered quiet kudos that deserves one slight amendment: "For our own part we share the opinion of the late Chief Justice Stone, who declared that the United States Army [along with the National Gallery] deserves the highest praise for the care exercised in salvaging these great works of art and in making provision for their safety until they can be returned to Germany. Art is the possession of the world and all men are its custodians." And when all was said and done, the record was, in fact, incredible. Contrary to the traditions of war, British and Americans ultimately made good their pledges not to claim as victors' spoils the cultural riches of the vanquished. ⁊

One Sunday, Gallery guards count 67,940 visitors, said to be an all-time high. On another Sunday, Gallery nurses count sixty first-aid cases. After the exhibition leaves Washington, it tours a dozen cities and is seen by another million people. Thereafter, the Berlin pictures are crated up and returned to Germany, where they land in Bremerhaven (above).

The Middle Years: Chester Dale

Chester Dale, once a
runner on Wall Street,
watches others run at his
bidding. He enjoys his well-
earned wealth to the hilt,
makes the pursuit of art a
contest, thrives on collecting,
and serves the Gallery
generously.

According to his *New Yorker* profile,

Chester Dale was "the only man in the world who has had his portrait painted, *seriatim*, by Robert

Reid, George Bellows, Jean Lurçat, Diego Rivera, Miguel Covarrubias and Salvador Dalí." To say this

proved his insatiable interest in art or self is to sell him short. He had the stamina of a fireman as suit-

ed the honorary member of a Manhattan firehouse; the metaphorical punch of a middleweight fighter

as he had boxed professionally; the nerve of a Wall Street runner, which was his first job; the luck of a

gambler who kept playing the odds and hitting jackpots. He also had the drive, wealth and eyes to

buy an unparalleled collection of nineteenth- and twentieth-century art. Eyes in the plural? Yes, his

own and those of a wife Maud, a lady of exceptional learning about art and of unusually discriminat-

ing taste.

Dale "met life head-on and enjoyed it hugely," wrote art critic Aline B. Louchheim (later

Saarinen). "I know of no other collector who delights in his paintings with such gusto or who: "speaks

237

of them with so little egocentricity and so much hearty pleasure." Further, and great names aside, she found that he possessed a great collection worthy of that title, a coherent gathering of pictures that reflected the collector's informed taste and sensitive perception.

The homogeneity of the pictures…is that they are the kind of modern paintings visibly connected with tradition; paintings in which emotion is gentle rather than violent; beautifully painted pictures, radiant rather than opulent. It is a well-tempered collection.

Yet Chesterdale (as he was called by wives, friends and victims alike) was himself not well-tempered at all. In fact, he was a terror. "I've had a few lunches with him. He catches my arm," Dalí complained, "and the next day it's blue, so violent is his touch." John Walker got chronic bursitis from taking his phone calls—long calls daily on a special line—during a particularly trying years-long period. He terrorized Walker and even Paul Mellon in an original manner: with the very real threat that he might recall his loans of numerous and fabulous pictures at any moment. So long as he lived, nearly all of the Gallery's vaunted Chester Dale Collection was only on

loan. Further these rich and varied treasures had come to the Gallery from the Art Institute of Chicago and the Philadelphia Museum of Art whose directors had come to believe that they had been loaned to them forever.

Lending a few early American portraits to the Gallery for the opening, the next year Dale provided a superb assortment of 126 nineteenth-century French pictures that might simply have made the Gallery his devoted beneficiary. Trouble was, this particular assortment of works by Matisse, Picasso and the like were only loans —as they had been loans in Philadelphia and Chicago. When Dale pulled his art from those distinguished museums, which had built their modern collections around his, he left rooms of bare walls in his wake. That was Dale's way, though needless to say both museums felt very much abused.

Were there mitigating circumstances, or is there a kinder light to shed on this? Finley's version of what happened vis-à-vis Chicago is sublime and characteristic in its understatement: "He decided he would like to see his paintings under one roof and proposed to me that he bring the Chicago loans to the National Gallery.

He explained to his Chicago friends why he was transferring his paintings to Washington and went ahead and did so, with the result that one can see French paintings of the nineteenth and twentieth centuries in Washington as in few places in the world." Period, paragraph. John Walker's published recollection is perhaps more candid: "In fairness... it must be stressed that he had made no [binding or legal] commitment to either institution, nor had he promised that his pictures would remain in Washington.... It has been said that Chester was unable to distinguish between the words 'gift' and 'loan,' that he used these terms interchangeably, that like Humpty Dumpty in *Alice in Wonderland* words meant what he wanted them to mean." But Dale had been elected to the boards of the Philadelphia and Chicago museums (the Museum of Modern Art as well) on the strength of his loans and the hope of his eventual gifts. Likewise, in February 1941 he became an "honorary officer" with the title of Associate Vice President of the Gallery, then succeeded Joseph Widener as a full board

member upon the latter's death in 1943, and became President of the Board in 1956. But he had never foresworn his penchant for barging like a bull to get his way and usually—not always—he got it.

Paul Mellon remembers visiting Dale in his Plaza Hotel apartment to discuss a pressing item on the Gallery's agenda. As usual in submitting to Dale-proof hospitality, the Board Member was plied with multiple martinis, then with wine, then with champagne after dinner when Mrs. Dale retired and her husband got down to serious business. In the course of that conversation, Dale produced a copy of his will and proceeded to read Mellon salient passages in order to make the point that the Gallery might not after all be the final repository of his collection. Mind you, his possessions included: Manet's *Old Musician*, Mary Cassatt's *Boating Party*, Renoir's *A Girl with a Watering Can*, Corot's *Agostina*, Van Gogh's *La Mousmé*, Gauguin's *Self-Portrait*, Toulouse-Lautrec's *Rue des Moulins*, Degas' *Four Dancers*, Monet's *Palazzo da Mula*, Rousseau's

Both boxers, Dale and Bellows become friends. The collector writes: "From the things I saw in his studio, he seems to be painting in a different manner than most of the others, furthermore they seem to have more of a wallop than paintings of other fellows."

George Bellows, *Both Members of This Club,* 1909
Chester Dale Collection

Equatorial Jungle, Modigliani's *Chaim Soutine,* Picasso's *Family of Saltimbanques,* Bellows' *Both Members of This Club,* to say nothing of other important works by the above and major pictures by Géricault, David, Ingres, Delacroix, Millet, Daumier, Boudin, Morisot, Pissarro, Fantin-Latour and many, many more.

The reason for Dale's lubricous twisting of Mellon's arm was simple enough: Chesterdale

wanted to name Huntington Cairns the next director of the National Gallery of Art. But he hadn't reckoned with David Finley nor with his heir apparent John Walker. Putting off that tempest for now, the question remains, how did Chester Dale get that way?

He was born the day after Christmas in 1883 to a cultured family on Madison Avenue. His father, a British-born scholar, sent the boy off to a military academy. That was enough formal education for Dale, who dropped out, preferring to go to work on Wall Street at the age of fifteen. He started out as a messenger delivering securities at five dollars a week. If he remembered it rightly in an unpublished stream-of-consciousness memoir that John Walker quoted, the job lasted only a week. It was too much work for too little reward. Going to the next job interview, he asked a telegraph messenger for directions, was called a "hick" for his pains and "took a swing at him" for his. In his youth Dale was a street fighter, too. The next job was easier on the feet, but at the same wage, and he wised up: Money was not made running other men's errands, though for the moment he had to settle for an office boy's slot. In an investment house that specialized in railroads, he studied the boss and realized that he more-or-less bought securities to resell at the highest markup he could get "without being too much of a robber." Dale thought that if he studied the real values of the stocks he could do better:

"I heard of White and Kemble's *Atlas and Digest of Railroads* with these maps [that] showed you the position of the various mortgages . . . all in concrete form. Well, I got so intensely interested in all that I couldn't even sleep nights." He learned the financial structure of all the railroads—what bonds they had issued, what they earned and what they were worth as negotiables. Before long, "I would make a boast that you can't name a railroad mortgage in the U.S. that I didn't know." One afternoon he saw "Mr. Harriman walking rather jauntily into Morgan and Co., wearing his specs and looking all serious and all of a sudden it occurred to me that there were five million Erie notes coming due in the

morning. . . . Mr. Harriman came out and looked to me as he had a kind of smile, a little bit like the cat that swallowed the canary. I said that smart guy beat Morgan and Hill and got the Erie." On the basis of reading Harriman's inscrutable look, the feisty wage-earner bought into the Erie himself. "Imagine me buying half a million notes. Supposing they'd gone off a couple of points . . . I'd have been washed up on Wall Street." But they didn't and he wasn't.

He opened the bond department in a new firm, became a partner and continued combining his knowledge of railroads with gutsy instinct. When two Canadian strangers appeared from an unknown place called Calgary ("sounded to me more like a cemetery than a town") Dale took in stride the fact that one man carried a brace of pistols in his belt. These cowboys had come to sell $750,000 in school bonds, and once Dale ascertained that Calgary was a boom town, he took their business—and then the business of towns like Moose Jaw, Medicine Hat and others, before Wall Street competitors realized there was money to be made in Western Canada municipals.

From there he went on to public utility

Another American inspired by study abroad, William Merritt Chase borrows impressionist colors and a French love of pure esthetics. He returns home to become an influential teacher and luminous painter.

William Merritt Chase,
A Friendly Call, 1895
Chester Dale Collection

holding companies and so forth, making millions and "retiring" from other people's employ at thirty-five, thereafter minding his personal affairs from a Wall Street office and managing financial matters for friends, whom he never forgot. John Walker reported that when the crash came, Dale held onto large blocks of one stock until friends who had followed his advice in buying it could bail out—though the waiting cost him $25 million. Worth $60 million before the 1929 crash, he escaped with less than $10 million. But, Walker continued, pictures he had bought for $2 million were appraised at $50 million when his estate was settled. If he had not recovered his entire paper fortune over the next thirty years, he had spent many millions in the interim while living as lavishly as possible and having a great deal of fun. "I was lousy in math at school, but this was making money and taking me places," Dale told *New Yorker* writer Geoffrey T. Hellman in 1958. "I was on the roof of the old Madison Square Garden when Stanford White was shot. Did you know that the first grapefruit in New York was served at the Astor, and the first avocado with French dressing at the Knickerbocker Hotel? It was the game! It was the fight! It was a challenge! All my life it's been a challenge, just as my collecting pictures is a challenge."

At the age of twenty-seven he married Maud Murray, a woman some years his senior, some inches taller, and head and shoulders above him in her knowledge of art (being an accomplished painter and art historian). "Mrs. Dale then began to lead me around to the various galleries about town," Dale recounted in another unpublished memoir. "By this time I really got myself hopped up about this art business, I thoroughly enjoyed it. I naturally began to ask questions of my tutor." In short order "Mrs. Dale and I had acquired the very bad and expensive habit of attending the picture sales in the New York auction rooms." They bought American modern works by Gilbert Stuart, Sully, Whistler, Morse, Chase, Ryder, then others including George Luks, Robert Henri and Arthur B. Davies.

Dale made many friends in diverse circles: cartoonist Rube Goldberg, sportswriter Grantland Rice, painters René Pène du Bois and George Bellows whose paintings, the budding patron thought, "have a lot more of a wallop." Bellows painted two portraits of Maud, and when Dale couldn't decide between them— "Naturally I didn't want somebody else to have a portrait of my wife"—he bought them both, the only portraits of women Bellows ever did on commission, Dale noted proudly.

I believe it was just about this time that Mrs. Dale said "If you are going to buy pictures like this and be a collector we had better talk over the situation a little more thoroughly and decide exactly what we will do.... I didn't realize you really wanted to start a collection."... Then I got the lecture about the French School particularly nineteenth century, what

great painters they were, what they had done. She began to talk to me about Renoir, Manet, Monet, Sisley, Courbet. I asked her why she had not mentioned this before and was told "I didn't know you were so interested in art."... She said, "Chester Dale, let us have some thing definite, I would suggest that you collect French art for the last 150 years with ancestors." I said what do you mean "ancestors"? What she meant was that Renoir was a great artist and came by way of and through Rubens, and Boucher. If you stop to think it over, you must understand it, Rubens had the color, Boucher, too, had all the flesh tints. I said what do we do about Cézanne, and she said, "Chester Dale, he came through Tintoretto and Greco." Then she tried to explain to me how Cézanne broke up form, and I wanted to know why he did it....

With Maud's advice he began buying wisely. "This picture business was really getting under my skin, I found that when I was downtown getting the wherewithal to buy pictures, my mind was on pictures. Perhaps all that was a good timing because you could not buy pictures with hay and I wanted more pictures." Frequenting Paris in the early 1920s, he bought presciently, but discovered that the art market there was as much a free-for-all as Wall Street in the wild and woolly decades before regulation. Anything went—if you could get away with it.

Not speaking French, he engaged a dealer to bid on a pair of Toulouse-Lautrecs for him at an auction. The paintings went for less than his limit, and he assumed they were his, when he realized that the dealer, in cahoots with an associate, had bought the better picture of the pair and for less than he offered. "He was furious," John Walker recounted, "and Chester's anger could be monumental. He threatened a lawsuit, hurled a few anathemas, and the terrified dealer delivered both pictures." Unwilling to remain an outsider, Dale bought stock in the Galerie Georges Petit, the French government's quasi-official art agent—enough stock to claim a seat

Rousseau, a self-taught artist, is part of the painters' "circle of Paris"— as Dale becomes part of the art buyers' circle in France.

Henri Rousseau,
The Equatorial Jungle, 1909
Chester Dale Collection

on the board, and membership in what he called
the French "Skindicate." Now he might "persuade the boys not to bid up against me on what
I wanted." The second memoir reveals many of
the French dealers' tricks, which Dale appreciated as only an old stock trader might. Much of it
simply boiled down to insider trading. Dealers
would agree in advance on which one would win
the bidding on choice works offered at Hotel
Drouet auctions. Or they would pool their
resources to beat outsiders.

Sometimes Dale played the game, as when
he hit on the novel idea (in those pre-electronic
times) of borrowing a New York bank's transatlantic teletype to make his bid, which then had
to be delivered by messenger to the auction in
progress. Evidently feeling the rich American's
breath on their necks even at that distance, dealers backed off, and Dale acquired Cézanne's portrait of his son. Sometimes he didn't play the
game. When Courbet's *Portrait of a Young Girl*
was on the block, lesser dealers deferred to an
eminence grise who was apparently supposed to

Family of Saltimbanques, *Picasso's first picture to fetch 10,000 francs, covers a huge canvas—too big for a struggling artist to waste— and conceals two other pictures.* Circus Family *and* Two Acrobats *were lost until Gallery scholars rediscover them (via x-ray) under this haunting troupe: The harlequin is Picasso himself; the fat jester his friend, poet Guillaume Apollinaire; the seated woman, his mistress Fernande Olivier. Most poignantly, the little girl is an orphan whom the barren Olivier adopted briefly, then returned to the orphanage over Picasso's objections.*

Pablo Picasso, *Family of Saltimbanques*, 1905
Chester Dale Collection

win the prize. When Dale kept bidding, "the auctioneer and the whole gallery started to laugh and... my competitor stood up and positively flounced out."

Dale was always bold as brass. Shaming a dealer into showing a treasure he was holding for another client, Dale decided he had to have *Madame Michel-Lévy*, Manet's pastel and oil portrait. Told that the other collector had an option on it until the next noon, Dale invited the dealer to lunch next day. Containing himself until nearly 2 P.M., he said the option must have lapsed. Still the dealer didn't want to offend the other buyer: "He said this was a very important client, Dr. Albert Barnes, to which I replied so am I." Dale got the portrait, then called on the sitter,

by now a septuagenarian who proudly showed off a footstool upholstered with material from the dress she wore in the picture.

After Maud saw Corot's *Agostina* in a home where they were dinner guests, Dale instructed his agent to offer a serious sum for it. The dealer said that one did not visit a house and offer to buy a picture. Dale replied, "'When you snap out of this... this nonsense, let me know whether you will or will not make the bid.' He admitted it was a substantial sum... and didn't see that it would do any harm to try." Dale said that the offer was good until 6 P.M.—not ten after. Again he got the picture.

In the early 1930s, Dale made a transatlantic offer on a Manet that Maud had recommended two years before. "What people wanted in those days was money; the demand for it was infinitely greater than for pictures…. Although the Depression was not any more useful to me than to any one else, I still wasn't broke and I was in the midst of making a collection," which *The Old Musician* would enhance mightily. Again, a dealer told him that making an offer on a picture not known to be for sale was gauche. Again Dale made a substantial offer, which was accepted before the short deadline passed. When it reached New York the picture proved too big to get into his apartment, so he loaned it to the Metropolitan. Picasso's *Saltimbanques* was too big, too, so he had it delivered to a 57th Street gallery —by crane through a window—in order to get a look at it.

Individual works aside, Dale's collection grew so large that he bought a townhouse on 79th Street to hold his art, while continuing to live in a hotel nearby. Dale lived all over the East Side of Manhattan, in apartments downtown and hotels uptown, in the Hotel Carlyle for years, finally at the Plaza. When art critic Aline Louchheim visited in 1952, she found "dozens of fine paintings completely masking the walls of the hotel apartment. Hung one above another, over doors, and even on a mirror, they leave 'no room even for a postage stamp.'" With a similar kind of concentration, he cultivated—stimulated or agitated might be the better word—a multitude of friends. These ranged from esthetes like John Walker to a Customs officer named Frank McCarthy who "saved him from double dealings on the docks." Having been burned out of two homes by fires, he courted firemen, getting an honorary badge from one fire house and dropping anything to attend a fire—in tails if need be and even if it meant then commandeering a fire truck to get to a dinner party.

Dale's neglected memoir shows that he had some tact too, as when he blurted out to Diego Rivera that his friend was wasting time on portraits of statesmen and such: "Then I stopped

Edouard Manet,
Madame Michel-Lévy, 1882
Chester Dale Collection

Dale puts off buying Manet's The Old Musician *for two years after Maud tells him it is a world-class picture. After he buys Manet's* Madame Michel-Lévy *he takes tea with the sitter, by then an old woman.*

Edouard Manet,
The Old Musician, 1862
Chester Dale Collection

After Salvador Dalí paints a Crucifixion, Dale virtually dares him to take Christ's Last Supper as a subject. The surrealist agrees, paints a tour de force, and grandly attends the picture's installation when Dale presents it to the Gallery. Later, Dalí paints Dale (with Coco).

Salvador Dalí, *The Sacrament of the Last Supper,* 1955
Chester Dale Collection

Salvador Dalí,
Chester Dale, 1958
Chester Dale Collection

short, and thought I may probably have stepped over a bit, but I was so in earnest that I had not considered how strongly I spoke. I hoped I hadn't made him mad." Rivera forgave him, and to prove it painted his portrait. Josef Stransky, formerly the conductor of the New York Philharmonic and then a Wildenstein dealer, owned Picasso's *Gourmet.* Dale offered to buy it during a dinner party in Stransky's home: "'I'll pay you a hell of a price, then you can buy from your firm something you may like better.' He laughed, wasn't a bit offended," though Dale himself was taken aback that he had "uttered a thing like that." He had to wait until Stransky died to buy the Picasso from his estate.

He also inspired some pictures in a manner of speaking. When Dale saw Dalí's *Crucifixion,* he was so entranced that he bought it—for the Metropolitan. Then, brooding about the painting over breakfast with Maud, he had the brainstorm that Dalí might paint a scene barely reinterpreted since Leonardo: The Last Supper. Dalí took to the idea, and though Dale was pleased to say he had not commissioned the work, he got first look. He didn't need a second. "Dale is very intuitive, very quick, very decisive," the flamboyant surrealist said. "Most collectors seek advice and wait; he falls in love with a picture and then he takes it. He is a passionate man for this kind of thing, and a passionate man in general."

In this case, Dale bought the enormous canvas and gave it to the National Gallery with great éclat. Dalí himself came for the unveiling, and the huge visionary canvas began a sort of migration through the building. Since then the work has hung in several places where it is often the only canvas in sight—usually in lonely and overwhelming splendor. The trouble was—and is—that at the Gallery it had no "ancestors," to use Maud's term.

Chester Dale lies in a cemetery in Old Greenwich, Connecticut, with his parents and first wife. The small family plot is reportedly overgrown with weeds; perpetual care was something he reserved for art. "I have little or no family, and why should I save and scrimp, accumulate eight or ten dollars, when by concentration, a little exploration and having an awful lot of fun I may be able to contribute something.... It's very little that any one individual can do and if by any possible chance you have an opportunity to do something for posterity, with everything we have taken from this world I intend to try to do it."

The *New Yorker* profile noted that Dale's collection "'is not just the backbone,' John

Walker... has said, 'it's the whole rib structure of the modern French school here. The quality is fantastically high.'... The Gallery's president [Dale], who is childless, knows that art, judiciously handled is a more likely vehicle of fame than common stocks, or even public-utility bonds. If his rib structure in the National Gallery settles down there permanently, his name, like the names of Mellon, Kress and Widener... may well be a household word, at least in households of culture and refinement, a hundred years from now." That was only a third of a century ago, but the point was well taken. ✷

A glossy magazine declares that Dale, "who has no family, considers every one of his paintings his children"—as Le Gourmet *might attest.*

Pablo Picasso,
Le Gourmet, 1901
Chester Dale Collection

A Succession and Its Successes

During the summer of 1955, Chester Dale

hatched the novel notion that Huntington Cairns, the Gallery's secretary-treasurer and general counsel, should become director. Thus began a sequence of events that threatened the Gallery's organization, its precious independence, and the gentlemanly rule by consensus of the five citizen trustees.

Cairns was one of the most distinguished minds ever to come to the Gallery, a polymath who had earlier entered the Treasury Department through a side door—as a censor who vetted books and works of art presented to U.S. Customs officers for import. ("Someone had to do it," he said. "Most of the Customs people did not know a Vatican mural from a French postcard. I was once shown a book which a Customs man regarded as highly suspicious. It was a Spanish version of the Bible.")

Born in Baltimore in 1904, the prodigy sailed through high school, skipped college and earned a law degree at the University of Maryland when he was twenty. For a time he practiced law, then was recruited as a legal advisor (that is, censor) in Morganthau's Treasury, and became assistant general

John Walker, scion of Pittsburgh wealth, student of Berenson's, husband of British nobility, and the Gallery's first chief curator.

counsel. He came to the Gallery as secretary-treasurer and general counsel in 1943 when Donald Shepard, showing signs of illness or infirmity, resigned to become Advisor to the Board.

Cairns was, save the mark, a man of letters. He was a friend of H. L. Mencken and corresponded with Aldous Huxley and Bertrand Russell. His own literary product was prodigious: books on legal theory, tax policy, French literature, criticism, esthetics, even Shakespeare's herbs. He collaborated with Edith Hamilton on *The Dialogues of Plato*, with Mencken on *The American Scene, a Reader*, with John Walker on *Masterpieces of Painting from the National Gallery of Art*. His anthology of *summa* literature from Homer onward, *The Limits of Art*, was a landmark collection of poetry and prose. He won august kudos—membership-at-large in the American Council of Learned Societies, the Rockefeller Public Service Award and an offer from Harvard to teach whatever he pleased at the price he named. He turned it down; the Gallery was his vineyard.

Cairns was an able administrator who somehow attended to his manifold duties and still found time for the censoring, as he ripped

through novels in ninety minutes each. He banned some serious art in both painting and literature—novels by his friend Henry Miller, among others, because they violated his personal definition of obscenity by belonging in a "class of sexual stimulants not customarily brought into public view." He was a bibliomane who spent all his leisure time reading—when he wasn't writing the essays and books that his wife, Florence, edited. He and Paul Mellon traveled to London with their wives, and the Mellons were somewhat surprised that when the Cairnses were not actually engaged in Gallery business they closeted themselves in their hotel room to read.

Cairns was also a diplomat, or the perfect subordinate. Paul Mellon once remarked he hated being interrupted by phone; Cairns promised never to call him again. If a trustee vacationing in Florida needed his advice or counsel, he jumped on a train and was there the next day, because he would not fly. He adored the Outer Banks, where he vacationed (and eventually retired) and boasted of reading Virgil to the waves. For all his gifts, however, the art of office politics was not one of them.

His lack of finesse came to light when he announced during the summer of 1955 that he

had been duly chosen to succeed David Finley as director. Finley had no plans to retire just then, and didn't want to be succeeded by Cairns in any case. But by jumping the gun, Cairns was again being the good subordinate—of Chester Dale in this instance. Dale had summoned Paul Mellon to Southampton and read him his will, threatening to remove his collection from the Gallery. The Louvre was really the best place for his French pictures, he said. The threat was all too real, Mellon decided, and reluctantly agreed to placate Dale by endorsing Cairns as the next director. But to make their decision stick, they needed a third Trustee and evidently enlisted Vice President and acting President F. Lammot Belin, who soon left the country for a European vacation. It was then recorded that a quorum of three had made a decision that was binding on the entire board of five General Trustees and the four ex-officio members. When Cairns let that cat out of the bag, a particularly polite form of hell broke loose.

Dale and Mellon had played a card earlier by advising Finley that he was due to retire when he turned sixty-five, since the Gallery had experienced some unpleasantness when age had overtaken Donald Shepard's acuity, and a compulsory retirement policy seemed wise. Ever the persuasive diplomat, Finley had begun marshal-

ling his own forces. Now, with Cairns' memo making very confidential rounds, Finley went into action. He found ready allies in Duncan Phillips, who believed that Finley should pick his own successor, and in Rush Kress, the surrogate for brother Sam who was still president of the Gallery several years after a stroke left him speechless and immobile. Finley then ascertained that the ex-officio members of the Board—notably Treasury Secretary George Humphrey and Chief Justice Earl Warren—were completely in the dark about these goings-on and were quite willing to insist that the full board consider the matter of the director's succession. In effect, the Southampton decision was deemed inconclusive and Finley did not step out of harness on his birthday in September, the month that Sam Kress mercifully died. Finley had too much to do to retire—for one thing to plan the fifteenth-anniversary celebration for the following March when new Kress gifts would be unveiled and the entire Kress Collection splendidly rehung; for another, he meant to choose his own successor.

In the meantime, Sam Kress' demise meant a reshuffling of the board. In what can only have been a political compromise of Solomonic wisdom, Sam's brother Rush Kress was elected to the board and Chester Dale elevated to the presidency—men who were like oil and water. But

the matter of the directorship still hung fire, and before the December trustees meeting Finley played an ace. He drafted an unmistakably clear letter for Rush Kress' signature. Addressed to the Chief Justice as chairman of the board, it reviewed the importance of the Kress Collection, and expressed the opinion that Cairns was not qualified for the director's job but that Walker was. Further, it stated "we [the Kress interests] shall take no part in the proposed Anniversary celebration" and would instead withdraw planned gifts "unless we have been reassured as regards the future Director." Should there have been any doubt, Kress Foundation officer Franklin Murphy delivered the message personally to the Chief Justice.

In polished form the letter said, "It is the unanimous feeling of [Kress Foundation Trustees] that no more paintings should come to the Gallery until we have assurances of the highest type of official management and an attitude on the part of the Board of Trustees...." The letter suggested a review of appropriate laws and bylaws, specifically the provision "that three members of the Board can constitute a working quorum to decide matters of important policy.... This is not a private Gallery. The paintings are the possession of the American people; consequently it seems to me [Kress as ghosted by Finley] that the four government

members of the Board should have a definite, active and continuing responsibility for the basic policies and activities of the National Gallery of Art." It might even do to consider expanding "so small a Board"—all of which would open questions that had not been contemplated since Roosevelt reviewed the terms of Andrew Mellon's proposed gift.

In his cover letter to the Kress advisors, Finley noted that his draft of the letter to the Chief Justice might be too strongly worded. "We must be firm and courageous, and not pussyfoot, but we are part of this great American people's museum. We must be careful not to put in writing and deliver to the Chief Justice a letter which will result in Messrs. Mellon and Dale becoming so angry and ashamed of their wrong actions that they will take it out on the Gallery, Mr. Mellon by withholding any future gifts and Mr. Dale by withdrawing his large Collection of paintings which are regarded with favor by a considerable section of the public." Again, Dale's Damocletian sword hung over the whole affair—and it bears mention that Paul Mellon admits regret over his part in the whole affair. But he felt at the time that continued stewardship of the Dale Collection had overwhelming importance to the Gallery's long-term interests.

Cairns had "a capacious mind" but in Mellon's view he had no soul—and, worse for a museum director, no taste. Walker, on the other hand, had informed taste, though Dale thought he lacked administrative talent, which the lawyer Cairns possessed. The fact was, as Mellon remembers it, quite simply, "We were all brainwashed by Chester because we were all frightened of losing the collection."

In the end, when Dale began to see that he lacked the votes, he called in his lawyer, Stoddard M. Stevens, who would later serve as Mellon's personal attorney and as a Gallery trustee. Said Stevens, then a senior partner of Sullivan and Cromwell: "Chester never calls me in until he is in trouble." Gallery Vice President Mott Belin invited the warring factions to dinner—including Secretary of State John Foster

Dulles—and by the time coffee and cigars came around Dale had backed down.

Sometimes as petty as he was expansive, Chester Dale had even objected to posting Duncan Phillips' name with the other major benefactors on the wall of the Sixth Street lobby. He harangued Mellon and threatened to retract his loans once again. This time Mellon said that Phillips' gift of Daumier's *Advice to a Young Artist* qualified him as a major donor; beside he had been Andrew's friend, an original member of the board of trustees, and Paul meant to see his name included with the others and that was that. This time Dale backed down. Dale hated Phillips, Mellon said, because he was a great collector and a gentleman; it was a matter of simple jealousy.

In any case Dale failed in his coup to promote Cairns and the majority of general trustees proved they could manage Gallery affairs without intervention by the ex-officio members. But as John Walker remembers it, there was another reason that the row was resolved happily. Walker said Cairns made it abundantly clear that he

would faithfully support the trustees' decision whichever way it went. Walker said he made it equally clear that if he wasn't named to succeed Finley, he'd go back to Berenson and I Tatti! In any case, the fifteenth-anniversary gala unveiled new Kress gifts of great distinction, and Finley, though he still didn't want to retire, stepped down on the last day of June 1956. John Walker became director, a post he would fill with distinction, and the matter of the succession was over.

Walker would serve as director for thirteen years, in the course of which he identified his own successor and groomed him for the task. His term marked a period of internal growth and consolidation, several spectacular events that raised the Gallery's profile, and a decision of monumental importance to the future of the National Gallery of Art. Parenthetically, it bears mention that Chester Dale took his defeat with all good grace, as Walker was the first to admit. He was not an easy president, generally speaking, but an active one who had Walker on the phone daily with opinions and instructions. When he died, in 1962, he bequeathed his col-

Friends during younger Pittsburgh days, Paul Mellon (left) and John Walker find common cause at the Gallery as President and Director respectively.

lections to the Gallery at last and forever, and Walker confessed that he slept a great deal better than he had in years. The dynamo also left a sum of money to Walker, which the surprised legatee used to purchase a summer house on Fishers Island—a little estate he gave a name that barely rates a second glance from passersby but which has a certain resonance. Walker christened the place "Will o' Dale."

Outstanding among the events that occurred during John Walker's administration was a "blockbuster" show—an unfortunate term but

one that sticks. The happening that raised the Gallery's profile in the public eye was the loan in 1963 by the French Government and the Louvre of Leonardo's *Mona Lisa.* It occurred in a manner as unlikely as the event itself, the Gallery's next director remembers:

Edward T. Folliard had covered national affairs for the *Washington Post* for decades. At a National Press Club luncheon, where French Cultural Affairs Minister André Malraux was the speaker, Folliard sent up a card with the question, "Mr. Minister, why don't you lend the *Mona Lisa* to the National Gallery?" Malraux's quick reply was "I will." The painting came as a personal loan from President de Gaulle to President Kennedy, who in turn called on John Walker to cope. Over the objections of the director of the Louvre, who resigned over the issue, the painting was taken down, crated up and shipped across the Atlantic on a luxury liner. It got its own first-class stateroom, and Folliard sailed with it, filing daily reports of the lady's voyage.

The Walker administration's most epochal decision came with the reminder that the Gallery had an explicit option to expand. But the Mall was becoming very precious real estate, in part thanks to the Gallery itself, and in part due to the visionary leadership that S. Dillon Ripley brought to the Smithsonian as its new secretary. Thus the trustees agreed to accept the most beneficent offer from Paul Mellon and Ailsa Mellon Bruce to enlarge the Gallery with a new building (of which more later). This brings to mind one of the unsung achievements of John Walker's career at the Gallery: his tutelage of Ailsa Mellon Bruce as a patron.

"If about Paul there is an aura of happiness, about his sister, Ailsa, there was always one of sadness," wrote Walker in his memoirs. "It was as though a wicked fairy had appeared at her christening, waved a wand, and blighted all future enjoyment of her wealth and beauty. Yet those of us lucky enough to have penetrated her shyness knew a woman who could be as gay and amusing as her brother. But we also realized that for years she was in constant pain from a form of arthritis, and that in her personal life there were repeated tragedies." For one thing, her marriage to David Bruce languished, and though it is said she was content to live apart and remain married in name only, the union ended in divorce, however amicable. Bruce, who then married Evangeline Bell, a diplomat's daughter as outgoing as Ailsa was reserved, went on to matchless distinction as a diplomat. For another thing, Ailsa's only child, Audrey, vanished in a chartered plane on a Caribbean flight with her husband Stephen

Currier, leaving three small children who were then raised by guardians outside their grandmother's rather rarefied circle.

Ailsa Mellon Bruce not only suffered pains in her joints, but as she aged her inborn shyness increased incrementally with the passing years. Though she was barely known to the staff, she is widely and justly honored as one of the museum's principal benefactors—in part thanks to Walker himself. He cultivated Ailsa and encouraged her to participate in the Gallery as best she was able. Theirs was a unique relationship—fraternal, tutorial, sycophantic.

While Walker subscribed to the mandate that "the museum director follows the hearse," that was not his only watchword. He also led

During John Walker's watch, Ailsa Mellon Bruce —here in her Founders' Room portrait by Philip de László—bestows wonderful gifts and names the Gallery in her will. Within five days after her unexpected death in 1969, a special memorial exhibition is mounted to honor one of the Gallery's most generous if unseen benefactors.

Philip Alexius de László, *Ailsa Mellon Bruce,* 1926
Ailsa Mellon Bruce Collection

patron and patroness by the hand, and he led no one with deeper understanding and affection than Ailsa Mellon, who repaid his attentions with marked generosity to the Gallery. (Walker's relations with Paul Mellon were less sublime, perhaps more jealous. Sitting in his fire-engine-red wheelchair in the dappled shade of the Chevy Chase Club, he once told me, flashing his trademark grin: "Paul's friends all like him more than he likes them." Two years later in a *New Yorker* article, Calvin Tomkins quoted the same remark, only with the verbs escalated to "love," so Walker must have meant it.)

It was Ailsa Mellon's husband who appeared to have been most actively involved in the Gallery during the planning stage and early years of

operation. Perhaps at the start she bore a ladylike grudge: When her father arranged to set aside the cream of his collection for the museum, he did not consult the children about details. Her favorite picture, which hung in her bedroom throughout her youthful years, was the sweetly haunting Reynolds portrait of *Lady Caroline Howard*: An ethereal and serious little girl sits on the ground in a somber landscape; she wears a bombazine cape and white silken dress with a lace cap and blue sash as she tentatively touches a rose bush. When Ailsa learned that this, too, was going to the National Gallery and "was not eventually going to belong to her, she was very, very upset," brother Paul remembers. Years later she yearned to acquire it—by loan, trade or purchase—if only it were done quietly. Even if an exchange could have been possible, the inevitable publicity would have been anathema to her, and the painfully shy art lover never got Lady Caroline back.

"Father's explanation of it to me was that he felt very badly about it," Paul Mellon told an interviewer. "But on the other hand he felt that Ailsa especially and maybe I too, didn't understand that we were creating a National Gallery

really as a family gift—that it wasn't just a gift from him but that it was a gift from all of us." Notably, it became just that when Walker gently drew her into the Gallery's thrall, as her generosity proved beyond doubt. As her brother and champion points out, she personally bore one-third of the monumental costs when the Gallery expanded.

In terms of smaller things Ailsa gave a treasury of pictorial gems, both directly and through her Avalon Foundation which endowed a special fund for American pictures. Devoted to certain acmes of symbolic femininity, she gave the lush, rococo Fragonard portrait of *A Young Girl Reading*, and most spectacularly funds to purchase the only Leonardo da Vinci painting in the western

Two portraits mark a gamut in Ailsa's experience: The English girl kneeling is her favorite picture from her father's collection, one she wishes desperately to take back; The French girl reading, one of her many gifts to the Gallery, is given in memory of her father.

Sir Joshua Reynolds, *Lady Caroline Howard*, 1778
Andrew W. Mellon Collection

Jean-Honoré Fragonard, *A Young Girl Reading*, c. 1776
Gift of Mrs. Mellon Bruce in memory of her father, Andrew W. Mellon

The one-hundred-thirty-six
art works that Ailsa Mellon
Bruce wills to the Gallery
include French paintings
that surround her in her
late rather reclusive years: a
bright Renoir cityscape, a
breezy Boudin beach scene,
a tranquil Morisot harbor-
side (opposite below).

Auguste Renoir,
Pont Neuf, Paris, 1872
Ailsa Mellon Bruce Collection

Eugène Boudin, *Beach
at Trouville,* 1864/1865
Ailsa Mellon Bruce Collection

*Ailsa Mellon Bruce leaves
funds which make possible
such purchases as the 1970
coup of acquiring Thomas
Cole's allegorical quartet,*
The Voyage of Life.

Thomas Cole, *The Voyage of
Life: Childhood,* 1842
Ailsa Mellon Bruce Fund

Berthe Morisot,
The Harbor at Lorient, 1869
Ailsa Mellon Bruce Collection

Pictures from Ailsa's own collection, such as the Degas pastel and the Vuillard, appear in exhibitions of "Small French Paintings," a series of shows as popular as they are frequent. The Ailsa Mellon Bruce Fund acquires a major landmark in modern art, Picasso's Nude Woman, *the manifesto of a new artistic order, analytic cubism.*

Edouard Vuillard,
The Conversation, 1891
Ailsa Mellon Bruce Collection

Edgar Degas, *Dancers at the Old Opera House,* c. 1877
Ailsa Mellon Bruce Collection

Pablo Picasso,
Nude Woman, 1910
Ailsa Mellon Bruce Fund

hemisphere. This is the celebrated *Genevra de' Benci,* presumably a wedding portrait painted in the 1470s. Certainly when bought from the Prince of Liechtenstein in 1967 it was inch-for-inch one of the most expensive pictures in the history of cultural commerce. Its purchase per se, ending two centuries of ownership by a single family, was a coup, and one that could never have happened without the reclusive donor's regal gen-

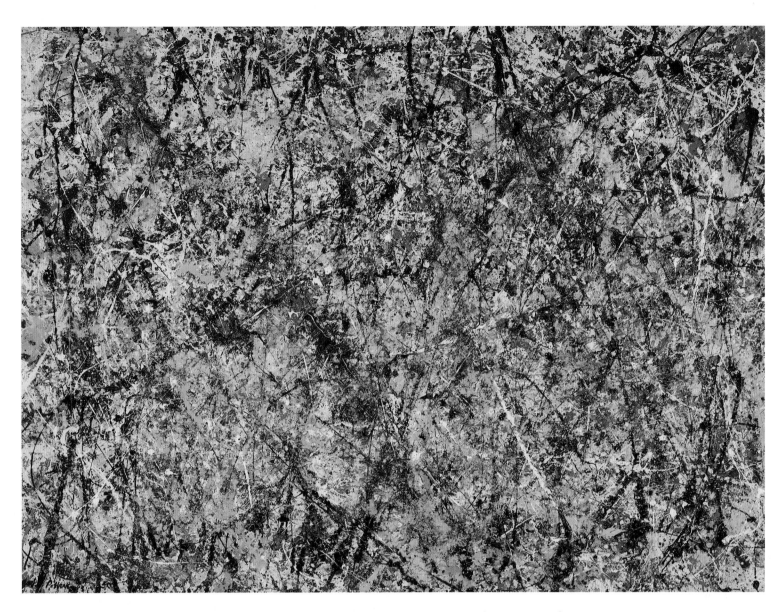

erosity. Walker explained its magic: "This is the first psychological portrait ever painted."

Ailsa Mellon told Walker repeatedly, "You know, John, you mustn't think you are going to get everything I have for the National Gallery." But in the end he did; when she died after a brief illness in 1969, her will bequeathed all her pictures to the Gallery. Fond of pictures of children, Ailsa had owned and left to the Gallery Goya's *Condesa de Chinchon* and Monet's *Artist's Garden at Vétheuil*, showing the painter's son. Especially rich in the works of French artists, her bequest included nine Bonnards, five Boudins, two Cassatts, a Cézanne, three Corots, a Daumier, a Degas, two Derains, three Dufys, another Fragonard, two Gauguins, four addi-

tional Manets, a Matisse, five Monets, four Morisots, five Pissarros, a Redon, twenty-two Renoirs, a Rouault, a Seurat, two Toulouse-Lautrecs, three Utrillos, ten Vuillards. Her legacy included drawings by Winslow Homer, the elder Brueghel, Tintoretto, Rubens, Van Dyck, Gainsborough, Delacroix, and many other major works on paper.

After her death, the funds she established made possible some of the Gallery's great acquisitions, including Thomas Cole's allegorical quartet, *The Voyage of Life*, the haunting Georges de la Tour *Repentant Magdalene*, dazzling cut-outs by Matisse, the Picasso *Nude Woman* of 1910, and *Lavender Mist*, the last great Jackson Pollock drip painting in private hands. ❧

When Lavender Mist *comes up for sale, Ailsa Mellon Bruce's posthumous fund provides the wherewithal to acquire this last major Jackson Pollock drip painting in private hands —a masterpiece by America's most original painter.*

Jackson Pollock, *Number 1, 1950 (Lavender Mist)*, 1950
Ailsa Mellon Bruce Fund

The Gallery's Lorenzo, The Pericles of Pleasure

Andrew Mellon made the National Gallery a grand museum, his gift to America. He conceived it, collected its first priceless array of art treasures, then posthumously paid for its monumental edifice, and endowed it handsomely. Paul, his son, made the National Gallery a great museum.

After succeeding his late father on the board of trustees for a very brief term, he went off to war, then returned to play a decisive role in the Gallery's affairs and to donate splendid gifts of money and art while serving an apprenticeship of sorts and even admittedly making a few mistakes. Once he rose to the Gallery's presidency, he inspired and directed its substantial transformation. Thanks to David Finley's fidelity to his mentor's vision, the original Gallery made manifest Andrew Mellon in its somber dignity and august dedication to the old masters. So too the transformed National Gallery makes manifest Paul Mellon the man, the most giving patron, the lover of art and servant of pleasure.

"I think this Gallery is a reflection of the love of one man for his country, and the love of

Family themes continue at the Gallery under the stewardship of the founder's son. Witness the shimmering Woman with a Parasol—*a picture of Monet's wife, with their young son hovering behind the brow of the hill. Bought in Paris in 1965, the picture hangs in Paul and Bunny Mellon's New York dining room before they give it to the Gallery in 1983.*

another man for his father. Andrew [for] the country; Paul for his father." So said Dr. Franklin Murphy, current chairman of the board, in an oral history interview shortly before the semicentennial year began. The love he attributes here is an original thing with each of them. Just as Andrew had never been a garden-variety flag-waver, neither was Paul a fawning scion striding (or tippy-toeing) in his father's footsteps. Rather he became his own man and his father's son most clearly in marching to his own drum.

Servant of pleasure? Or pleasure's presiding patron, its Pericles. In any case, here too he is an original—neither wizened esthete nor rampant hedonist, but a philophile abiding in an entirely different realm. Paul Mellon sees pleasure as one of life's necessities. Famous for his wealth and his philanthropy, he may have been most widely quoted for a quip about the pleasure of dreaming. His homily inspired editorial writers across the land one spring a quarter-century ago: "What this country needs is a good five-cent reverie."

He made the remark in the fiftieth-anniversary commencement address at Foxcroft School, the elegant girls' boarding academy near his home in Virginia's hunt country. And therein lies his credo:

For your own sakes, for your children's sakes, there is an inherent duty to be aware, to do something, to care. The only thing that I want to add today is something I think many people tend instead to subtract. This is the element of, the principle of, Pleasure....

I would say it was just as important to enjoy yourselves today as ever before, to plan your leisure as you should plan your work and responsibilities, so that fun, laughter, the contemplation of beauty, and relaxed loving-kindness become just as important as boring social conventionality or hard-won financial security....

You hear a lot these days about the expansion of leisure time and the need to use it well, but so often the suggestions seem to imply a desperate substitu-

Claude Monet, *Woman with a Parasol—Madame Monet and Her Son*, 1875
Collection of Mr. and Mrs. Paul Mellon

tion of unmeaningful labor for what was satisfying work. What we often really need is an hour alone to dream, to contemplate, or simply to feel the sun. What this country needs is a good five cent reverie....

My other category of pleasures I call cultural. I refer not only to the practice of and enjoyment of the arts and literature, but also to the enjoyment of any intellectual complex or body of knowledge which is alive and meaningful.... This can include everything from music, painting, sculpture, the dance, to a flirtation with the newer mathematics, or even a serious romance with the astounding and seemingly unreal world of physics and astrophysics....

None of you a year from now, or perhaps even a day from now, will remember what I have said. It's like writing on the surface of Goose Creek with a sycamore branch. But you may remember a kindly, greying man who said... that at least part of the purpose of life was enjoyment. And that beauty, in all its many forms, whether in nature or in art or in science, has a great deal to do with it.

It was a credo because Paul Mellon has given much of his inner life to pleasure, while devoting his external life, his very active career, to philanthropy. Inevitably he became a public figure long ago, in part because he was born a celebrity but in larger part because his chosen work as a philanthropist was practiced on a singular scale. No individual has done more to endow the arts and letters in America. Justly, he became famous for it, while privately he admits almost apologetically that his philanthropy always followed the directions of his personal interests. How did he choose beneficiaries of his largess? That wasn't so difficult because while he possessed impressive wealth, he never had infinite amounts of time and therefore had to focus his energies. Thus, he decided that he could support responsibly only those things that interested him personally. These include literature, scholarship, science to an extent, ditto animal husbandry and the natural world. Above all, he has supported art—through Yale, the Virginia Museum of Fine Arts and the National Gallery of Art.

About the time of their parents' divorce, Paul and Ailsa Mellon each has the look of a charming child.

As the *New York Times'* art critic emeritus wrote in *Smithsonian Magazine* a few years ago, "Paul Mellon may cultivate anonymity, but his philanthropies in the world of art constitute a benefaction without equal." While there was something quite original in his active involvement with art, John Canaday reminded readers that Paul in part followed his father's example: "The Mellon family's gifts to the nation, beginning with Andrew's funds for the construction of the National Gallery, are thought to be the largest from any one source." How large has this largess been? In more than fifty years of fairly systematic giving, he has contributed roughly $1 billion to various causes.

The fact remains that he chose to become a philanthropist and chiefly a supporter of the arts and letters while making his very life a work of art. Perhaps learning to give charitably was partly a way out of a dilemma, for as Canaday summed up: "His problem as the possessor of a staggering inherited fortune has been to see that it does not possess him." Being the only son of one of America's richest men was not, one infers, entirely cakes and ale—though he has had his share.

His parents' marital situation notwithstanding, Paul's growing up had a dream quality about it. He and Ailsa rode off to nursery school in a horsedrawn carriage driven by a trusted groom. He had a Shetland pony by the time he was six and began to ride in earnest in his early teens. And there were the regular sojourns abroad; he had been christened in St. George's Chapel at Windsor Castle. His childhood shimmered with images of a painter's England—its lush landscapes, blooded horses and tailored gentry:

I remember huge dark trees in rolling parks, herds of small friendly deer, flotillas of white swans on the Thames, dappled tan cows in soft green fields, the gray mass of Windsor Castle towering in the distance against a background of huge golden summer clouds; soldiers in scarlet and bright metal, drums and bugles, troops of gray horses; laughing ladies in white with gay parasols, men in impeccable white flannels and striped blazers, and always behind them and

behind everything the grass was green, green... somehow at this great distance it all melts into a sunny and imperturbable English summer landscape. There seemed to be a tranquility in those days that has never again been found, and a quietness as detached from life as the memory itself.

Close friends would often say that he seemed to have more of his mother than his father in him, though his attachment to England came from both sides—Nora's birthright and Andrew's chronic anglophilia.

At twelve, Paul was sent off to one of New England's smaller, finer preparatory schools, Choate. Somewhat shy, he learned that some people sought him out because he was the son of a rich and famous father, while he feared that others might not befriend him because he was nothing except a poor little rich boy. Studious, he wrote poetry, and made a serious stab at poet's laurels but instead won a biography of Lincoln "for earnest and persistent effort." (One devoutly Christian poem of his youth was immortalized to the Anglican tune of "Duke Street" in the school hymnal.) Going on to Yale, he found it shining in a golden age. As he told his classmates at a reunion many years later, "Nothing I have ever done [for the arts and letters]...would have occurred to me—would even have had the slightest interest to me—were it not for the four years I spent here. My love of English literature, life, and art...all this was cherished, intensified, confirmed by...the Yale English Department."

A college anthem extolled "Bright College Years," and Paul lived them to the luminous hilt. He slavishly "heeled" the *Yale Daily News*, and shamelessly used Father's connections to win points by getting interviews with celebrities and statesmen alike through his special assistant. (David Finley kept him supplied—often by pages-long telegrams—with reams of speech texts, by Secretary Mellon and others, and government reports.) The year Paul became vice-chairman of the *News* board, it was hardly coincidental that the annual roast-beef-and-julienne-potato banquet was addressed by Deputy Secretary of the Treasury Ogden Mills.

Having graduated with honors from Yale in 1929, it was off to Cambridge and Clare College for a sojourn that confirmed Mellon's anglophilia and awakened him to a new passion. "My mother gave me a big Irish hunter, Dublin, comfortable, safe, a wonderful jumper.... He gave you a wonderful feeling at a fence. I took him to England, ran in a few point-to-points." Riding to hounds and racing would ultimately broaden his involvement with art and heighten his eventual reputation as a singularly gifted collector. He got interested in art through hunting prints. Paul had noticed pictures before (he slept beneath Raphael's large *Cowper Madonna* in the McCormick apartment), but his interest in them was passive. Reading history at Clare, he earned a B.A. degree while leading a picture-book student's life. He rowed for a winning crew, donned white tie and tails to dance the night fantastic, and nurtured a benign pastime into a lifelong passion: horses.

His father had approved his stay in Cambridge for one year, and when Paul proposed to remain for another, Andrew Mellon wrote his son an "unusually long letter" of three pages, urging him to come home and get started in business (though allowing him to make up his own mind). Paul stayed the extra year, then went back to Pittsburgh in the summer of 1931 and reported for work at the Mellon National Bank— with the press hard on his heels to cover the event as hard news. His mother had always hoped he wouldn't end up behind a desk, though she needn't have worried. He gave business a try, but it really didn't take and his banking career was short. His presence was sometimes called for in London while Andrew was ambassador there, and he often escaped then-gloomy Pittsburgh for New York as well.

He was there over Christmas in 1933, and got his name in the papers again—for riding a horse-drawn sleigh through the winter's first snow and winning a race to the Central Park Casino. His prize was a magnum of champagne;

his companions the writer Lucius Beebe and a pretty divorcee, Mary Conover Brown. The daughter of a distinguished Kansas City doctor, she had graduated from Vassar in 1926, studied at the Sorbonne and Columbia, then worked in an art gallery and as a fashionable photographer's assistant. Mary, called Mim during childhood, then Mima, was bright, curious, musical, effervescent. One friend said "when she walked into a room, you'd feel that the sunlight had come in." Another called her "a joyous spirit who jumped into all gaiety and gave enormously to it, with an instant laugh and a quick remark. Everybody loved her." Paul married her in Ailsa

As his father is rightly known for his somber mien, Paul Mellon wins a reputation for warmth and friendly wit as plain as the smile on his face.

and David Bruce's New York apartment a little more than a year later.

Mary was a woman of parts: Cultured, intuitive, inquisitive, and intelligent in a sparkling and undisciplined way that led some cerebral friends to conclude that she was not an intellectual. One admirer records, "She was so vivacious, just the opposite of quiet Paul, that [even] his father took right to her." At a birthday party for her the entertainment was a spider-web game in which each guest had to follow a different string through tangles, over tables and under chairs all through the house to find his or her prize at the other end. "So there we were, all of us, including Mr. Mellon, crawling on the floor and in and out of closets." Perhaps only Mary could get him on his knees in fun. She was gregarious and a talented singer and pianist (who would play the "Wedding March" at a friend's wedding, then slip into bee-bop). A Gallery associate who knew her from childhood still remembers most vividly how Paul regarded her: "Paul adored this woman. I mean *adored* her.... She certainly touched him. It was a *real* love affair."

The newlyweds took a long honeymoon

Mary Conover Mellon: as blooming youth from America's heartland, and (opposite) as the fashionably arty New Yorker in a portrait by George Platt Lynes, the celebrated photographer for whom she once worked.

abroad, chartering a houseboat to cruise up the Nile to Abu Simbel, then visited in Paris. (It was said that Paul might conveniently stay beyond the reach of subpoenas relating to his father's tax case.) Returning to Pittsburgh in 1935, they took up brief residence in Andrew's house, and rented a pied à terre in New York. Here they gained easy entree into art, social and intellectual circles, including an avant-garde group that was exploring the new psychology espoused by disciples of the Swiss analyst, Carl G. Jung. Smoking and drinking with fashionable abandon, Mary had a lively curiosity, yet her interest in psychology was not merely intellectual, for she suffered from a form of asthma as severe as it was chronic. Though she at first pooh-poohed the new psychoanalysis, she took it up and soon came to believe that her malady was psychosomatic. Though she tried couch therapy to cure it, the asthma came and went for years, often with frightening force.

Paul Mellon's recollection of his entry into Jung's circle is all the more intriguing for seeming inevitable, as a quick chain of emotional experiences led to a personal epiphany. In part, it appears an example of Jung's belief in the unity of human experience and the collective unconscious. It also seems to exemplify what several friends and associates have remarked about Paul himself: In many ways, as the elements of his experience intertwined and themes reinforced each other, his life came to resemble a work of art.

Intrigued by Jung's published work, Paul and Mary had consulted a psychologist who invited them to meet the master during his celebrated trip to lecture in New York. Then they pursued a growing interest in the Jungian world view, which involves psychology, comparative religion, ancient iconography, archetypal mythology, philosophy, the history of art and cultural history in general. This became a major intellectual pursuit, though not their only preoccupation. Late in 1936, their daughter Catherine Mellon Conover was born, and they settled at Rokeby Farm in Upperville, Virginia, the horse-breeding farm that Andrew had bought for his ex-wife Nora. They commissioned architect William A. Delano to design a Georgian house, modeled after the Hammond-Harwood house in Annapolis, for Oak Spring, the farm adjacent to Rokeby. Then in 1938 they went to Switzerland to participate in Jung's seminars and soon become disciples. They helped underwrite various research and publishing projects, hoping to see all Jung's writings translated and published in America. The following year they moved to Switzerland and set up housekeeping with little Cathy, a nurse and butler, becoming for nearly a year Jung's psychoanalytic patients as well as his advocates and patrons.

John Walker, who had known Paul growing up in Pittsburgh, would write much later that "perhaps as a result of Jung's analytical psychology, [Paul] became one of the best balanced and, as far as an outsider can ever know, one of the happiest of human beings." Paul himself discounts this, saying "Whatever my problems were, I did not think that it helped me very much." (By comparison, an analysis in another mode which he went through later was beneficial.)

In any case, the Mellons' work with Jung ended in May of 1940 when they left neutral Switzerland shortly before Hitler seized the surrounding nations and Europe tumbled into war. Before the year was out, Mary had organized the Bollingen Press, named for the hamlet that was the site of Jung's private retreat.

Back home, America was girding for war and Paul was putting his affairs in order. He had resigned the Gallery's presidency and his seats on other boards the previous spring. Now he established the Old Dominion Foundation, which would be incorporated days before Pearl Harbor and which became his primary vehicle for all sorts of philanthropy. His military future was uncertain while he cherished "the romantic idea that the horse cavalry would still be fighting in this war." Seeking advice, he followed Mary's rule "When you want something done, always go to the fountainhead," and sought the advice

of a foxhunter he had ridden with, General George S. Patton. Ultimately, in June of 1941, Paul simply enlisted through Selective Service, which still let volunteers choose a branch of service. Swiftly, the army sent Private Mellon through basic training, then on to OCS and Cavalry School; soon he was training other officers to ride.

A month after Pearl Harbor, the Bollingen Foundation was founded in New York with Mary as its president and its purposes were "to stimulate, encourage and develop scholarship and research in the liberal arts and sciences and other fields of cultural endeavor generally." It was hamstrung almost immediately by a national policy borne of paranoia. Mary was compelled to cut all ties with Jung and his associates in neu-

After riding to hounds in England, Paul Mellon develops a passion for horses. In Virginia (here in the lead) he competes in point-to-point races and develops Rokeby Farm as an admired breeding and racing stable.

tral Switzerland; the Foundation corporately, and its officers and trustees individually, might be deemed in violation of the new *Trading With the Enemy Act* if they continued to send food parcels and funds to foreign friends through the Red Cross, let alone to collaborate with them on the publication of books. Through attorney Donald Shepard the FBI warned the Foundation "unequivocally to cease all activities, correspondence and financing of its work in Switzerland. Unwittingly, these [activities] might give aid and comfort to the enemy with serious results and untold embarrassment." This despite the fact that Allen Dulles, OSS chief in Switzerland and later head of CIA, was frequently consulting Jung himself about the personalities of "sinister [Axis] leaders." Nonetheless Bollingen soon began its publishing program through Pantheon

Books, the house just founded by veteran German publisher Kurt Wolff and his wife Helen, who had managed to reach America as refugees. The Bollingen Series would, Mary wrote, issue "books in all fields which deal with Man in relation to himself."

Meanwhile the intermittent mails brought Mary a letter from Jung that said in passing, "I suppose Mr. Mellon is now in the army. I always had the impression that he had the psychology of somebody who is waiting to be picked up by something which wasn't yet in sight." He was still waiting, if no longer as a private soldier. Paul had won a lieutenant's commission in the cavalry and, tiring of teaching horsemanship, applied for duty overseas. Shipped to England, he found himself reclassified as a gardening instructor, hardly his cup of tea. Never shy about contacting friends in high places, he finagled a billet with his brother-in-law's outfit, the OSS. As an intelligence officer, he briefed and debriefed agents working with resistance groups on the continent. He saw duty near the front in France and Belgium, but says the greatest danger he faced was during Nazi air raids in London— unless it had been surviving a three-week Atlantic crossing in a troop ship.

At the war's end he got a wire from David Finley asking him to return to the Gallery's board; David Bruce was resigning as president, his marriage to Ailsa in a state of suspended animation after years of separation. By this time, the Mellons' plans seemed crystal clear and twice as bright. The house in Upperville was finished; they would live there principally, breeding horses, hunting foxes, and raising Cathy and her little brother, Tim, in the country. Mary had delivered a son in the summer of 1942, and named him Timothy, "because, in the New Testament, Timothy is Paul's companion and friend," according to a Bollingen memoir. Upperville was within reasonable reach of Pittsburgh and New York, where Paul would regularly attend to major interests in family enterprises and foundations respectively. It was also in commuting range of Washington, where he would make a headquarters; yes, now he would go back to the Gallery—the family enterprise—and take up its work with a will. As for Mary, she would turn her boundless energy and contagious enthusiasm to directing the metamorphosis of a newly reorganized Bollingen Foundation and launching its "programs of fellowships, scholarly publications and contributions to humanistic learning."

The single cloud on these halcyon horizons was Mary's erratic asthma. One known cause of it was her sensitivity to horse dust, but even this was highly inconsistent over the years, and she took to riding and driving about the farm in a horse cart. She had also long since sworn that she would not let a little allergy prevent her from sharing her husband's favorite leisure activity. William McGuire, editor of the Bollingen Series and its historian, described what happened all too soon:

On October 11, 1946, a pleasant autumn day, Mary and Paul went fox-hunting early in the morning. For a year or so, she had been enjoying riding, though she always carried an atomizer containing medication. After the hunt they were on their way back home when Mary suffered an asthma attack. The atomizer had broken, and the attack grew more severe. At Oak Spring, she was put to bed and seemed to improve. But in the early afternoon she had another attack that was too much for her heart. Her last words to Paul were, "And I had so much to do." She was forty-two at her death.

When John Barrett [a friend from Yale days and soon Bollingen's mainstay] arrived at Oak Spring the next day, Paul told him immediately: "Jack, if you'll stick with me, what happened will not prevent our going on together to create what Mary wanted."

The funeral was held at Oak Spring.... The plain coffin, covered with flowers from the farm, rested on a small spring wagon, which was drawn by Mary's two ponies. The pallbearers walked beside the wagon, and the others walked in an uneven procession behind, Paul and [nine-year-old] Cathy first. Dr. and Mrs. Conover were driven in a car. The burial was under an old tulip tree in a little cemetery that had been on the farm for many years. [It is Nora and

Andrew's resting place as well.] The minister of the local Episcopal church read the service, which included a text that was inscribed on Mary's ring and was a favorite of Jung's: "And as Moses lifted up the serpent in the wilderness, so must the Son of Man be lifted up."

Needless to say, Paul was good to his word. He would sustain the Bollingen enterprise that his wife had inspired and directed. Led by Barrett, this remarkable academy without walls would go on to aid hundreds of scholars. Through its liter-

Paul Mellon's hippophilia leads him into the cavalry in the brief belief that horses may play a gallant role in World War II. Later posted to England, he is assigned in error to tending victory gardens before he escapes into the OSS.

ary centerpiece, the Bollingen Series (first issued by Pantheon and now by Princeton University Press) it would publish one hundred scholarly titles in nearly three hundred volumes: classics, translations, and original theses in the fields of esthetics, archaeology, cultural history, ethnology, literary criticism, mythology, philosophy, poetry, psychology, religion, symbolism. By 1952 it would launch a series within a series, publishing the annual A. W. Mellon Lectures in the Fine Arts, which are delivered each spring at the Gallery. Among other volumes, The Mellon Lectures comprise: Kenneth Clark's *The Nude: A Study in Ideal Form,* Herbert Read's *The Art of Sculpture,* Anthony Blunt's *Nicholas Poussin,*

John Pope-Hennessy's *The Portrait in the Renaissance,* J. Bronowski's *Art as a Mode of Knowledge,* Ludwig H. Heydenreich's *Leonardo da Vinci,* Jacques Barzun's *The Use and Abuse of Art,* H. W. Janson's *Nineteenth-Century Sculpture Reconsidered,* Joseph Alsop's *The Rare Art Tradition* and John Rewald's *Cézanne and America.*

Landmark scholarship aside, doubtless the most popular titles were two spectacular surprises for a purportedly academic press, Joseph Campbell's comparative study of godheads through the ages, *The Hero with a Thousand Faces,* and the Taoist best-seller *The I Ching, or Book of Changes.*

In 1948 Paul married again, making a match that would animate the Gallery both in its collections and its ambience. Bunny, née Rachel Lambert, a Listerine heiress and hunt country neighbor, had been Mary's friend, and her marriage to Paul produced new cultural progeny (if not human offspring; they each had two children already). There was Trinity Episcopal Church in Upperville, which they built as a memorial to Mary. Designed by H. Page Cross in the manner of French medieval churches, it is a sublime testament to Paul and Bunny's sense of exacting excellence, with stained glass from Holland, some ironwork rescued from a thirteenth-century church near Dresden, and interior carvings executed by Virginia craftsmen working in native stone and woods. There was also "the farm"—Oak Spring and Rokeby Farm augmented by surrounding acreage—which now resembles a sort of Eden.

Delano's neo-Georgian residence with its all-too-resonant center hall proved a noisy home for four growing children, and Bunny Mellon supervised its conversion into "The Brick House," which now serves as a library for Paul's rare books and as a museum and private gallery. Here, for example, is a room devoted to the display of his incomparable collection of Degas wax statues—dancers and horses—along with Degas' monumental painting *Steeplechase—The Fallen Jockey.* The family moved over the brow of a hill to a home that evolved from eighteenth-century

In later years wherever Paul Mellon lives or works he will be surrounded by art of exceptional quality, such as this cluster of his own pictures in his office. His passion for art— especially French pictures— is kindled by Bunny, whom he marries in 1948.

beginnings and that Bunny transformed into a country house fit to entertain the Queen of England and the Prince of Wales—yet a disarmingly modest-looking dwelling set in as artful a landscape as Constable or Pissarro ever dreamed of capturing on canvas.

Approached along a winding drive bordered by pruned apple trees, it sits amid fenced pastures and young orchards. The whitewashed stone and shingled house seems cradled by the land, yet it in turn shelters an enclosed acre of gardens dark with herbs, bright with flowers and bordered by espaliered fruits. Beyond the garden is a greenhouse, its glass-roofed wings joined by a room whose walls are all cabinets with trompe l'oeil doors seeming to display Bunny's own pruning shears, sun hats and such. A "basket shed," which doubles as a playhouse when children visit, has a Braque still-life on the wall, and nearby lily ponds murmur with the lilt of flowing water.

At Oak Spring, the Gallery's next director J. Carter Brown would encounter "the realization of an ideal I had sensed as a student at I Tatti: life lived as a work of art." Art is everywhere at the farm. Not just on the walls and occasional pedestals, art lies in the arrangements of things —in the eighteenth-century French game table in a powder room, in the statue of Paul's legendary horse, Mill Reef, in front of the brood mare barn, in the vistas that invite one from room to room taking in here a Van Gogh on the wall and there a garden beyond the window.

Like their Washington house off embassy row, Oak Spring displays Bunny's exceptional gifts for visual arrangement and Paul's special appreciation of beauty and amenity. Thus, it is hardly surprising to read a corollary in an art

An amateur gardener of exceptional gifts, Rachel Lambert Mellon tends fruit trees at Oak Spring, now the family's principal country home in Virginia, where Henri Cartier-Bresson photographs her. In 1961 President Kennedy asks Americans to discover "What you can do for your country;" then he recruits Bunny to redesign the White House Rose Garden.

critic's view of the East Building: "The kindness of the staff, the understated elegance of the galleries—it's a little like being in one of the Mellons' houses. [In the Gallery] he has tried to make our lives more like his." Oak Spring is the acme of the rustic estate: several farms combined into 4,000 fertile acres of fenced meadows cleaved by streams and bounded by woods. The pastures support cattle, and the cows produce cheese for Bunny's larder. The rolling fields are nurseries of foals for Paul's racing stables in South Carolina and England; the woodland edges are home to foxes. (There is an airstrip, out of sight of course, to respect the mise en scéne. Even the cabin of the private jet has small pictures framed on the bulkheads: Braque again, Ben Nicholson and a vibrant little Dufy of Buckingham Palace.) Paul declares with a combination of gratitude and

awe that Bunny made this idyll, a place that seems enchanted.

Bunny's special gifts would be felt at the National Gallery which, thanks to her influence, in time forsook the puritan aversion to entertainment in favor of splendid receptions and elegant dinners. But before that happened, her special interests transformed her husband as a connoisseur. Heretofore he had focused on English sporting art; Bunny introduced him to the delights of collecting nineteenth-century French pictures particularly (much as Maud inspired Chester Dale, and with Dale's collaboration). The Mellons had several homes—in Washington, Upperville, Cape Cod, Manhattan and Antigua—and all demanded decoration. Thus they began to buy pictures that happened to appeal to them. "Neither Bunny nor I have ever felt a driving urge to own any picture just because it is important," Paul has written in a forthcoming memoir, "and certainly not because either considered it to be a good investment." They have bought what they liked, and avoided whatever put them off (among other things, pictures of windmills and landscapes with more than three cows).

Nonetheless, in the fifties and sixties they bought some very important pictures: Manet's *George Moore in the Artist's Garden* and Monet's *Bridge at Argenteuil*, Cézanne's *Boy in a Red Waistcoat*, Van Gogh's *Green Wheat Fields, Auvers*, Monet's *Woman with a Parasol—Madame Monet and Her Son*, Manet's *The Plum*, Seurat's *The Lighthouse at Honfleur*. They began to give some of these treasures to the Gallery with the approach of its twenty-fifth anniversary. While most of their gifts would be French paintings, the Mellons have contributed an astonishing variety of objects and images, from the wax original of Degas' *Little Dancer, Fourteen Years Old* to a spectrum of shimmering Rothko canvases.

Once he became known as a serious collector, an indicative bit of wisdom spread quietly among knowledgeable dealers: never bargain with Mr. Mellon. That is, if he liked a picture and thought it worth the price, he would place a hold on it for a few days while he thought it over. If a dealer got anxious and volunteered a lower price, according to dealers' lore, Paul would very likely not do business with him again. While perhaps foregoing a few "bargains," this policy probably saved him money in the long run by encouraging dealers to price their goods realistically. By the same token, he does not bargain when selling works of art, which he has done a couple of times when culling his collection. If a picture doesn't fetch its "reserve" price at auction, he usually does not entertain lower offers. Each work of art has a value, in his view, and he will hold on to a picture or sculpture if he can't get what it's worth.

Paul's first major gift of art came to the Gallery in 1965. This was a group of 351 paint-

One Paul, son of the founder and now president of the Gallery, unveils another Paul's powerful portrait of his father (see page 282).

ings by George Catlin, the singular portrayer of American Indian life; and these pictures became a mainstay of the museum's National Lending Service. In 1966, the Gallery mounted an exhibition of French paintings from his and Bunny's collections along with Ailsa's nineteenth-century paintings. Then the major gifts began to arrive: Cézanne's portrait of his father in 1970; then Manet's *The Plum,* Degas' *Woman Ironing,* Cézanne's landmark *Houses in Provence* and Gauguin's dreamlike *Te Pape Nave Nave.* In 1983, the Mellons gave another 93 paintings, sculptures and drawings including two works by Mary Cassatt, five by George Bellows and their most important Hogarth. Still, the gift was largely French impressionists and post-impressionists: six Monet works, Renoir's *Flowers in a Vase,* Vuillard's haunting *Woman in a Striped Dress,* the Seurat *Lighthouse* and ten Boudins. In 1985, the Mellons gave 186 more pictures.

Paul's own collecting began at Cambridge— illustrated books of English country life, then a canvas: George Stubbs' 1774 equestrian portrait, *Pumpkin with a Stable-Lad.* In time, as art historian Edmund P. Pillsbury has written, he "spurned the sort of formal British portraiture"—the full-length images by Reynolds, Gainsborough, Romney, Hoppner, et al. who followed in traditions that Van Dyck imported and which in turn pursued Renaissance ideals. "In contrast, Paul Mellon's predilection was for an indigenous and more intimate form of British art, one that exploited the careful draftsmanship and tonal subtleties of Dutch seventeenth-century art and manifested itself in small-scale portraits, sporting subjects and landscapes." In 1959, Leslie H. Cheek, director of the Virginia Museum, seized upon this interest and invited Mellon to organize a landmark exhibition, "The Horse in Art." This project inspired Paul to expand his sporting pictures into what became a comprehensive collection of English pictures and books—a collection he would give to Yale, along with a building to house it.

Paul's gift for giving has ranged wide for over half a century and reached beyond the realms of art as he found a vocation in the business of serious and systematic philanthropy. He has given personally and corporately—through his own Old Dominion Foundation and in partnership with Ailsa's Avalon Foundation (which then combined to form The Andrew W. Mellon Foundation) and through the E&C Trust which was only disbanded in 1980. To the nation, he and Ailsa gave the start of Cape Hatteras National Seashore, when they matched state funds to buy the original lands. To Virginia, he gave Sky Meadows, a little wilderness in the Blue Ridge which his purchase saved from development. To Yale, he gave the wherewithal for mental health programs, for several undergraduate seminar programs, for two residential colleges designed by Eero Saarinen, and works of art. To Cambridge, he gave the endowment for a professorial chair. To both universities he gave an exchange program for graduating seniors. To St. John's College, where he had taken courses after Cambridge, he gave a building by modernist architect Richard Neutra. To Choate, he gave a science and an arts building, both designed by I. M. Pei. To the Virginia Museum, with Sydney and Frances Lewis, he

gave a building wing and art to fill it.

Through gifts from his several foundations, he has created, or caused to be created, whole institutions, among them Bollingen, of course, and Harvard's Center for Hellenic Studies in Washington, and the Yale Center for British Art, which he housed in what proved to be Louis Kahn's last building. It now comprises the most comprehensive collection of English paintings, drawings and illustrated books to be found anywhere outside England. He has sustained old institutions, among them the Audubon Society and the Conservation Foundation, while he has contributed to the evolution of some institutions when time overtook their usefulness as independent organizations. Thus Paul oversaw the merging of the Mellon Institute of Industrial Research with the Carnegie Institute for Technology into more than the sum of their parts: Carnegie-Mellon University. Likewise, as president of the A. W. Mellon Educational and Charitable Trust, he directed its liquidation fifty years after it had been founded. He has supported equestrian

Equally revolutionary, a pointillist lighthouse and tranquil river also seize real instants, albeit en plein air. *Seurat explores natural light through the science of optics, recording solid objects such as buildings as he finds them. Monet takes more liberties in placing sailboats and even trees or buildings to enhance his composition.*

Georges Seurat, *The Lighthouse at Honfleur*, 1886
Collection of Mr. and Mrs. Paul Mellon

Claude Monet, *The Bridge at Argenteuil*, 1874
Collection of Mr. and Mrs. Paul Mellon

Gauguin incorporates Tahitian figures in his quest to limn spiritual truth. Bazille observes a flower seller with quiet dignity. Degas portrays one laundress' labor with the sublime simplicity of a Japanese print. Renoir infuses a bouquet with summer's spectrum of vibrant and fecund colors.

Paul Gauguin, *Te Pape Nave Nave (Delectable Waters)*, 1898
Collection of Mr. and Mrs. Paul Mellon

Edgar Degas, *Woman Ironing*, 1882
Collection of Mr. and Mrs. Paul Mellon

Frédéric Bazille, *Negro Girl with Peonies*, 1870
Collection of Mr. and Mrs. Paul Mellon

Auguste Renoir, *Flowers in a Vase*, c. 1866
Collection of Mr. and Mrs. Paul Mellon

Cézanne père, a banker like Andrew Mellon, sternly supports his son in a career he does not approve and wins homage in this portrait that seems both a monument and a diploma. Executed with palette knife, it is a new technique that blazes a path for the painter's later work.

Paul Cézanne, *The Artist's Father*, 1866
Collection of Mr. and Mrs. Paul Mellon

Painted fourteen years after the portrait of his father, *Cézanne's* Houses in Provence *exemplifies his ability to balance colors and masses in palette-knife landscapes. Young Vincent van Gogh uses a grid to get perspective as he experiments with impressionist dicta involving palette and choice of familiar subjects before moving to France. Edouard Vuillard, a deft colorist, will practice the lessons of post-impressionism well into this century.*

Paul Cézanne, *Houses in Provence*, c. 1880
Collection of Mr. and Mrs. Paul Mellon

Vincent van Gogh, *Flower Beds in Holland,* c. 1883
Collection of Mr. and Mrs. Paul Mellon

Edouard Vuillard, *Woman in a Striped Dress,* 1895
Collection of Mr. and Mrs. Paul Mellon

Grand Champion at seventy-one, Paul Mellon wins his fourth (of five) Hundred-Mile Ride in 1978. Likewise he serves the Gallery actively well past threescore years and ten, having been a general trustee, then president from 1963 to 1979, then chairman until 1985 and honorary trustee thereafter.

284

nutrition studies at Virginia Tech, a library at the University of the West Indies, the New York Shakespeare Festival, St. John's College....

In many instances he feels his own unique talent was inherited. As Andrew had the knack of backing able men in business ventures, Paul's contribution has been in picking the right people to run foundations and the cultural institutions in which he was interested. Not all his gifts have been seen as perfectly benign. When the Bollingen Poetry Prize was awarded to Ezra Pound in 1949, the *New York Times* headlined the story with the sort of accuracy that missed the real point: "Pound, in Mental Clinic, Wins Prize for Poetry Penned in Treason Cell." The poet, who had broadcast Fascist propaganda from Italy during the war, escaped prosecution for treason because he was deemed insane and confined in Washington's St. Elizabeth's Hospital. Public outcries were predictably noisy, and threatened to eclipse the prize jury's near unanimous view: that whatever his politics or mental health, Pound had written the best verse published the previous year.

Where does Mellon stand among other benefactors? "Harvard" magazine, no less, asked rhetorically, "What living philanthropist has been a greater personal force in American scholarship and letters than Paul Mellon?" Carter Brown writes: "What Paul Mellon has created in his first eighty years through the medium of the art museum represents a museum achievement without equal in our age.... The totality of his contribution is overwhelming."

Paul Mellon's service to the National Gallery is unequalled. He served as a general trustee for forty-one years in all and as president for sixteen years, from 1963 to 1979—notably the years that saw its remarkable expansion. In 1979, Chief Justice Burger begged off serving as chairman of the board because of the press of other duties, and Paul succeeded to the chairmanship, an opportunity he welcomed as he slowly phased into a manner of living that hardly resembles retirement. In 1985 he relinquished the chair and was named Honorary Trustee.

All things considered, the years have treated him well; he only gave up foxhunting when he was seventy (about the time he stepped down as president) though he was still winning Virginia's 100-Mile Trail Ride—a sort of marathon for equestrians—at seventy-two. Fully a decade later, when accepting the World Monuments Fund's Hadrian Award for leadership in preserving art and architecture, he confessed: "I am something of an ancient monument myself... in need of restoration." Speaking to a glittery audience, Mellon compared the pleasures "of ownership and donorship"—the savoring of beauty in his daily life and the joy of seeing people enjoy his gifts in museums.

The Hadrian Award was only the latest in an array that speaks volumes about the man and his achievements—in the eyes of others. Having commissioned buildings by Saarinen, Kahn, Pei and others, he was made an honorary fellow of the American Institute of Architects. Having served his alma mater so well, he has received the Yale Medal. He has also won the Horace Marden Albright Scenic Preservation medal, a National Institute of Arts and Letters award "for distinguished service to the arts," and Benjamin Franklin Medals from both the Royal Academy of Arts, and the American Philosophical Society. With Louise Nevelson and Georgia O'Keeffe, he was in the first class to receive the President's National Medal of Arts. A few years earlier, Queen Elizabeth II had bestowed on him knighthood as honorary knight commander, Order of the British Empire.

But characteristically, and with his famous modesty, he downplays his generosity. "I don't think of giving art as philanthropy" since it involves a motive that might have a self-serving element: having the pleasure of pursuing personal interests and seeing them perpetuated. He admits, "Still, you like to have the feeling that after your death someone will take care of them [the gifts] and others will enjoy them too." In any case, he says in a moment of rare personal justification, "I was not just sitting here foxhunting and eating bonbons." ❧

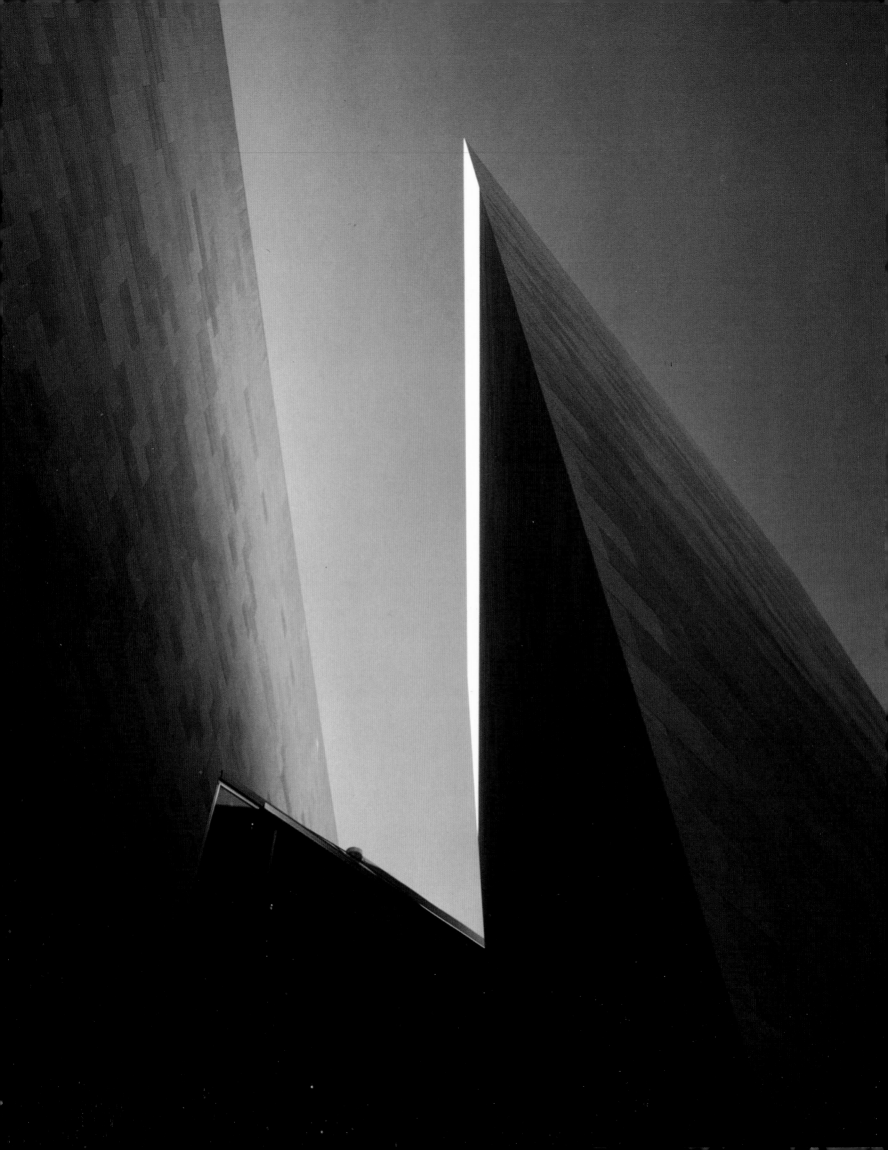

Third Director, Second Building, First Transfiguration

The active, personal interest that Paul Mellon dedicated to the Gallery after World War II enabled the museum that his father founded to find its stride and realize unimagined potentials. In all this, the Gallery built upon its original legacies and experience, making manifest an epigraph carved in the stone facade of John Russell Pope's nearest building: "What Is Past Is Prologue." Yet the evolution of a grand museum into a great one is neither a simple event nor an inevitable process. Here it involved several interdependent elements: the coming of J. Carter Brown who would be the next director; the construction of the celebrated East Building with its Center for Advanced Study in the Visual Arts; and the coming-of-age of the temporary exhibition as an art form of its own—a genre that enhances the meaning of art. While these elements were all related, there is no chicken-or-egg question of which came first—the third director did.

All appearances suggest that Brown was born to the job, but a colleague uses an entirely different metaphor to describe his role: Carter Brown "wears the place like a suit of clothes." It is pinstripe on many days of the week—hunting garb in the quest for new masterpieces to acquire or new angels to woo. Metaphorically speaking, he also has an outfit of white trousers, red tailcoat, top hat, and megaphone. Esthete and connoisseur, Brown is also innovator, orator, and by all intramural accounts, a kind of ringmaster. Whereas the director's office had been long on elegance, he gave it exuberance; where the Gallery prided itself on dignity, this Yankee aristocrat made it also remarkably democratic in its appeal. Certainly he encouraged things museological: development of the permanent collection through new acquisitions; expansion into new areas of collecting, notably modern paintings, sculpture and graphics; advancement of the publications program; establishment of a state-of-the-art conservation department; pursuit of major development efforts; the staging of remarkable exhibitions, and the development of innovative education programs. Yet while overseeing all these activities like a great impresario in the center ring, he would focus attention on the show itself and the tents.

J(ohn) Carter Brown was born in 1934 into the first family of Rhode Island, the clan of merchants and traders for whom Brown University was renamed in 1804 to honor many benefactions already bestowed. He was the middle child of John Nicholas Brown, the Renaissance man of his own time, who advised the army on cultural matters during World War II. Heir to several substantial fortunes, the elder Brown was at liberty to do anything he liked, and he liked doing many things very well. He knew Greek and Latin, led the New York Yacht Club as its legendary commodore, fostered cultural institutions of all kinds—artistic, scholarly, archeological, architectural—and served as their trustee, and collected art (drawings in particular) with exceptional discrimination. Carter's mother, Anne Kinsolving, an Olympian in her own right, was the daughter of Baltimore's preeminent Episcopal cleric, a professional violinist, columnist and music critic before her marriage. Parenthetically her sister (Carter's aunt) had been the first wife of Macgill James, the only experi-

enced museum hand on the original staff and one of David Bruce's ushers when he married Ailsa Mellon. In time Carter Brown would himself marry a Mellon (Paul's second cousin once removed). His second marriage, to Pamela Braga Drexel, took place in Westminster Abbey and produced two children before the parents separated fifteen years later. An outsider infers that Brown is really married to the Gallery.

Carter Brown's fit as director now seems so deft as to have been foreordained by birth and upbringing. Inheriting immaculate credentials (better than blue blood, blue genes) he grew up in a remarkably cultured household. Old master paintings hung on the walls; the summer estate at Newport had been landscaped by Frederick Law Olmsted; Toscanini was a friend of the family and chamber music was regular at-home entertainment—whether played by a professional quartet or by the children and their gifted parents. When John Nicholas Brown brought his family to Washington after the war, Gallery folklore relates, the boyish Carter glimpsed this new museum, glowing pink in the rain, from a taxi and declared he meant to be its director when he grew up. (He himself thinks he might have said only that he'd "like to have a job in a place like that someday.")

Carter's academic and intellectual achievements prepared him perfectly for his future career. Sent to boarding school at nine, he was expected to excel and did. He graduated first in his class from Groton at sixteen, spent a year at the Stowe School in England, and entered Harvard where he decorated his room with pictures by Matisse and Cézanne—originals from home. Buckling down to study history and literature, he followed the advice of a leading museum director to broaden his base by not majoring in art history which already seemed his forte. As an undergraduate he pursued serious interests in sailing, drama and music (as president of the Harvard Glee Club) and considered a career in theater or the concert stage. Graduating summa cum laude in 1956, he then led the Glee Club on a European tour which stopped in Florence

Directors' dynasty: In 1969 a boyish Carter Brown joins his elders, David Finley and John Walker, at the latter's retirement party. The trustees will ordain that the names be writ in stone by the Mall Entrance (opposite). Finley served as director for the first eighteen years; then Walker for thirteen after eighteen as chief curator. In all, Brown has served the Gallery for thirty years; as director, twenty-one and counting.

where Bernard Berenson's secretary heard them and invited a small ensemble to perform for B.B. at I Tatti. Presented to the nonagenarian afterwards, Brown engaged him in debate and was invited to study with him. He put off that honor for two years until he earned a masters degree at Harvard Business School, then joined the company of connoisseurs who had served as Berenson protégés, among them Kenneth Clark, John Pope-Hennessy and, of course, John Walker.

Brown stayed some months at I Tatti, then "realized there was a limit to what I could ac-

complish" there and decamped for Paris to take the prerequisite course for French museum professionals at the Ecole du Louvre. While Berenson made incalculable contributions to art history and connoisseurship, Brown says the sage "thought museum work was a lower form of life.... He used a German phrase, 'dumb as a museum director.'" But the student had by then decided on becoming a curator at least. After the Louvre, Brown embarked on a self-directed tutorial as he perambulated the art centers of Europe, seeing firsthand the masterpieces he

might have glimpsed in reproductions as an undergraduate. Returning to America, he enrolled in the doctoral program at New York University's Institute of Fine Arts, then *the* place for curatorial training, and passed his comprehensives in art history on the first day.

John Walker, who had known Carter since he was a boy, caught up with him there and heard of his ambition to direct "a museum that's the cultural center of its community." Walker responded that he might do that for the nation, and made an offer Brown couldn't refuse: the job as his assistant. He accepted and came to the Gallery in 1961, taking the summer off to write his masters thesis on Jan van Goyen, a seventeenth-century Dutch painter, and foregoing his long-range plan to earn a doctorate. (He has since received twelve honorary degrees and knighthood, or equivalent office, in nine noble societies: France's Legion of Honor and Order of Arts and Letters, Norway's Order of St. Olav, Egypt's Order of the Republic, Holland's Order of Orange-Nassau, Italy's Order of Merit, Austria's Order of Arts and Letters, Spain's Order of Isabel la Católica and Sweden's Royal Order of the Polar Star.) Succeeding Walker in 1969, he who would preside over the Gallery's fiftieth

anniversary was in harness for its twentieth and the museum's director by its twenty-ninth.

Coming to the Gallery, Brown made himself the museum's young-man-of-all-work with memorable energy and thoroughness. One retired staff member recalls being especially impressed by the manner in which the apprentice carried himself in those early years. He did his homework, handled all manner of seemingly minor projects for his seniors, while also becoming a regular at the staff table in the cafeteria. He studied the place systematically and tirelessly, learning about each part of the museum and how it worked. There was no debate over John Walker's successor when it came time for him to step down; here was the heir apparent chosen by the director himself being groomed and fitted for office.

Brown studied the place so well that he perceived a way that would eventually turn one of the Gallery's limitations into a remarkable strength. The deficit lay in the fact that at its inception this museum staked out a very clear, even confined bit of turf for itself—as delimited a territory as that of the rarest burgundy. The National Gallery collected European and American painting, as well as sculpture and works of art on paper from the middle ages to the early twentieth century; further, following Andrew Mellon's mandate, it restricted its holdings to works of the highest esthetic quality. That gave it rich realms to explore but excluded many others that were absent from the programs and collections of the city's other museums. If the National Gallery could not deal with the art of the wider world in its permanent collections, it certainly could do so through temporary exhibitions, which could bring the finest art from every period to America's national museum. It could not only present great works from other cultures but provide new opportunities for the appreciation of art in the Western tradition. As a corollary to this ambitious vision, Brown realized that the presentation of great works of art, even in temporary exhibitions, should be done properly. This led to the Gallery becoming a virtual laboratory for research and development in

T. Davies,
Ship in Full Sail, 1827
Gift of Edgar William and Bernice
Chrysler Garbisch

William Matthew Prior,
Little Miss Fairfield, 1850
Gift of Edgar William and Bernice
Chrysler Garbisch

Anonymous American
19th century, *The Cat*,
probably 1850/1899
Gift of Edgar William and Bernice
Chrysler Garbisch

Joshua Johnson, *Family
Group*, c. 1800
Gift of Edgar William and Bernice
Chrysler Garbisch

Edward Hicks, *Peaceable
Kingdom*, c. 1834
Gift of Edgar William and Bernice
Chrysler Garbisch

As the Gallery matures and fewer grand collections remain in private hands, singular acquisitions made possible by special donors continue to enrich its American holdings: Cropsey's epic allegory purchased through the Avalon Fund, and Heade's hummingbirds given by the Morris and Gwendolyn Cafritz Foundation. Peale's bespectacled son is the first purchase made from the Patrons' Permanent Fund, from the Gallery's campaign for an endowment, raised under trustee and president John R. Stevenson's leadership.

Rembrandt Peale, *Rubens Peale with a Geranium,* 1801

Patrons' Permanent Fund

Thomas Eakins, *Baby at Play,* 1876

John Hay Whitney Collection

Martin Johnson Heade, *Cattleya Orchid and Three Brazilian Hummingbirds,* 1871

Gift of The Morris and Gwendolyn Cafritz Foundation

Gifts of many kinds—
outright, partial, memorial,
—augment the collections.
Fitz Hugh Lane's sublime
bayscape is partly given by
Mr. and Mrs. Francis W.
Hatch, Sr.; Thomas Eakins'
rapt child is given by John
Hay Whitney and Winslow
Homer's sailboat by Ruth K.
Henschel in memory of her
husband, Charles.

Jasper Francis Cropsey, *The Spirit of War*, 1851
Avalon Fund

Winslow Homer, *Key West, Hauling Anchor*, 1903

Gift of Ruth K. Henschel, in memory of her husband, Charles R. Henschel

Fitz Hugh Lane, *Lumber Schooners at Evening on Penobscot Bay*, 1860

Andrew W. Mellon Fund and Gift of Mr. and Mrs. Francis W. Hatch, Sr.

soul-searching about its place in the nation, the world and its future in general. Five years later Carter Brown landed the task of soliciting ideas from respected colleagues elsewhere as to what roles the Gallery might assume. Should it expand its teaching role and affiliate with a nearby university? Might it serve a consortium of established academic departments? An art historian at Johns Hopkins University in Baltimore reported that his colleagues and students were forever coming to Washington to visit the libraries and to study various collections (not the least of them the Gallery's) but they had no place to work, and no single institution provided common ground—the grove sacred to all. This sparked an old idea that the young administrator seized with the ardor of a true believer; it was a very old idea after all.

This was to build a center of learning like the great library of antiquity at Alexandria, the city founded by Aristotle's pupil, Alexander the Great. Berenson for one, who considered his own I Tatti essentially a library, had espoused the Alexandrian example not only to Carter Brown but to John Walker a generation earlier. In any case, Brown says he explained the Baltimore professor's plight to Walker who hardly needed a refresher course in Berensonian ideals, since he had been B.B.'s executor and had overseen I Tatti's annexation to Harvard.

The idea could not have been more timely. Andrew Mellon had presciently insisted that the Gallery's charter provide room for expansion; the museum's "second site" lay across Fourth Street on ground occupied by tennis courts, a tract that looked riper for development with each passing season. The Mall was very choice real estate, and, with the arrival of S. Dillon Ripley as the new and energetic secretary in 1964, the Smithsonian began to expand rapidly. The Museum of History and Technology (now the National Museum of American History) was under construction; the National Air and Space Museum and Joseph Hirshhorn Museum and Sculpture Garden would follow, as eventually, would an underground complex comprising the National

state-of-the-art exhibition installations and their educational interpretation.

When Brown arrived, John Walker was nearly half-way through his thirteen-year tenure. The Gallery was on a steady course of collecting great works of art but it was running out of wall space. The collections had been growing thanks to the generosity of the founding donors, of course, but also with the accumulation of purchases, smaller gifts and bequests from other individuals. Often a "little" benefactor gave just a few pictures or a single ancestral portrait by a Copley, Stuart or Trumbull. In the aggregate these gifts helped the Gallery's pictorial wealth amount to far more than the sum of its parts. By now in its twenties, the Gallery was ready to do some institutional

Museum of African Art and the Sackler Gallery. All this left precious little Mall acreage not spoken for; anyone with a claim to an unused site had better use it or lose it. With little prompting, "the trustees asked me to detach myself from staff duties," Brown remembers. "I found new space with a secretary and, as one trustee said, 'set sail' for the East Building."

At first the idea seemed to center exclusively on a library of art per se with scholar's offices attached. Yet through the foreshortening lens of 20/20 hindsight, it appears that several ideas and purposes fell smoothly into alignment. When the Gallery's future needs were examined, the Alexandrian/Berensonian idea gained relevance. A community of scholars might be attracted to a library and the new building could evolve into a major research center that would both serve the National Gallery and its professional staffs in their public museum functions and enhance the Gallery's stature as a scholarly institution. A nucleus of such a community already existed in the Gallery's curatorial staff, and in the coterie of visiting scholars brought in by the professorial chair endowed by the Kress Foundation, by the Kress and Dale Fellowships and by the Andrew W. Mellon Lectures. (This program, conceived by Huntington Cairns, brought an outstanding scholar to give a series of lectures each spring— Kenneth Clark on the nude, for instance. The lectures were then published by the Bollingen Foundation.) To these intellectual seats were added the Finley Fellowships, which provided stipends from the Andrew Mellon Foundation for up to two and a half years. This program would eventually train, for instance, the present director of the department of painting and sculpture at the Museum of Modern Art and the director of the Museum of Fine Arts, Boston, as well as six of the Gallery's own curators.

Scholarship aside, the Gallery staff was in tight quarters in the West Building. While its library was bursting at the seams, a newly chronic shortage of space kept temporary exhibitions very much to a kind of second-class citizenship. Before the brainstorming was done, the plan for

The Ailsa Mellon Bruce Fund provides many masterpieces both profane and sacred such as Tacca's bronze Pistoia Crucifix, *named for the town in which it adorned a church, and the portrait of devout contemplation by Georges de La Tour.*

Pietro Tacca, *The Pistoia Crucifix*, c. 1600/1616
Ailsa Mellon Bruce Fund

Georges de La Tour, *The Repentant Magdalen*, c. 1640
Ailsa Mellon Bruce Fund

Henri Rousseau's fantasy is a gift from John Hay Whitney; Paul Cézanne's valley landscape and Picasso's gesturing lady (opposite) are gifts from W. Averell Harriman in memory of his wife Marie.

Henri Rousseau, *Tropical Forest with Monkeys,* 1910

John Hay Whitney

Paul Cézanne, *Mont Sainte-Victoire,* c. 1887

Gift of the W. Averell Harriman Foundation in memory of Marie N. Harriman

Pablo Picasso, *Lady with a Fan*, 1905

Gift of the W. Averell Harriman Foundation in memory of Marie N. Harriman

René Magritte, *La condition humaine*, 1933

Gift of the Collectors Committee

Edouard Manet, *Ball at the Opera*, 1873

Gift of Mrs. Horace Havemeyer in memory of her mother-in-law, Louisine W. Havemeyer

The Collectors Committee presents this René Magritte perplexity. Manet's gala entr'acte is the gift of Mrs. Horace Havemeyer in memory of Louisine W. Havemeyer.

an addition would include office space for curators, administrators and support personnel, thus freeing up room in Pope's building for conservation, exhibition design, and principally for the display of the Gallery's own collections of sculpture and works on paper. It also appeared that a major new structure should include additional exhibition space as well—indeed flexible exhibition halls that would be suitable for the presentation of art of all kinds, including modern art. In short, an ambitious and complex program was under discussion, and the discussion was encouraged by Paul Mellon who had become president of the Gallery in 1963. He decided to fund the construction of a new building with his sister Ailsa's equal participation, and late in 1967 President Lyndon Johnson announced their planned gift to enlarge the National Gallery. As in 1937, the project would require Congressional endorsement but LBJ chortled that unlike his Great Society programs, this building project

would not require "the expenditure of one dollar of Federal funds."

The idea called for a building as distinguished as Pope's edifice in its own right, but Director John Walker told the assembled press corps at the White House that it might not necessarily be neoclassical in style. In preparation for the ambitious effort, the board of trustees had been strengthened by the election of John Hay Whitney, art collector, newspaper publisher and diplomat, along with Stoddard M. Stevens, formerly Chester Dale's personal attorney, reigning partner of Sullivan & Cromwell, and now Mellon's lawyer. In addition, the board comprised two seasoned trustees in Franklin D. Murphy, president of the Kress Foundation and Chancellor of U.C.L.A. (and later chairman of the Times Mirror Corporation), and Lessing J. Rosenwald, the major benefactor and distinguished collector who had been chairman of Sears, Roebuck. Members of the building com-

Architects' sketches show the evolving design of an edifice to house activities as disparate as public exhibitions and advanced research. I. M. Pei's scrawl (left) reveals two triangles for the East Building and, notably, a vertical line to mark the West Building's all-important axis. The circle denotes his early plan for a round fountain in a plaza. In a later drawing, the exhibition building takes clearer form while the Study Center remains vague—and vaguely connected.

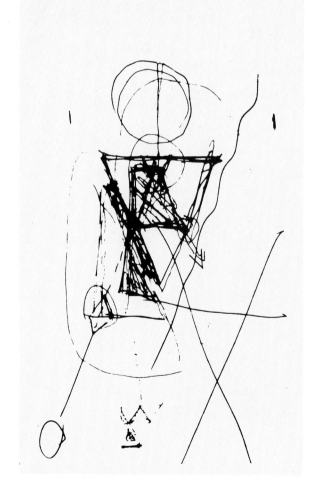

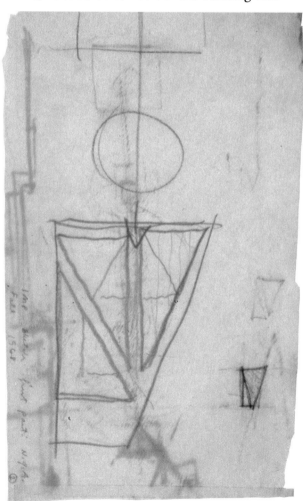

298

mittee, led by Paul Mellon, studied major museums abroad and embarked on a quest for the right architect in America. Using Mellon's personal jet, they hopscotched the country inspecting monumental buildings.

An annex for John Russell Pope's neoclassical masterpiece would be a choice commission for any architect even in the heyday of modernism, and to design a building for the Mall was a coveted honor. Yet the challenge was compounded by a host of complicating conditions. Being on the Mall meant that ironclad height limits and setbacks had to be respected. Further, the location meant oversight by the National Capital Planning Commission and the Fine Arts Commission as well as an unusual degree of critical attention. The building's complex purposes added another layer of design problems. Then there was the immutable fact that the new edifice had to honor and enhance Pope's masterpiece while being of an entirely different style and standing on its own architectural feet. Finally there was the site's shape, as unique as it is awkward—a trapezoid aligned with the original site along only one side, whose central axis does not match that of the original building.

In due course I. M. Pei was chosen for the manifold challenge, which he addressed with characteristic originality. (Introduced to Mellon over lunch, "Pei didn't crack an egg," Brown remembers. Born in China, the Harvard-educated architect was, like Paul Mellon, the son of a banker who once signed his country's currency as had Mellon's father.) Doodling on the back of an envelope while flying back to New York one day, Pei sketched the site's inelegant trapezoid, then split it into two triangles, which then suggested the solution he pursued. One triangle would house the library, offices for curators, and scholars' community—the Center for Advanced Study in the Visual Arts. The other triangle would contain ten separate, flexible exhibition areas on four levels, varying in size from 2,000 to 7,000 square feet. In an inspired stroke, Pei linked the two initial triangles with a third that embraced and unified the whole while providing

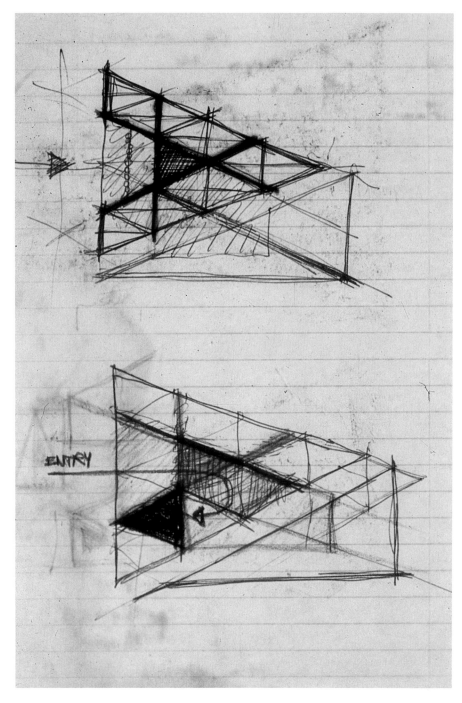

an awesomely inviting central space—a room that is a wonder in its own right as well as being an orienting atrium crossed by bridging walkways and punctuated with balconies. The entire building would provide offices for curators, visiting scholars and the Gallery's support staff; carrels for students, pro tem associates and independent researchers (deliberately intermixed); reading rooms with publications ranging from new periodicals to rare books; a library of photographs that would grow to become an unexcelled

Below the rough schematic, a more careful drawing suggests the final plan: The large triangle now has three shaded parallelograms — towers for "house museums." The central shaded triangle represents the space frame linking the exhibition spaces with the Study Center, which is the right triangle.

Groundbreaking: May 6, 1971. Hard-hatted and silver-shoveled, the dignified diggers are Chief Justice and Gallery Chairman Warren Burger, Gallery President Paul Mellon, and J. Slater Davidson, Jr., president of Chas H. Tompkins Co., the general contractor.

visual archive of art; restaurants for staff and visitors alike; two auditoriums, and an array of exhibition spaces that could be linked in endless and variable combinations.

To establish an explicit relationship with the Pope building, Pei called for facades composed of the same pink marble (which meant reopening the closed quarries in Tennessee). Yet a stronger link between the proposed modernist building and the existing neoclassical monument derived from Pei's two-triangle scheme. This allowed the axis of Pope's rechristened "West Building" to bisect the apparent front of the new "East Building." Here was an instance of magnificent architectural illusion: In fact the overall width of the new building does not line up with the West Building. Part of that width was established by the south edge of the study center and the apex of the smaller triangle. It is the base of the larger triangle that would be split by the West Building's axis to create a visual marriage. In turn, the space between the East and West

buildings would be designed as a unifying outdoor plaza of Belgian block, as Pei called it, a sort of "carpet of stone" (despite the passage of car traffic along Fourth Street). Finally, beneath this space there would be an underground concourse linking the two buildings and making them one in terms of access, security and environmental integrity.

This time there was a groundbreaking—on May 6th, 1971—with silver shovels wielded by Chief Justice Warren Burger, ex-officio trustee and board chairman, and Paul Mellon. Then on June 1, 1978, Mellon presented the gift of the completed building to President Jimmy Carter who accepted it on behalf of the nation in a ceremony that recalled the one of thirty-seven years earlier. Between the ground-breaking and dedication lay an epic series of adventures. In budgetary terms there were misadventures, in part because a series of strikes delayed the work and because construction occurred during one of the most inflationary periods in American history when basic indices for the building industry rose by three-digit percentages. There was no threatening the enviable record of the West Building which had been budgeted at $15 million and in the end cost barely $35,000 more. The East Building project was originally estimated to cost $20 million; in the end it comprised a greatly expanded program and cost upward of $95 million. The entire price would be shared by Mellons—first and foremost by Paul, almost equally by Ailsa before her death and then by the Andrew W. Mellon Foundation that Paul and Ailsa created.

The opening of the East Building in 1978 marked the metamorphosis of the nation's art museum: once the National Gallery added its second building it grew by an entire order of magnitude. In one stroke the expansion doubled the Gallery's physical size, which in turn enabled the doubling of its annual attendance, which prompted the near doubling of its staff before long. And as these forms of growth were underway, the Gallery's ken broadened to embrace the entire world of art. Importantly, the new building was designed as a foil to the old. Pope had designed the West Building as a temple for the great art of the past, a sanctuary of the classic; Pei designed the East Building as a pavilion for today and tomorrow, a place of adventure, of exploration and experiment.

The Pei structure was constructed with exceptional care and attention to detail. (Instead of carpenters, master cabinetmakers were employed to build the wooden forms to receive the poured concrete; instead of ordinary concrete the mix was colored with marble dust of the exterior's pink Tennessee stone.) It won twenty-four craftsmanship awards, a record of its kind. The East Building proved to be a great structure of exceptional energy, beauty and flexibility. Its office spaces, however, soon became filled to overflowing by the growing staff. Consequently, areas designed as open space became work stations or desks and one-person triangular offices were added here and there by closing off the end of a larger room. On some floors "islands" con-

In Tennessee, members of the Building Committee inspect marble samples extracted from newly-reopened quarries. They are (from left) Paul Mellon, Stoddard Stevens, Carter Brown and I. M. Pei.

taining office space for several people were added simply by installing glass walls and placing furniture inside.

In manifold ways the building was a spectacular success. In its first two months it received more than one million visitors, many of them coming to see the edifice itself as word spread of its attractions: the careful stonework, the soaring atrium, the "knife edge" of the study center's apex. At 19.5 degrees, this is surely the sharpest corner of any building in the world, which passersby could not resist touching until their fingers turned it black. Clad in the same pink Tennessee marble as its august predecessor, the addition shared another crucial element with it. Each building was the apotheosis of its era. When the Pope building was unveiled, it was both praised and panned as the greatest and latest example of neoclassicism. Even as it was being built in the late 1930s, a new architectural look had started to cover the country in glass and concrete masses. But this was brief as archi-

Progress Report: By May 1974 construction is well underway; deep underground a six-foot-thick slab has been laid and girded with waterproofed walls, a sort of underground boat floating in a virtual marsh. Six months later, underground construction has occurred between the East Building and the near side of the roadway. This is the "connecting link" — two vast levels comprising a garage, public concourse and cafeteria, kitchens, workshops, office suites, storage ranges and more, indeed nearly a mini-city underground.

By January 1976, the East Building's superstructure rises — steel framing and masonry walls to be clad in slabs of pink marble taken from the same quarries that provided stone for the West Building. Pei devises a method of hanging each slab independently with plastic gasketing to avoid unsightly expansion joints. Six months later the entire plaza has been covered anew, and what was planned as a round fountain has become a sloping, diagonal waterfall amid a cluster of pyramidal skylights.

Third Director, Second Building, First Transfiguration

Alexander Calder and Paul Matisse, the painter's grandson and an artful engineer, study a model of the great mobile that will grace the atrium. At center, workmen assemble the red, blue and black creation. Working with the model, Gallery savants advise Calder of a problem and he requests "a map indicating where the mobile bangs, or rubs, the walls." Bottom, it flies freely in the building's grandest public space, though its creator writes, "Personally, I might be in favor of a little rubbing or bumping. But I guess the clients are never happy about that."

Alexander Calder,
Untitled, 1976
Gift of the Collectors Committee

tectural fashions go, because even as Pei's East Building was being completed in the late 1970s, critics were sounding the death knell for the international style, and Pei's construct was hailed as its last and greatest monument in America. The end of an architectural era notwithstanding, Pei's building was voted one of America's ten greatest buildings by the American Institute of Architects.

When the executive offices moved to the East Building, they moved to the best new address in town, and one that maintains its cachet years later as an architectural icon which is pleasant to inhabit. Traditionally, art historians had done their research in crowded quarters; this new building housed a reading room with measureless elbowroom and inspiring spaces whose light changed every hour with the passing of the sun. In 1941 Director Finley could look out of his office through windows covered with bronze grills onto a surrounding "moat." Director Brown could gaze through his office's glass wall and across its balcony to the Capitol's West Front. One of the great views in a city of monumental vistas, this prospect is shared by lucky occupants of all window offices on this side of the building.

Moving the executives and curators to the East Building obviously freed-up long needed space in the West Building—for expanded conservation facilities, analytic laboratories, photography (including x-ray and infrared), study rooms for bronzes and works on paper, a lecture hall, a proper archives storage range and the like. Of almost equal esthetic import, the east end of the West Building was renovated with a viable entrance facing the East Building.

Completion of the East Building also allowed the redesign of much of the ground floor of the West Building, work carried out in two phases during Paul Mellon's presidency. (In the aggregate all this increased the exhibition space in the West Building to more than 230,000 square feet.) Most important perhaps—and more simply said than done—was the linking of the two ends of the West Building via an axial passage along the ground floor. This ground level concourse running the length of the West Building was built after the Herculean task of removing the old auditorium and relocating such utilities as the air conditioning equipment. When finished, this link made circulation on the ground floor clear and logical.

Then at the west end of the West Building, galleries were renovated and new ones opened in formerly non-public spaces. Most of the ground floor—which had been given to offices and staff operations—was put to new uses. A double suite of galleries was converted to a "museum-within-a-museum" for the graphic arts. The old treasurer's office, with its walk-in vault, became a facility for the permanent storage and study of the Gallery's matchless collection of Renaissance bronzes. The old library became a lecture hall, and new galleries were designed for the exhibition of sculpture and decorative arts, including the precious Widener gifts of French furniture, Chinese porcelains and medieval objects. This newly converted Ground Floor nearly doubled the number of objects on view from the permanent collection.

After the completion of the Ground Floor renovations, a second phase of design and construction began on the Main Floor and at the Sixth Street entrance. Undeveloped spaces at the east end and storage areas at the west end of the West Building were redesigned as paintings galleries. The new galleries are identical in detailing to the original ones. The project also involved piercing an "oculus" in the low ceiling of the Constitution Avenue entrance to give people entering a dramatic glimpse of the Rotunda above. The idea of this opening had been considered by Pope, who recognized the problem of the low ceiling, but had not been carried out because the Mall was seen as the principal entrance to the building.

Meanwhile, the Pei building added 110,000 square feet of public space to the Gallery and allowed a quantum leap in exhibition activity. Without doubt, greater attention would be paid to temporary exhibits though the change was in

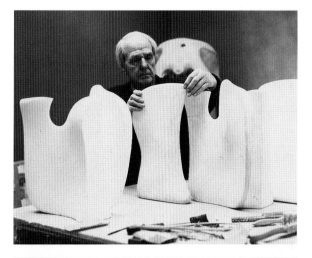

In his studio in England, Henry Moore weighs possible elements for his sculpture on the porch of the new building before settling on two. At center he oversees the installation of the finished bronze, Knife Edge Mirror Two Piece, *which requires a crane to set in place.*

Henry Moore, *Knife Edge Mirror Two Piece,* 1977/1978
Gift of The Morris and Gwendolyn Cafritz Foundation

some ways more perceived than real since temporary shows began with the Gallery's opening in 1941. (More than six hundred of them have been put on over the past five decades.) The Pope building had been the site of what would come in the 1970s to be called "blockbusters"— perhaps to mean art events of such artistic impact that they shook our cultural foundations. Notably there had been *Paintings from the Berlin Museums* which attracted more than 24,000 people a day for six weeks in 1948; and *Mona Lisa,* the month-

long one-painting, one-smile show in 1963.

Perhaps undue attention has been paid to the numbers of visitors drawn to landmark exhibitions at the expense of remarking on the new substance. Certainly the enlarged National Gallery, with its two buildings, has attracted increasing numbers of visitors—because it has presented more art: more in terms of numbers of objects and numbers of exhibitions, more in terms of variety and quality as well. "Blockbusters" aside (Brown for one detests the term), the

results might rival the invention of a series of better mousetraps.

In its first two months the East Building received more than one million visitors, many of them doubtless come to see the building itself as word spread of its unique central space with its 16,000-square-foot skylight—the soaring atrium that fulfills at least two functions. First, it awes incoming visitors, then it orients them as it provides an enormous reference point whence to embark into specific galleries and thence to return. The atrium itself contains unforgettable art in the building's own particular icon: Alexander Calder's enormous red, black and blue mobile, which was finished only a week before the death of the artist, himself an American original.

The day the East Building opened, six separate exhibitions filled the new spaces and suggested the scope of things to come. The lead exhibition was the ambitious *Splendors of Dresden*, a landmark documentation of five centuries

The new building takes shape (left to right): The study center's open corridors and library stacks; the space frame that spans the atrium; the study center's towering space.

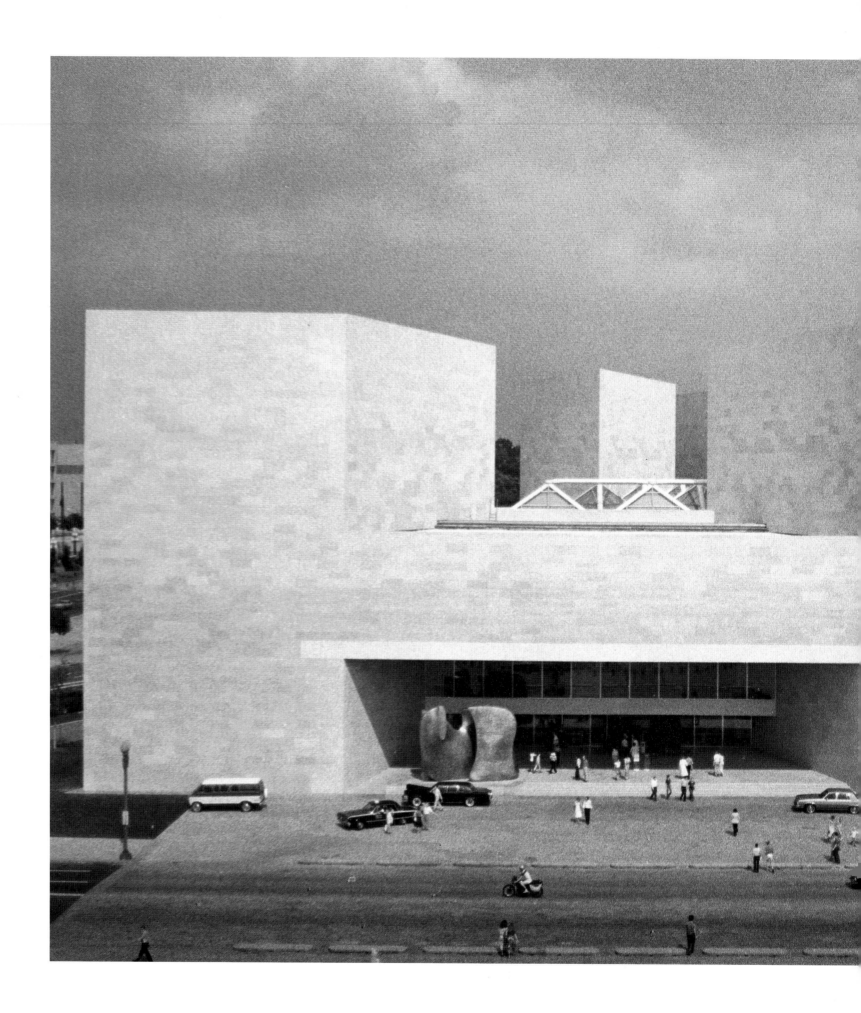

of art collecting by the rulers of Saxony. Filling 18,000 square feet on the concourse level, the exhibition comprised more than seven hundred objects: paintings, drawings, prints, porcelains, scientific instruments, arms and the like from eight museums in Dresden. Next, *American Artists at Mid-Century,* the second largest exhibition of the lot, placed the works of seven abstract artists over 12,000 square feet reaching into the North Tower where sculpture by David Smith was mounted to recall their display at Spoleto two decades earlier. Next, there were two smaller shows that could hardly have been more different. One displayed graphics from the twelfth century to the modern day—an array of drawings from the Gallery along with promised gifts. The other offered the first of a serendipitous tradition that would become perennially popular: *Small French Paintings from the Bequest of Ailsa Mellon Bruce.* Much of this material came from the collection of Paris couturier Captain Molyneux, which Ailsa purchased intact and combined with her own pictures. Additionally, an array of Piranesi's *Early Architectural Fantasies*—prints, books, drawings and copper plates—celebrated the bicentennial of the Italian designer's death. A final exhibition was *Aspects of Twentieth Century Art,* a look at three very different aspects of modern European art.

These exhibitions broke ground in two respects. The East Building's opening card gave unprecedented attention (for the Gallery) to contemporary art and premiered the multi-level show—the exhibition that used the building vertically as well as horizontally, distributing parts of the same shows on different floors. In all this, the six opening shows presaged the Gallery's agenda for years to come. At the very least, the art world and public at large were alerted to the fact that something new was happening in the museum that once prided itself on collecting old masters and hanging them in suitably sedate surroundings. Here, all at once were: a historical survey of particular connoisseurship, a group show of American abstractions, a finely-focused examination of European modernism, a celebra-

The mighty facade as seen from the West Building: Note the three towers containing exhibition "pods" on several levels; the Henry Moore sculpture; and the offset apex of the study center with its "knife edge."

Dedication Day: June 1, 1978. At right, Paul Mellon presents his and sister Ailsa's gift to the nation. With him on the podium are the Right Reverend John Walker, Episcopal Bishop of Washington who delivers the invocation, and President Jimmy Carter who accepts the gift as his predecessor Franklin Roosevelt accepted the Pope Building two score years earlier. In the front row (center picture left to right): Pamela Brown, Carter Brown, Eileen Pei, I. M. Pei, Bunny Mellon, Joan Mondale, wife of the Vice President. Below, architect Pei greets President Carter, flanked by Carter Brown and Paul Mellon.

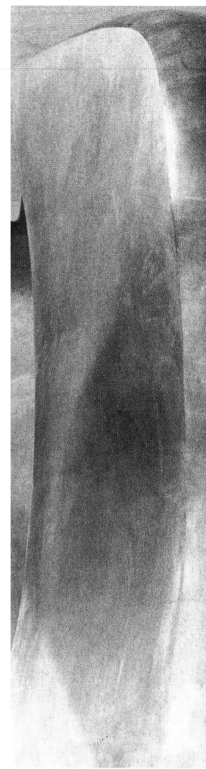

tion of Piranesi, an array of master drawings, and a major donor's legacy. Clearly the augmented Gallery had a broader agenda, a freer range.

The apparent departure from earlier tradition was really an extension of what had been going on since Carter Brown took the helm in 1969 in his search for new substance, new vari-

ety, new horizons, new rules and even policies. Previously, the notion of closing an exhibition space, even briefly, had been frowned upon. Temporary shows were hung quickly by a museum virtuoso, one man who was art handler, framer and master gilder like his father and grandfather before him. A member of the ancien

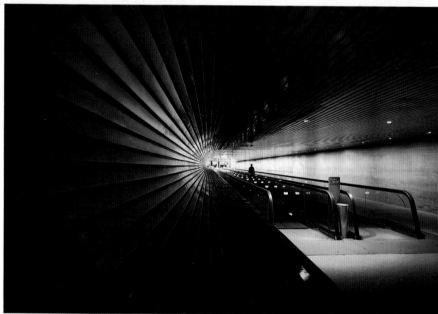

Within the "connecting link," the underground concourse has a waterfall and skylights (top) and moving sidewalk. At right, the atrium boasts an exhibition of sculpture from the Nasher Collection, while the Indian archer advertises folk art from the Shelburne Museum.

régime reported that with two assistants Fred Rieth "installed and dismounted many of the exhibitions, often within one day since John Walker...did not wish any exhibition area to be vacant" for long. Doubtless Rieth was very good at his manifold jobs; his services were often required at the White House and the homes of prominent lenders, and, indeed, there was only one way to hang a temporary show in those days: very plainly. The Central Gallery had gray fabric walls broken up by wedge-shaped parti-

Third Director, Second Building, First Transfiguration   313

The new building, especially hospitable to modern work, encourages the display of art rarely contemplated at the Gallery before: Morris Louis' Beta Kappa *(top), an example of Washington's contemporary color school; Alberto Giacometti's existential sculpture,* The Chariot, *which reduces a vehicle to an essence; Joan Miró's* The Farm, *which blends his provincial Spanish roots with the new Parisian vogue, cubism.*

Morris Louis,
Beta Kappa, 1961
Gift of Marcella Louis Brenner

Alberto Giacometti,
The Chariot, 1950
Gift of Enid A. Haupt

Joan Miró, *The Farm,*
1921/1922
Gift of Mary Hemingway

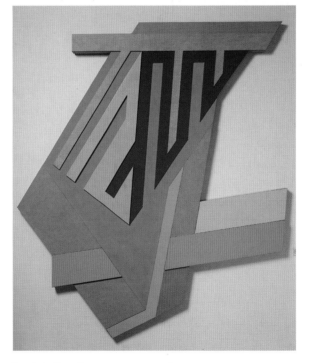

Henri Matisse,
La Négresse, 1952
Ailsa Mellon Bruce Fund

Mark Rothko, *Untitled*, 1956
Gift of The Mark Rothko Foundation

Frank Stella, *Chyrow II*, 1972
Gift of the Collectors Committee

Constantin Brancusi, *Bird in Space*, 1925
Gift of Eugene and Agnes E. Meyer

Other contemporary acquisitions include La Négresse, *one of the famous cutouts from Matisse's last years. Mark Rothko's green and red canvas comes to the Gallery as part of a wealth of pictures and papers donated by The Mark Rothko Foundation. Frank Stella's* Chyrow II *is one of the so-called Polish Village series of reliefs. The marble* Bird in Space *(above), the first of the Gallery's three Brancusi birds, is a subject central to the sculptor's work.*

tions that could only be positioned at different intervals along the walls. (Alas, they could not be removed; they were too big to fit through the doors.) Further, these walls were all lit with permanent banks of ceiling lights. Thus the art handlers were restricted to only deciding roughly where to put the partitions, and then would hang the pictures symmetrically on the wall segments and partitions. When more light was needed, desk lamps with cone reflectors were placed on the floor in front of a painting, their wires held down with tape.

This simplicity of presentation changed early in the Brown administration as the new director brought new excitement and spontaneity to bear—as several shows exemplify. Within a year, he had displayed contemporary art on the West Building's main floor—a Gallery first—in *British Painting and Sculpture 1960–1970*, which celebrated the fiftieth anniversary of the English Speaking Union here. When the embassies of thirty-four African nations sponsored a sculpture show, Brown commissioned the building of a special environment in the Central Gallery (for the first time ever) and the installation of special spotlights. Before his second year was out, *Dürer in America* marked the artist's five hundredth anniversary with the largest exhibition of its kind ever shown in the New World: selected from the finest of Dürer's graphic works in American collections. This show also marked the arrival of Gaillard F. Ravenel, an art historian and former Kress Fellow who had shown a flair for exhibit design.

Ravenel chaired a new Design and Installation Department which, with architectural designer and artist Mark Leithauser and lighting designer Gordon Anson, began to set the standard for art exhibitions in museums throughout

America. Instead of just hanging pictures on gray walls, the group cogently *designed* each exhibition with several simultaneous purposes in mind: To present the show's thematic and scholarly message, to highlight its individual objects, to let the separate pieces be seen in relation to each other. This in turn reflected a new emphasis on the didactic purposes of specific exhibitions. No longer content just to display art, the Gallery meant variously to illuminate a finely focused topic for the cognoscenti and to present a grand panorama for students of art and the excitement of the public at large.

With *Rodin Drawings, True and False*, 1972, a traditional graphics exhibition was transformed into a participatory experience in which the viewer was asked to first learn points of connoisseurship and then test his eye and understanding in a final room where thirty originals and fakes were juxtaposed.

In Ravenel's words, "works of art speak to each other," thus different juxtapositions enable different conversations between them, and exhibitions organized by different curators or planned with different theses in mind evoked unique dialogues.

The East Building offers unprecedented flexibility, as proven by these three exhibitions that utilize identical space: Art of the Pacific Islands, The Search for Alexander *and* Splendors of Dresden, *an examination of the history of collecting.*

Now, just about every exhibition area was architecturally designed to suit the art that was being shown. When a theme show included small sculpture, these were no longer placed in vitrines borrowed from the Smithsonian like a poor bride's hasty trousseau. Now special cases were designed and constructed to hold each object, and all objects were placed or hung with a clear awareness as to their relationships to each other. During these years, the educational and scholarly components of the exhibitions continued to gain in importance. Exhibition texts, brochures, recorded tours and especially the exhibition catalogues, became models of their kind. Under Carter Brown, the Gallery embarked upon the publication of catalogues which were major scholarly publications, produced to the highest standards of scholarship and design.

In 1973, an exhibition of spectacular breadth transformed the Gallery. *The Far North: 2000 Years of American Eskimo and Indian Art* married ethnography (usually reserved for museums of natural history) and pure art (albeit not of an old

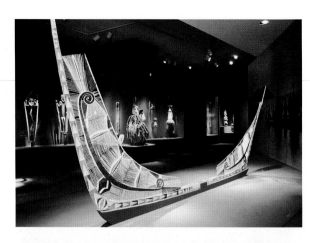

Over the years, another space undergoes many transformations to accommodate art of spectacularly contrasting kinds: (clockwise from top) American folk art from the Shelburne Museum; a sacrificial Aztec altar in the shape of a jaguar; spectacular objects from Japan; a vault from the Royal Swedish Armory.

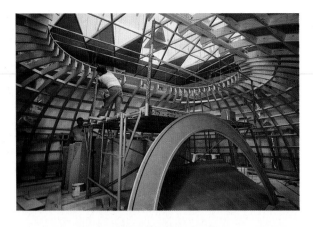

Architectural settings created for Treasure Houses of Britain *exemplify the versatility the new exhibition spaces allow. Walls and ceilings are built within the East Building's huge volumes to provide appropriate contexts—like these that evoke English interiors of five centuries. The sculpture rotunda, lower left, synthesizes the experience of a number of historical precedents and illustrates the grouping of antique to eighteenth-century sculpture. The Waterloo gallery, upper right, draws its inspiration from a single grand model, the picture gallery at Attingham.*

masters school). The show presented masks, helmets, headdresses, amulets, chests and ivories made by the diverse peoples of Alaska and the Pacific Northwest. Loans came from twenty-three North American museums and eight national collections abroad. The design team provided settings that reflected the four cultures' distinct coastal environments in order to provide contexts for these arrays of artifacts.

While the finishing touches were being put on the *Far North* exhibition, negotiations between Armand Hammer and the Soviets came to a successful close: *Impressionist and Post-*

Impressionist Paintings from the U.S.S.R.—forty-one canvases including seven Matisses, seven Gauguins, six Picassos, five Cézannes and three Van Goghs—were on their way to America. This was an unconventional event in that Hammer, by now widely famous for effectual dealings with Soviet leaders, was then also the principal owner of M. Knoedler and Co. The loans were actually made to the art dealership as quid pro quo for paintings Hammer had loaned to the Russians. In any case, the National Gallery staff had only thirty-six days to prepare for this exhibit which, in less than one month, attracted nearly 11,000

For the first section of a mammoth retrospective, Rodin Rediscovered, designers find photographs of Paris salons in the 1870s. The interior of the salon—down to decorative wrought iron work—was recreated in wood, plaster and paint to give the impression of the sculpture's historical milieu.

visitors a day. Though a traditional show in many respects, the Russian paintings heralded an extraordinary event—these works of art had not been seen outside the Soviet Union since the Revolution. This exhibition signaled an important aspect of Brown's directorship: his ability to negotiate for major international exhibitions.

African Art and Motion, 1974, presented the then-radical thesis that African art could only be understood by experiencing African dance and ritual through the special language of body motion: implied, arrested or expressed. The visitor's delight in the works of art was enhanced by

multiple audio-visual stations that documented the same or similar objects in the context of dance and ritual. *The Exhibition of Archeological Finds of the People's Republic of China*, brought together extraordinary objects in the context of a significant change in political climate: the opening of relations between the People's Republic and the United States.

In 1981, *Rodin Rediscovered* presented the largest exhibition of the French sculptor's works ever assembled—some 366 of them. From drawings and small marbles to an eight-ton bronze, the spectrum of Rodin's oeuvre could be presented in a series of contexts. The show used all four levels of the East Building, and a special two-story space was created for the mighty *Gates of Hell*. (The exhibition received a million visitors.) What could be more dramatically different from hanging pictures on gray walls and flipping on the lights?

In 1985 *Treasure Houses of Britain: 500 Years of Private Patronage and Art Collecting* set a new

standard. The biggest and most complex exhibition to that date, it included seven hundred objects from more than two hundred country houses in the British Isles. There were paintings by Rubens, Velazquez, Van Dyck, Canaletto, Sargent; sculpture from Praxiteles to Henry Moore; porcelain from Chelsea and the Orient; drawings, tapestries, jewelry, armor and the decorative arts. All this was displayed in seventeen rooms evoking various periods designed and built within exhibition spaces in 36,000 square feet of the East Building. Thanks to the flexibility of the galleries, and the ingenuity of the designers and its curator, Gervase Jackson-Stops, the Gallery staged an event that rocked the cultural landscape and changed people's perception of the world they inherited.

Meanwhile there would be exhibitions of gentler impact: a small display of sublime artifacts left by America's stone age Woodland Indians, an event that proved their remarkable facility as workers in stone, clay, wood and shell. There would be exotic shows: *The Search for Alexander* and *The Art of Suleyman the Magnificent* that brought national treasures from countries of the near east to North America for the first time. Similarly *The Sculpture of Indonesia* and *Japan: The Shaping of Daimyo Culture* introduced Americans to ancient art traditions on a scale not encountered before in this country. Conversely, *An American Sampler: Folk Art from the Shelburne Museum* celebrated native creativity. There were one-man surveys: of masters the likes of Titian and Gauguin, and finely focused looks at familiar painters who suddenly appeared in new light, like *Matisse in Nice*. There have been tributes to artists from Ansel Adams to Anthony van Dyck, the latter all the more revealing since it showed the great English court painter as master of much more than the flattering portrait. *A Century of Modern Sculpture: The Patsy and Raymond Nasher Collection* championed two things at once—the array of objects and the hall that showed them off, the atrium of the East Building. The list goes on....

Large and small, these exhibitions attracted a

broader range of people to the Gallery: some of them scholars of a particular period who had never been to Washington before, many more of them tourists who had never been to an art museum before. But increasingly the exhibitions served the Gallery's growing constituency even as newcomers became regulars. While a vastly expanded audience is beating a path to the National Gallery, an enlarged community of scholars, technicians and even scientists has been at work out of public view—both in the study

Third Director, Second Building, First Transfiguration

A wealth of new treasures heralds the start of the Gallery's second half-century, witness a sampler from the fiftieth anniversary gifts: The gift of Kirchner's street scene opens the door to German expressionism, a school only slightly represented before. The fantastic landscape is by Roelandt Savery, who spread the influence of the elder Bruegel to seventeenth-century Holland.

Ernst Ludwig Kirchner,
Green House in Dresden,
1901/1910

Gift (Partial and Promised) of Ruth and
Jacob Kainen

Roelandt Savery,
*Landscape with Animals
and Figures,* 1624

Gift of Robert H. and Clarice Smith

One of the crown jewels among fiftieth-anniversary gifts, Ribera's St. Bartholomew fills a rare gap in the Gallery's collections with a Neapolitan masterpiece in remarkable condition. New prints, such as Edward Weston's near-abstract dunescape, continue to expand the museum's relatively young photography collection. Fittingly, the new gifts include one of Winslow Homer's most spectacular early watercolors and one that pushes the medium to its limits, a portrait of a favorite yet mysteriously anonymous model.

Jusepe de Ribera,
*The Martyrdom of
St. Bartholomew*, 1634
Gift of the 50th Anniversary Gift
Committee

Edward Weston,
Dunes, Oceano, 1936
Gift (Partial and Promised) of Katherine
L. Meier and Edward J. Lenkin

Winslow Homer,
Blackboard, 1877
Gift (Partial and Promised) of Jo Ann
and Julian Ganz, Jr.

center and in the more conventional spaces of the West Building.

Whereas originally the Gallery relied upon consultants to clean its precious pictures, it has since developed a full conservation laboratory with a staff whose abilities are the equal of any museum in this hemisphere.

Whereas scholarship was limited to the labors of a few transient fellows, now the Center for Advanced Study in the Visual Arts has become an academy of wide renown and the venue for symposia of international importance.

Whereas a one-room library contained a miscellany of titles donated by officers and trustees, in fifty years the Gallery's collection of books, both rare and commonplace, and its photo archives have grown to become major, world-class resources.

Whereas once America's capital city had a paucity of art, a single man combined cultural philanthropy with patriotic pride to create what has become one of the world's distinguished museums.

Whereas the example of one philanthropist inspired a half-dozen others to give major collections to the nation, over time, thousands of giving individuals have followed suit.

Thus the National Gallery of Art became

supra-national—in the richness of its collections,

in stature and in breadth of ken. Thus it gave to

the nation and the world a new lease on art.

Offering myriad opportunities for people to bring

art into their lives, it has instructed millions,

enlightened millions, enabled millions to answer

affirmatively the grand old question, "Oh say,

can you see...." ❧

Allegorically speaking, the sun sets on the National Gallery's first half-century —the nation's bicameral museum of universal art at the foot of Capitol Hill. Bring on the millennium.

Third Director, Second Building, First Transfiguration

Donors to the Collections of the National Gallery of Art
1937–January, 1991

Sabatino J. Abate, Jr.
Gordon Abbott
Maida and George Abrams
Harry N. Abrams Inc.
Vito Acconci
Elisabeth Achelis
Keith Achepohl
Theodore C. Achilles
Virginia B. Adams
Mrs. George Cotton Smith
Adams
Mr. and Mrs. George Matthew
Adams
Mr. and Mrs. William Howard
Adams
American Federation of Labor
and Congress of Industrial
Organizations
Daniel Aladjem
Josef Albers
Mrs. Edward K. Aldworth
Thomas Alexander, III
Natalie Fuller Allen and Her
Children
W.G. Russell Allen
Elsie Alsberg
Arthur G. Altschul
American Curator Fund
Winslow and Anna Ames
Copley Amory
Helen and Paul Anbinder
Leonard E.B. Andrews
Walter H. Annenberg
Aperture Foundation
Arakawa
Larry Dale Arnold
Mme. Jean Arp
Art Center, Inc., South Bend,
Indiana
Artemis Fine Arts (UK) Ltd.
Dr. and Mrs. Joseph Aschheim
Jeffrey Atlas
Martin and Liane W. Atlas
The Atlas Foundation
The Australian Legal Group
Avalon Foundation
Sally Michel Avery
Dr. Catherine Lilly Bacon
Mrs. Robert Low Bacon
Mr. and Mrs. Franz Bader

Dr. and Mrs. George M. Baer
Barbara Baird
Mrs. Charles Baird
Gwendolyn Baptist
Edna L. Barbour
Mr. and Mrs. Will Barnet
David Baron
The Barra Foundation, Inc.
Mr. and Mrs. Jacques Z. Baruch
Jacques Baruch Gallery
Leonard Baskin
Katherine A. Batchelder
Margaret R. Battle
Patricia Bauman
Rudolf L. Baumfeld
Charles Ulrick and Josephine Bay
Foundation, Inc.
Mrs. Williams Beale
John W. Beatty, Jr.
The Bechtel Foundation
Mathilde Q. Beckmann
James O. Belden
Ferdinand Lammot Belin
Mr. and Mrs. Daniel Bell
Larry Bell
Katrin Bellinger
Mrs. Alfred Bendiner
William and Ruth B. Benedict
Thomas Hart Benton
William Benton
Bernard and Audrey Berman
Mrs. Earle E. Bessey
Mrs. Albert J. Beveridge
Galerie Beyeler
Dr. and Mrs. Malcolm W. Bick
Horace Binney
Mona Bismarck
Mr. and Mrs. William Draper
Blair
Mr. and Mrs. Donald M. Blinken
Mr. and Mrs. Robert Woods Bliss
Nelson Blitz
Charles Blitzer
Charlotte Bloch
Fritz Blumenthal
Ruth Blumko
C. G. Boerner
Dr. and Mrs. Samuel Bogdonoff
Walter L. Bogert
Leslie Bokor

John and Louise Booth
Mrs. Ralph Harman Booth
Jonathan Borofsky
Margaret Bouton Memorial Fund
Otis T. Bradley
Warren and Grace Brandt
Employees of Braniff Airways, Inc.
Peter M. Brant
Marcella Louis Brenner
Mr. and Mrs. Sam R. Broadbent
Ruth and Joseph Bromberg
Bernard Brookman
Mr. and Mrs. Harry Brooks
Dr. and Mrs. Harrison Brown
J. Carter Brown
Nicholas Brown
Robert L. Brown
The Brown Foundation, Inc.
Ailsa Mellon Bruce
Michel de Bry
Mildred Gott Bryan
John L. Bryant, Jr.
Ellen T. Bullard
Syma Busiel Fund
Charles Terry Butler
Mrs. Mellon Byers
Lewis Cabot
Mr. and Mrs. William N. Cafritz
The Morris and Gwendolyn
Cafritz Foundation
Mrs. Holger Cahill
B. Gerald Cantor Art Foundation
Mrs. Andrew G. Carey
Mrs. Calvert Carey
E.A. Carmean, Jr.
Mary Endicott Chamberlain
Carnegie
Anthony Caro
Mrs. Charles S. Carstairs
Elizabeth O. Carville
Edward William Carter and
Hannah Locke Carter
Leo Castelli
Vija Celmins
Mrs. E.C. Chadbourne
Dorothy Jordan Chadwick Fund
Pierre Chahine
Nathan Chaikin
Marian Corbett Chamberlain
Mrs. Gilbert W. Chapman

Charlottesville-Albemarle
Foundation for the
Encouragement of the Arts
Sandro Chia
The Circle of the National
Gallery of Art
Addie Burr Clark
Michael Clark
Stephen C. Clark
Alice W. Clement
Mr. and Mrs. David Cleveland
Chuck Close
Dr. and Mrs. G.H. Alexander
Clowes
William Robertson Coe
The Coe Foundation
Richard J. Coffey
Mr. and Mrs. Ralph F. Colin
Collectors Committee
Mrs. Philip Connors
Elizabeth Miles Cooke
Thomas Jefferson Coolidge, IV
Mrs. Edward Corbett
Dr. and Mrs. Ronald H.
Cordover
Elizabeth E. Cornwall
Harrison Covington
The Cowles Charitable Trust
Mr. and Mrs. John Hadley Cox
Mrs. W. Murray Crane
William D. Crockett
William Nelson Cromwell
Fund
Estate of Frank Crowninshield
William Crutchfield
Madeleine R. Cury
Catherine Gamble Curran
Mr. and Mrs. B.J. Cutler
Ann Cylkowski
Mrs. Peter D'Albert
Chester Dale
Leslie Dame
John B. Davidson
Mrs. L. G. Davidson
Gene Davis
Pauline Sabin Davis
Ron Davis
Mr. and Mrs. George W.
Davison
Carley Dawson

Larry Day
Frederic A. Delano
Mrs. Ludwell Denny
Mrs. Gordon Dexter
Mrs. Watson B. Dickerman
Mr. and Mrs. Richard
Diebenkorn
Mrs. Gerhard Heinrich Dieke
John Dimick
Jim Dine
Lamar Dodd
Alice L.C. Dodge
Robert Donner
Mr. and Mrs. Jeff Dorfman
Mary Paschall Young Doty
Mrs. Charles D. Draper
Dr. and Mrs. Arthur E. Dreskin
Werner Drewes
Mrs. Cooper R. Drewry
Donald Droll
Louisa C. Duemling
The Dunlevy Milbank
Foundation
Mr. and Mrs. Ernest du Pont, Jr.
Andre Dunoyer de Segonzac
John L. Eastman
James T. Dyke
Lee V. Eastman
Kerr Eby
Dr. and Mrs. Richard Edelstein
Dorothy Braude Edinburg
Samuel Efron
Mrs. Michael H. Egnal
Mr. and Mrs. Robert B. Eichholz
Lewis Einstein
Anne Eustis Emmet
Louise Thoron Endicott
Julia B. Engel
Estate of Sir Jacob Epstein
Lionel C. Epstein
Sarah G. Epstein
Epstein Family Fund
George Erion
Dorothea Tanning Ernst
Estate of John Nichols Estabrook
Mr. and Mrs. Thomas M. Evans
Kathleen Ewing
Frank R. and Jeannette H. Eyerly
Beatrice Beck Fahnestock
Dr. and Mrs. Henry L. Feffer

Julia Feininger
Lorser Feitelson
Mr. and Mrs. Stuart P. Feld
Mr. and Mrs. Sidney M. Feldman
Mr. and Mrs. Daniel Fendrick
Robert Fichter
Barbara Fiedler
The Fiftieth Anniversary Gift
    Committee
Ruth Fine
David Edward Finley
David Edward and Margaret
    Eustis Finley Fund
Angela B. Fischer
Harry and Wolfgang Fischer
John George Fischer
Dr. and Mrs. Robert Fishman
Dan Flavin
Aaron I. Fleischman
John Fleming
Henry Prather Fletcher
Family of Wanda Flynn
The Ford Foundation
Xavier Fourcade, Inc.
Mrs. Edward Fowles
Foxley Leach Gallery
Rita and Daniel Fraad
Sam Francis
Robert Frank
Helen Frankenthaler
Enriqueta Frankfort
Joanne Freedman
William C. Freeman
Bert Freidus
Mrs. Peter H.B. Frelinghuysen
French Navy
Albert M. Friend, Jr.
Angelika Wertheim Frink
Grey Froelich Memorial Fund
Clements C. Fry
Samuel L. Fuller
The Fuller Foundation, Inc.
Carol and Edwin Gaines
    Fullinwider
Elizabeth Merrill Furness
Dr. and Mrs. Robert J. Futoran
Mr. and Mrs. John R. Gaines
R. Horace Gallatin
Galerie Cailleux
Galerie Arnoldi-Livie
Mrs. John E. Gallois
Jo Ann and Julian Ganz
Kate Ganz
Edgar William and Bernice
    Chrysler Garbisch
Emily Floyd Gardiner
Martin Gardner
Fernando Garzoni
Mr. and Mrs. Anthony Geber
Dr. and Mrs. Webster Gelman
Gemini G.E.L.
David Gensburg
Friends of Georgia Museum
    of Art
Leola S. Gerhart
The German People
Edith Stuyvesant Gerry
Ann and Gordon Getty
    Foundation
Rose and Charles F. Gibbs

Jean and Kahlil Gibran
Frederica R. Giles
The Howard Gilman Foundation
Mr. and Mrs. Ira Glackens
Michael Glier
Lucien Goldschmidt, Inc.
The Horace W. Goldsmith
    Foundation
Joe Goode
Robert Gordy
Adolph and Esther Gottlieb
    Foundation, Inc.
Katharine Graham
Robert Graham
Graphicstudio
Michael Graves
Nancy Graves
Olga Roosevelt Graves
Mr. and Mrs. Edward R. Gray
Mr. and Mrs. Gordon Gray
Dr. and Mrs. George Benjamin
    Green
Theodore Francis Green
Lucia T. Greenway
David Grinnell
Grinstein Family
Mr. and Mrs. Winston F.C. Guest
Guest Services, Inc.
Mrs. Irving Gumbel
Helena Gunnarsson
Philip Guston
Evelyn and Walter Haas, Jr. Fund
Mrs. Najeeb E. Halaby
Michael E. Hall, Jr.
Edward J.L. Hallstrom
Mr. and Mrs. Nathan L. Halpern
Brian Halsey
The Armand Hammer
    Foundation
Charles E. Hammond
Margaret I. Handy
Mr. and Mrs. Gordon Hanes
Elodie Hanson
Elizabeth Donner Hanson
Ione Bellamy Harkness
Pamela C. Harriman
W. Averell Harriman
W. Averell Harriman Foundation
Janet C. and Charles U. Harris
Mrs. Leland Harrison
Sheigla Hartman
Jane Haslem Gallery
Mr. William T. Hassett, Jr.
Mr. and Mrs. Francis W.
    Hatch, Sr.
John Davis Hatch
Olivia Stokes Hatch
Enid A. Haupt
Mr. and Mrs. Robert A.
    Hauslohner
Harry Waldron Havemeyer
Horace Havemeyer
Mrs. Horace Havemeyer
Horace Havemeyer, Jr.
Joseph H. Hazen Foundation,
    Inc.
Louis J. Hector
Mrs. Rudolf J. Heinemann
Mrs. Arthur William
    Heintzelman

H. John Heinz, III
Michael Heizer
Julius S. Held
Heller Foundation
Mr. and Mrs. Joseph Helman
Mary Hemingway
George F. Hemphill
The Henfield Foundation
Mrs. Charles R. Henschel
John D. Herring
Paul L. Herring
John Hill
Margaret Mellon Hitchcock
David Hockney
Mr. and Mrs. Philip Gibson
    Hodge
Myron A. Hofer
Philip Hofer
Martha Hogan
Hom Gallery
Mr. and Mrs. Jem Hom
Mrs. Robert Homans
Janet A. Hooker Charitable
    Trust
Anne Horan
Mr. and Mrs. Raymond J.
    Horowitz
Vladimir Horowitz
Katherine Husson Horstick
Andrew Hudson
Lesley Hughes
The Christian Humann
    Foundation
Mary S. Humelsine
George H. Hurwitz Enterprises
Barbara Hutton
James Hazen Hyde
Dora Donner Ide
Dahlov Ipcar
Ernest Iselin
Arata Isosaki
Istituto Nazionale per la Grafica-
    Calcografia, Rome
Billy Morrow Jackson
Patrick T. Jackson
Sidney and Jean Jacques
William B. Jaffe
George and Janet Jaffin
Mrs. Walter B. James
Jasper Johns
Gerald L. Johnson
James A. Johnson, Jr.
Oscar Doyle Johnson
Samuel Josefowitz
Rupert L. Joseph
Peter W. Josten
Louis and Jean T. Joughin
Addie W. Kahn
Harry and Margery Kahn
The Children of Mr. and Mrs.
    Otto H. Kahn
Roger W. Kahn
Ruth and Jacob Kainen
Kaiser Aluminum Fund
Otto and Franziska Kallir
Mrs. Jacob M. Kaplan
Hilda Katz
Andrew S. Keck
Katharine Campbell Young
    Keck

Mr. and Mrs. Stephen M. Kellen
Ellsworth Kelly
Mary Kelly Memorial Fund
David Keppel
Alice Hall Kerr
Edward Kienholz
Mrs. Kenton Kilmer
Kimbell Art Foundation
Mr. and Mrs. Gilbert H. Kinney
Ivo Kirschen
Lincoln Kirstein
Mr. and Mrs. Richard A.
    Kirstein
J.R. Kist
Mr. and Mrs. Antony J.
    Trapnell Kloman
Oscar Kokoschka
Robert P. and Arlene R. Kogod
Elizabeth Gottschalk Krakauer
Werner Kramarsky
Rush H. Kress
Mrs. Rush H. Kress
Samuel H. Kress
Samuel H. Kress Foundation
Jeff Kronsnoble
Brenda Kuhn
Mr. and Mrs. Sidney K. Lafoon
David Landau
Loula D. Lasker Fund
Mr. and Mrs. Earl M. Latterman
Evelyn and Leonard A. Lauder
Mr. and Mrs. Ronald S. Lauder
Alexander M. and Judith W.
    Laughlin
Frederic C. Lawrence
Children of The Rt. Rev.
    William Lawrence
Sylvia Benson Lawson
Mr. and Mrs. Harry Le Bovit
Joan Lees
Sarah Barney Lefferts
Halleck Lefferts
The Leger Galleries Ltd.
Adele Lewisohn Lehman
Marilyn and Leonard Lehrer
Mark and Bryan Leithauser
Madeleine Chalette Lejwa
The James H. and Martha McG.
    Lemon Foundation
Edward Lenkin
Sara L. Lepman
Parker Lesley
Alfred Leslie
Fern D. Letnes
Bertha B. Leubsdorf
Karl Leubsdorf
Janice H. Levin
Mr. and Mrs. Benjamin E. Levy
Adele R. Levy Fund, Inc.
Albert Lewin
H.H. Walker Lewis
Margaret Seliman Lewisohn
Sam A. Lewisohn
Dorothy and Roy Lichtenstein
Robert M. Light
R.M. Light and Co., Inc.
Ella Fillmore Lillie
Charles L. Lindemann
Denise Lindner
Lotte Walter Lindt

Seymour Lipton
Louise Alida Livingston
Mrs. John E. Lodge
Mr. and Mrs. Earl H. Look
Eleanor Lothrop
Dr. and Mrs. Ronald R. Lubritz
Mrs. Pym Lucas
Asbjorn R. Lunde
Mr. and Mrs. Harry H.
    Lunn, Jr.
Edward E. MacCrone
    Charitable Trust
Christina Macomb
Nannie R. Macomb
Laura T. Magnuson
Paul Magriel
Florence Mahoney
Bryn Manley
Mr. and Mrs. Robert Manning
Robert Mapplethorpe
Toni Marcy
Mr. and Mrs. John C. Marin, Jr.
Maritime Administration,
    United States Department
    of Commerce
Louise Marock
Maud Marriott
The Mars Foundation
Bruce Marsh
Michael Marsh
Martha J. Martin
Maryland Institute
G. Grant Mason, Jr.
John Russell Mason
Thomas A. Mathews
Marian B. Maurice
Mr. and Mrs. Frederick R.
    Mayor
Mrs. Hyatt Mayor
Mrs. James McBey
Florence S. McCormick
Margaret McCormick
Joseph F. McCrindle
Ethelyn McKinney
Mrs. Alexander H. McLanahan
Katherine L. Meier
Andrew W. Mellon Fund
Paul Mellon
Richard King Mellon Charitable
    Trusts
A.W. Mellon Educational and
    Charitable Trust
W.L. and May T. Mellon
    Foundation
Vincent Melzac
Ana R. Menapace
Lois and Georges de Menil
Mrs. Houghton P. Metcalf
Dieter Erich Meyer
Agnes E. Meyer
Robert and Jane Meyerhoff
Mme. R.G. Michel and Family
Mickelson Gallery
Middendorf Gallery
Christopher and Alexandra
    Middendorf
Liselotte Millard
Mark Millard
Adolph Caspar Miller
Edward S. and Joyce I. Miller

Harvey S. Shipley Miller
Mr. and Mrs. Myron Miller
Mr. and Mrs. N. Richard Miller
Ralph T. Millet, Jr.
Mr. and Mrs. Abbot L. Mills
Pepita Milmore Memorial Fund
Kent and Marcia Minichiello
Ellin Mitchell Works of Art
Matthew J. Mitchell
Jan and Meda Mladek
Modern Master Tapestries
Eunice Mohri
Agnes Mongan
Beatrice Monk
Mr. and Mrs. Paul Shepard
  Morgan
Malcolm Morley
Dr. and Mrs. Harold P. Morris
John Morton Morris
Stanley Mortimer
Robert Motherwell
John W. Mowinckel
Dr. and Mrs. Frederick Mulder
Judith H. and Franklin D.
  Murphy
Henry A. and Caroline C.
  Murray
Mr. and Mrs. Iain Nasatir
Graham Nash
Raymond D. Nasher
Bruce Nauman
John and Evelyn Nef
Mr. and Mrs. Morton G.
  Neumann
Annalee Newman
Mrs. George Nichols
Mrs. Robert B. Noyes
John O'Brien
Georgia O'Keeffe
The Georgia O'Keeffe
  Foundation
William B. O'Neal
Mrs. Harold Ober
Mrs. Seymour Obermer
Frederick C. Oechsner
Motoi Oi
Cloes Oldenburg
Violet Organ
John T. Overbeck
Isabel Padro
Joan Palevsky
Clarence Y. Palitz
George Pappas
Charles Parkhurst
Patrons' Permanent Fund
Ambrose and Viola Patterson
C. Michael Paul Memorial Fund
Frank Pearl
Philip Pearlstein
Cecil Charles Pecci-Blunt
Herbert and Claiborne Pell
Family Petschek (Aussig)
Duncan Phillips
Ivan and Jacqueline Phillips
Neil and Sharon Phillips
Neill Phillips
Gustave Pimienta
Robert S. Pirie
Dr. and Mrs. Julius S. Piver
Eugene S. Pleasonton

Helen H. Plowden
J. Randall Plummer
Peter Pollack
Dr. and Mrs. David S. Pollen
Cynthia Hazen Polsky
Mrs. John Russell Pope
Mr. and Mrs. Meyer P.
  Potamkin
Kimiko and John Powers
Herbert L. Pratt
Herbert L. Pratt, Jr.
Mrs. John Lockwood Pratt
Eugénie Prendergast
Alice Preston
Ken Price
The Prince Charitable Trusts
Prince George's Docents
Princeton Club of Washington,
  D.C.
Professional Art Group I
Paul Proute
Mr. and Mrs. B.H. Pucker
Esther W. Putnam
Ethel Gaertner Pyne
Robert Rauschenberg
Mrs. Henry R. Rea
The Reader's Digest Association,
  Inc.
Mark Reinsberg
Curt H. Reisinger
Edith Reynolds
Mrs. Charles Edward Rhetts
Malcolm Rice
Mr. and Mrs. John Ridgely
Mrs. Fred Rieth
Rijksmuseum
Elinor Roberts
The Roberts Foundation
Murry and Selma Robinson
Andrew Robison
Dorothea Rockburne
Mrs. John D. Rockefeller, III
Mrs. Huttleston Rogers
Mrs. Joseph W. Rogers, Jr.
Cornelius Van S. Roosevelt
James Rosati
Stanley Roseman
Arthur G. Rosen
Martin N. Rosen
Alexandre P. Rosenberg
James N. Rosenberg
Paul Rosenberg
James Rosenquist
Nan Rosenthal
Lessing J. Rosenwald
Mrs. Lessing J. Rosenwald
Robert L. Rosenwald
Susan Rothenberg
The Mark Rothko Foundation,
  Inc.
Herbert and Nannette
  Rothschild
Felix Rozen
Daryl and Lee Rubenstein
Mr. and Mrs. Lawrence Rubin
Nancy and Miles Rubin
William S. Rubin
Willis E. Ruffner
Mr. and Mrs. Helmut H.
  Rumbler

Edward Ruscha
David E. Rust
Mrs. John Barry Ryan
Charles Ryskamp
Arthur Sachs
Paul J. Sachs
Michael S. Sachs
Arthur M. Sackler
Mortimer D. Sackler
John H. Safer
Saff Tech Arts
Ruth and Donald Saff
Mrs. Walter Salant
Mark Samuels Lasner
Gerhard and Christine Sander
Lili-Charlotte Sarnoff
Eleanor Whittlesey Kotz
  Savorgnan
Albert Scaglione
Richard M. Scaise
William H. Schab Gallery, Inc.
Mrs. H.S. Schaeffer
Morris Schapiro
Mrs. Paul Scheerer
Hugo B. Schiff
Leonard and Mary Schlosser
Rita Schreiber
The Schreiber Family
  Foundation
Mrs. Robert W. Schuette
Mr. and Mrs. Marvin Schwartz
Seymour and Iris Schwartz
Virginia Steele Scott
Sculpture and Decorative Arts
  Curators Fund
Jean-Pierre Seguin
Elmar W. Seibel
Mrs. William C. Seitz
Eleanor Selling
Richard Serra
Donald D. Shepard
Katharine Shepard
Herman and Lila Shickman
Mrs. John Farr Simmons
Mr. and Mrs. Robert Hilton
  Simmons
Richard A. Simms
Lucille Ellis Simon
Jean W. Simpson
Mrs. John W. Simpson
Robert Peet Skinner
Regina Slatkin
Helen Farr Sloan
Candida Smith
Dorothy J. and Benjamin B.
  Smith
Mr. and Mrs. Gerard C. Smith
Joshua P. Smith
Rebecca Smith
Robert H. and Clarice Smith
Sherwood B. Smith, Jr.
Smithsonian Resident Associate
  Program
Gerald B. Snedeker
Mr. and Mrs. Roger P.
  Sonnabend
Keith Sonnier
Julia Marlowe Sothern
Mrs. Richard Southgate
Southwestern Bell Corporation

Stephen Spector
William M. Speiller
Natalie Davis Spingarn
Leonard R. Stachura Fund
Mrs. McFadden Staempfli
Grace C. Steele
Saul Steinberg
Mr. and Mrs. John H. Steiner
Frank Stella
Stoddard M. Stevens Memorial
  Fund
Ruth Carter Stevenson
Mark Stock
Lauson H. Stone
Marshall H. Stone
James C. Stotlar
Michael Straight
Mrs. Irwin Strasburger
Mrs. Herbert N. Straus
Mrs. Jesse Isidor Straus
Mr. and Mrs. Philip Straus
W. S. Stuckey, Jr.
Frederick Sturges, Jr.
Howard Sturges
Friends of Esther Stuttman
Mary Swift
Yvonne tan Bunzl
Sheldon J. Tashman
Prentiss Taylor
The Ruth and Vernon Taylor
  Foundation
Horton and Chiyo Telford
Mr. and Mrs. E.W.R. Templeton
Joseph Ternbach
Daniel J. Terra
John S. Thacher
Mr. and Mrs. Eugene Victor
  Thaw
Alexander D. Thayer
John E. Thayer
Robert H. Thayer
Virginia Pratt Thayer
Mrs. Sigourney Thayer
Wayne Thiebaud
Clarence Van Dyke Tiers
Mrs. Paul Tillich
Lillian S. Timken
Dr. and Mrs. Walter Timme
Josip Broz Tito
Mrs. Walter Tittle
Ethel G. Tolman
Josephine Tompkins
Mr. and Mrs. Burton Tremaine
Friends of Anne Truitt
Allen Tucker Memorial
Mr. and Mrs. David Tunick
Tunisian Government
James Twitty
Ukrainian Art Academy
United States Army Forces,
  Middle Pacific
Universal Limited Art Editions
University of South Florida
  Foundation
Gertrude Mauran Vail
Roxana Wentworth Vereker
Versailles Foundation, Inc.
Alexander Vershbow
Ann Vershbow
Arthur and Charlotte Vershbow

Maude Monell Vetlesen
Philippe Visson
Mrs. William D. Vogel
Dr. and Mrs. Maclyn E. Wade
Robert M. Walker
DeWitt Wallace Fund No. 3
Lila Acheson Wallace
Frieda Schiff Warburg
Eleanor Ward
Mr. and Mrs. George W. Ware
Martha E. Warner
Washington Print Club
Washington Printmakers Inc.
C. Malcolm Watkins
June Wayne
Mr. and Mrs. J. Watson Webb
Dr. and Mrs. John C. Weber
Mr. and Mrs. Hans W. Weigert
Marcia S. Weisman
Mrs. Sumner Welles
W.G. Wendell
Mr. and Mrs. Alex Wengraf
Barbara Harrison Wescott
Dr. and Mrs. Robert Wetmore
Monroe Wheeler
Arthur K. and Susan H.
  Wheelock
Mrs. E. Laurence White
John C. Whitehead
Betsey Cushing Whitney
Mr. and Mrs. Cornelius
  Vanderbilt Whitney
Trustees of the John Hay
  Whitney Charitable Trust
William C. Whitney Foundation
J.H. Whittemore Company
Thomas Whittemore
Angus Whyte
George D. Widener
Joseph E. Widener
Malcolm Wiener
Daniel Wildenstein
John Wilmerding
John Wilmerding Fund
Emily M. Wilson
Harriet Winslow
Lenore A. Winters
Howard Wise
Wolfgang Wittrock
Edwin Wolf, II
Emile Wolf
Edward D. Wolski
Mr. and Mrs. William Wood
  Prince
Ian Woodner
The Woodward Foundation
Eleanora M. Worth
Hermann Wunderlich
Eric M. Wunsch
Z-Bank of Vienna
Zeitlin & Ver Brugge Booksellers:
  Los Angeles
Mr. and Mrs. Jacob Zeitlin
Anita and Julius Zelman
Lawrence Zicklin
Dorothy Zimmermann
Emma P. Ziprik Memorial
  Fund
Zorach Children
Tessim Zorach

Notes and Sources

THE SHRINE AND THE METROPOLIS

This section's data, such as they are, come largely from the Gallery's annual reports. The impressions are my own, gleaned in the process of doing the research for this book and as an ordinary visitor for more than three decades.

A GRAND OPENING

News magazine reports reflect the disparate goings-on in the spring of 1941; newspapers covered the opening in detail. Two prime sources disagreed on the number of guests at the opening: the *Washington Post* stated in the next day's paper that 6,000 guests were invited but 7,962 noses counted at the door. The Gallery's annual report later put the gate at over 8,000 "invited guests"—a statement of model politesse if dubious veracity.

The President's address appears in *The Public Papers and Addresses* of Franklin D. Roosevelt, in many press reports and was quoted extensively by David Finley in his memoir, *A Standard of Excellence, Andrew W. Mellon Founds the National Gallery of Art at Washington, D.C.* (Smithsonian Institution Press, 1973). Paul Mellon's speech is found in the National Gallery Archives, which proved to be a rich source of information for me.

The anecdote about Dr. Adolph Miller in a caption comes from John Walker's memoir, *Self-Portrait with Donors: Confessions of an Art Collector* (Little, Brown and Company, 1974).

BEFORE THE CREATION

An account of John Varden's museum comes from *The National Gallery of Art*, an official history by its first director, William H. Holmes, and published in 1922 by the Smithsonian Institution. (It was this "National Gallery" that ceded its name to Andrew Mellon's project and was itself transformed into the National Museum of American Art.) Another book entitled *The National Gallery of Art* (Bulletin No. 70 of the U.S. National Museum), by the museum's director Richard Rathbun describes the Harriet Lane Johnston bequest. My thanks to Smithsonian archivists William A. Deiss, James Steed and Bill Cox for their assistance.

For general information about the city, I consulted Constance McLaughlin Green's standard history, *Washington, A History of the Capital, 1800-1950* (Princeton University Press, 1962). Kathryn Smith's *Washington at Home* (Windsor Publications, 1988), a history of the city's neighborhoods, is informative. The Junior League's illustrated *The City of Washington* (Alfred A. Knopf, 1977) has intriguing photographs. Franklin W. Smith's promotion publication survives in the personal collection of Gallery art historian William J. Williams.

CAPITAL AND CHARACTER

Andrew Mellon has not lacked for biographies, and I have at least scanned more than half a dozen, from Harvey O'Conner's polemic *Mellon's Millions* (Blue Ribbon Books, 1933) to Philip H. Love's fawning *Andrew W. Mellon, The Man and His Work* (F. H. Coggins & Co., 1929) which reads too sweetly by half. A few years after Mellon's death, his children commissioned Burton K. Hendrick to write the sound and stolid *Andrew William Mellon, 1855-1937, A Biography*, but it was never published. Perhaps by coincidence, two unauthorized histories of the family appeared in 1978 and each paid Andrew considerable attention. They are Burton Hersh's *The Mellon Family* (William Morrow) and David E. Koskoff's *The Mellons* (Thomas Y. Crowell), which covers the same ground with more grace and straightforward literacy.

I am indebted to each of the authors above for adding at least one piece to the puzzle, but I think that none of them got it all or got it right in terms of Mellon's crowning achievement, the National Gallery. Mellon aide and NGA founding director David Finley botched the best opportunity in his exegesis *A Standard of Excellence* , because of all-too-good

intentions. What went awry is accidentally expressed in a letter Finley sent with a few pages of typescript to the widow of a very minor player in the book; he asked her to recall some fifty-year-old trivia, then "tell me whether you agree with it and approve. I would not want anything to go into the manuscript about you or anyone else unless they were pleased with it." Both Mellon and the Gallery deserve better than that.

For information about Mellon's town per se, I consulted Stefan Lorant's *Pittsburgh, the Story of an American City* (Doubleday, 1964), and I am grateful to the University of Pittsburgh Library staff for verbal help. Joanne B. Moore of the Helen Clay Frick Foundation in Pittsburgh provided information about Henry Clay Frick and kindly allowed me to browse in the Foundation's informal archives. I also appreciate the courtesy of Edgar Munhall, curator of the Frick Collection in New York. The collection published a glowing biography of its founder, George Harvey's *Henry Clay Frick, the Man* (1936), which I also consulted.

Andrew's father's memoir, *Thomas Mellon and his Times*, was privately printed "for his family and descendants exclusively" in Pittsburgh in 1885. A short version, *Selections from Thomas Mellon and his Times*, was edited by Matthew T. Mellon for the opening of the restored family homestead, part of the Ulster-American Folk Park in County Tyrone, Northern Ireland. It was published in Belfast in 1970.

THE MAN OF FAMILY

Sources for this chapter include those mentioned immediately above. The letters between Andrew and Nora are quoted in Burton Hendrick's unpublished biography; other letters are found in family files. Nora Mellon's statement was made public during the divorce proceedings.

MR. MELLON GOES TO WASHINGTON

Charles F. Rotchford, building management consultant, showed me around National Trust for Historic Preservation headquarters, formerly the McCormick apartment house. I am grateful to Trust President J. Jackson Walter for guidance. In addition, I thank restoration architect Nicholas A. Pappas, now of the Colonial Williamsburg Foundation, for his recollections of the building and its renovation.

The guest list for Ailsa Mellon's wedding is among David Finley's papers in the Gallery Archives. Additional information about Mellon son-in-law David K. E. Bruce came from his widow, Evangeline Bruce.

The Mellon biographer mentioned on page 67 is Burton Hendrick.

The effect of Mellon's car on traffic comes from *The Age of Moguls*, Stewart H. Holbrook (Doubleday, 1958).

MR. MELLON'S FOREIGN AFFAIRS

S. N. Behrman's book, *Duveen* (Harmony Books, 1952), previously appeared in *The New Yorker*.

Colin Simpson's book is *Artful Partners* (Macmillan, 1986). His charge that Mellon employees sold information to Duveen's man is confirmed by John Walker in his *Self-Portrait*. Kenneth Clark's account of the Duveen dinner party is found in his memoir *Another Part of the Wood* (Harper and Row, 1974).Slightly different versions of the transfiguring illumination are found in Walker and Finley's repective memoirs.

Letters noted on pages 88 and 89 are in the Mellon family files.

A TAXING CASE

The latest summary account of Mellon's tax case appears in David Burnham's weighty text *A Law Unto Itself; Power, Politics and the IRS* (Random House, 1989). I regret mis-stating the title on page 110.

Elmer L. Irey's memoir is *The Tax Dodgers: The Inside Story of the T-Men's War with America's Political and Underworld Hoodlums* as told to William J. Slocum (Greenberg, 1948).

continued on page 332

The Compact

President Roosevelt's letters to Andrew Mellon now reside in the Gallery Archives. Attorney General Homer S. Cummings' diary is in the Alderman Library at the University of Virginia, Charlottesville.

Inevitably, the font of New Deal memoranda and such—presidential papers in particular—is the Franklin D. Roosevelt Library in Hyde Park, N.Y. I am indebted to Mrs. Newman A. Townsend, Jr., of Raleigh, North Carolina, for generously providing information about her late husband's father, Judge Newman A. Townsend.

The Master Builder and His Masterpieces

Assessments of John Russell Pope's work and stature come from a variety of standard sources, including the *Dictionary of American Biography*. Pope scholar Steven Bedford, a doctoral candidate at Columbia University, provided additional information to me verbally. Theodore Young gave an extensive interview to A. C. Viebranz for the Gallery's oral history project. Edwin B. Seastad Olsen of Blauvelt, N. Y., who worked for Pope's firm, responded to a notice in the *New York Times Book Review* and kindly provided interesting information. A copy of Alexander Reed's informal memoir is in the Gallery Archives.

The Finley quotation on pages 138-139 is from his memoir.

Construction and Dedication

Cited above, the published memoirs of David Finley and especially John Walker provide first-hand information, as does the unpublished reminiscences of Alexander Reed. Articles describing the building around the time of its opening are too numerous to mention.

The First Director

David Finley's own memoir, of course, was a principal source. The Gallery Archives offered a wealth of material in his office papers and official correspondence, which include the letters from Jacqueline Kennedy Onassis who kindly gave me permission to quote them.

Jonathan Daniels' social history *Washington Quadrille* (Doubleday, 1968) offers more information about Finley and his in-laws, the Eustis family.

The senior curator quoted on page 164 is Andrew Robison.

The Brothers Kress: Following the Leader

Sources include the Finley and Walker memoirs. The Gallery Archives files on Samuel and Rush Kress contain a variety of press clippings including several interviews from the *Washington Post* and profiles filed in 1937 by Associated Press and in 1946 by National News Service. A full biography of Sam in particular is long overdue.

Kenneth Clark's review of Walker's book appeared in the *Washington Post*.

The Wideners' Most Manifold Gift

Young P. A. B. Widener's autobiography is *Without Drums* (Van Rees Press, 1940).

Aline Saarinen offered additional background in her classic *The Proud Possessors* (Random House, 1958).

Edith Standen's oral history interview is in the Gallery Archives.

The Fourth Pennsylvanian

Augmented by press reports, my principal source was curator Ruth E. Fine's substantial biography in her exhibition catalogue *Lessing J. Rosenwald, Tribute to a Collector*, published by the National Gallery in 1982.

In addition, a chance meeting in the Gallery's cafeteria with Brother Patrick Ellis of La Salle University provided a unique glimpse of the collector.

Wages of War

The Gallery Archives contain ample documentation of early exhibitions, and Richard Bales provided much information to me in a lengthy interview. Elise V. H. Ferber's summary chronicle of Gallery exhibitions, compiled ex post facto for the Archives, is now an authoritative, if terse, source.

Lynn Nicholas, who is writing a book on art matters during World War II, generously shared background material on the MFA&A and German art controversy. Finally, the controversy was covered aggressively by the daily press and the art press.

The Middle Years: Chester Dale

"B OOK...by Chester Dale," (sic) the engaging if unfinished source of many Dale quotations, is in the Archives of American Art. Since this document was clearly the hasty transcription of oral dictation and had received only the most cursory proof-reading, I have taken the liberty of correcting obvious errors of typography and, occasionally, syntax.

Geoffrey T. Hellman's profile of Dale, *Custodian*, appeared in *The New Yorker* of October 25, 1958. Well remembered in both the Finley and Walker memoirs, of course, "Chesterdale" was also recalled for me by both Paul Mellon and Carter Brown.

For the glimpse at the Dale family gravesite in Connecticut, I thank A. C. Viebranz.

A Succession and Its Successes

Huntington Cairns' persona and career are documented in the Gallery Archives, which also contains documents reflecting the controversy over his candidacy to succeed David Finley. In addition, obviously, I interviewed John Walker on the subject.

Ailsa Mellon, a very private person, is sensitively described by Walker in his memoir. She is also remembered in interviews by Walker, Mellon, Brown and some staff members.

The Gallery's Lorenzo, The Pericles of Pleasure

Augmenting material in an oral history in the Archives, I had the pleasure to interview Paul Mellon on many occasions. In addition I interviewed others about him. My evaluation of his influence on the Gallery is my own—based upon and bolstered by the views of colleagues and observers.

As for documentation, the Gallery Archives are rich in papers involving Mellon, and articles about him have appeared in numerous periodicals ranging from *Forbes* and *Fortune* to *Smithsonian* and *Sports Illustrated* to *Time* and the *Yale Alumni Magazine*. In addition to popular sources, I consulted *Bollingen: An Adventure in Collecting the Past* by William McGuire (Princeton University Press, 1982).

Third Director, Second Building, First Transfiguration

Carter Brown's career has received wide exposure. He was the subject of a profile by Calvin Tomkins in *The New Yorker* of September 3, 1990, as well as one in the *Washingtonian* of April, 1988. I also was able to interview him at length, and benefited from his oral history interview, conducted by John Harter.

The story of the Pei building draws on special sources, including Benjamin Forgey's essay in the Gallery's *A Profile of the East Building*, 1989, and Carter Wiseman's book on I. M. Pei (Harry N. Abrams, 1990).

Index

A

Adams, Ansel, 322
Adams, John, 28
Adams, John Quincy, 28
Agostino di Duccio, 183
Ailsa Mellon Bruce Collection, 257, 263, 277
Alsop, Joseph, 274
Altdorfer, Albrecht, *The Beautiful Virgin of Regensburg*, 208 (illus.)
Alverthorpe, 206, 207, 208, 210, 211, 213, 214
American Academy in Rome, 170, 173
American Commission for the Protection and Salvage of Artistic and Historic Monuments in Europe, *See* Roberts Commission
American School, *The Cat*, 291 (illus.)
Anderson, Marian, 221
Andrew W. Mellon Collection, 21, 22, 90-97, 100-101, 107-110, 157, 158, 166, 168, 249
Angelico, Fra, 183
Adoration of the Magi, 185, 189 (illus.)
Anson, Gordon, 316
Apollinaire, Guillaume, 246
Art Institute of Chicago, 238, 239
Audubon, John James, 168
Avalon Foundation, 259, 292, 293

B

Bales, Richard, 219, 220 (illus.), 221-222
The Confederacy, 222
Baltimore and Potomac station, 19, 75, 77
Barbizon School, 47, 67
Barnes, Albert, 193, 246
Barrett, John, 273
Barzun, Jacques, 274
Bazille, Frédéric, *Negro Girl with Peonies*, 280 (illus.)
Bedford, Steven, 133
Beebe, Lucius, 269
Behrman, S.N., 97, 99, 108, 177
Belbello, da Pavia, *Annunciation to the Virgin*, 208 (illus.)
Belin, Ferdinand Lammot, 147, 149, 253, 254
Bell, Evangeline, 257
Bellini, Giovanni, 180, 183
The Feast of the Gods, 194, 195, 198, 202, 203 (illus.)
Portrait of a Venetian Gentleman, 183 (illus.)
Bellows, George, 237, 243, 277
Both Members of This Club, 239 (illus.), 240
Chester Dale, 238 (illus.)
Maud Dale, 238 (illus.)
Berenson, Bernard, 96, 170, 173, 176, 180-181, 255, 289, 294
Berenson, Mary, 96
Berlin museums exhibition ("202"), 218, 226-235
Biltmore House, 222, 223
Birley, Sir Oswald Hornby Joseph, *Andrew W. Mellon*, 40 (illus.)
Blake, William, 213
Christ Appearing to His Disciples after the Resurrection, 212 (illus.)
Bliss, Robert Woods, 66
Blum, John Morton, 104
Blunt, Anthony, 274
Boggis, Bert, 97, 99

Bollingen Foundation, 271, 272, 273, 278, 285
Bollingen Series, 272, 273, 274
Bonnard, Pierre, 263
Boskerck, Robert W. van, *Sunset, Pulborough, Sussex*, 67
Botticelli, Sandro, 228
Adoration of the Magi, 90, 91 (illus.)
Boucher, François, 243
Boudin, Eugène, 240, 263, 277
Beach at Trouville, 260 (illus.)
Bowman, John G., III
Brancusi, Constantin, *Bird in Space*, 315 (illus.)
Braque, Georges, 276
Brenner, Marcella Louis, 314
Bronowski, Jacob, 274
Brown, Anne Kinsolving, 288
Brown, J. Carter, 135, 275, 285, 287, 288-290, 289 (illus.), 294, 304, 311, 316
Brown, John Nicholas, 225, 226, 234, 288
Brown, Mary Conover, *See* Mellon, Mary Conover
Bruce, Ailsa Mellon, *See* Mellon, Ailsa
Bruce, Audrey, 124, 257
Bruce, David K.E., 71 (illus.), 71, 72, 86, 113, 131, 139, 147, 155, 168, 169, 198, 219, 257, 258, 272, 288
Bruegel, Pieter, the Elder, 228, 263 324
Buchanan, James, 32
Bullard, Ellen, 214
Burger, Warren, 300 (illus.)
Burnham, Daniel, 77, 78
Burnham, David, 110
Byzantine School, *Madonna and Child on a Curved Throne*, 157 (illus.)

C

Cairns, Huntington, 72, 224, 226, 227, 230, 240, 251-253, 252 (illus.), 254 (illus.), 295
Calder, Alexander, *Untitled*, 304 (illus.), 307
Calhoun, John C., 28, 122
Cameron, David Young, 206
Campbell, Joseph, 274
Canady, John, 268
Canaletto, 322
Carnegie Institute, 79
Carnegie, Andrew, 45, 48, 96
Carstairs, Charles S., 53, 55, 69, 97
Carter, Jimmy, 225, 300
Cartier-Bresson, Henri, 275
Cassatt, Alexander, 78
Cassatt, Mary, 35, 263, 277
The Boating Party, 239, 240 (illus.)
In the Omnibus, 212 (illus.)
Catlin, George, 277
Cazin, Jean-Charles, *Moonlight Effects*, 67
Cellini, Benvenuto, 195
Center for Advanced Study in the Visual Arts, 287, 294, 295, 299, 327
Cézanne, Paul, 243, 263, 320
The Artist's Father, 277, 282 (illus.)
Bathers, 193
Boy in a Red Waistcoat, 277
Le Château Noir, 165 (illus .)
Houses in Provence, 277, 283 (illus.)
Mont Sainte-Victoire, 296 (illus.)

Still Life with Apples and Peaches, 165 (illus.)
Chadbourne, Thomas L., 56
Chalice of the Abbot Suger of Saint-Denis, 196 (illus.), 200
Chardin, Jean Baptiste Siméon, 91
The House of Cards, 92 (illus.)
Chase, William Merritt, 35, 243
A Friendly Call, 241 (illus.)
Cheek, Leslie H., 278
Ch'ing Dynasty, *Tall White Beaker with Red Blossoms*, 197 (illus.)
Ch'ing Dynasty, K'ang-hsi, *Deep Apple-green Crackle Jar*, 197 (illus.)
Church, Frederic Edwin, 35
Clark, Kenneth, 98, 100, 176, 181, 182, 189, 218, 274, 289, 295
Clay, Lucius, 226, 227, 228, 230
Clodion, Claude Michel, 158
Coates, Robert M., 143
Cole, Thomas
The Voyage of Life, 263
The Voyage of Life: Childhood, 261 (illus.)
Colnaghi, 86, 88
Connally, Tom, 122-123
Conover, Catherine Mellon, 270, 272, 273
Constable, John, 35
Contini-Bonacossi, Count Alessandro, 176, 183
Coolidge, Calvin, 41, 63, 71, 75, 78, 79, 81
Corcoran Gallery of Art, 30, 31, 96, 107, 151, 163, 167
Corcoran, W. W., 163
Corot, Jean Baptiste Camille, 53, 263
Agostina, 239, 246
Cosimo, Piero di, *The Visitation with Saint Nicholas and Saint Anthony Abbot*, 156 (illus.)
Costanzo da Ferrara, *Mohammad II. Sultan of the Turks*, 181 (illus.)
Courbet, Gustave, 243
Portrait of a Young Girl, 245
Covarrubias, Miguel, 237
Cowan, Frank, 46 (illus.), 47
Cropsey, Jasper Francis, *The Spirit of War*, 293 (illus.)
Crosby, Sumner, 228
Cummings, Homer, 104, 116, 117, 120, 121
Curphey, Alfred George, 58
Currier, Stephen, 257
Curtis, Charles, 68
Cuyp, Aelbert
Herdsman Tending Cattle, 54 (illus.), 55, 73 (illus.)
The Maas at Dordrecht, 156 (illus.), 158

D

Dale, Chester, 146, 171, 219, 236 (illus.), 237-249, 251, 253, 255, 276, 298
Dale Collection, 238, 239-240, 242-249, 254, 255-256
Dale, Maud, 171, 237, 239, 243, 246-247, 249, 276
Dalí, Salvador, 237, 238
Chester Dale, 248 (illus.)
Crucifixion, 249
The Sacrament of the Last Supper, 248 (illus.), 249
Daniels, Jonathan, 163
Daumier, Honoré, 240, 263
Advice to a Young Artist, 255

Photographic Credits

Unless otherwise noted, photographs of works of art in the Gallery collections have been taken by the Photographic Laboratory, National Gallery of Art and are not listed below. Photographs from the National Gallery of Art, Gallery Archives are designated as NGA Archives. NGA Photo Archives identifies images from the National Gallery of Art Photographic Archives. Credits are listed by chapter; the numbers refer to pages on which the illustrations appear. All illustrations © copyright 1991, Board of Trustees, National Gallery of Art.

End papers: View from above, Rotunda, West Building, with Ames-Haskell Azaleas, Dennis Brack/Black Star; i: West Building, view looking south, down Sixth Street, Library of Congress, photo by Theodor Horydczak; ii-iii: North elevation, West Building, drawing by Otto R. Eggers, NGA Archives; iv-vi: Sculpture Hall, West Building, NGA Archives, photo by Samuel H. Gottscho; viii: Visitors in the Rotunda, West Building, photo by Toni Frissell. Courtesy, Frissell Collection, Library of Congress

THE SHRINE AND THE METROPOLIS

2-11 (top): Dennis Brack/Black Star; 12-13: Dennis Brack/Black Star

A GRAND OPENING

14: © *Washington Post*; Reprinted by permission of the D.C. Public Library; 16-17: The Bettmann Archive; 18-19: The Bettmann Archive; 20-21: NGA Archives; 23: José Naranjo; 24-25: NGA Archives

BEFORE THE CREATION

26: Library of Congress; 28-29: Smithsonian Institution; 30-31: Smithsonian Institution; 32-33: Courtesy William J. Williams; 34-35: Smithsonian Institution

CAPITAL AND CHARACTER

38-39: Carnegie Library of Pittsburgh; 42: The Bettmann Archive; 43 (top): Carnegie Library of Pittsburgh, (bottom): Courtesy Mellon Bank; 44-45: Courtesy Mellon Bank; 46-47: Carnegie Library of Pittsburgh; 48: Courtesy Mellon Bank; 49: The Bettmann Archive

THE MAN OF FAMILY

50: Courtesy Paul Mellon; 52: Mary Evans Picture Library; 53 (top): Carnegie Library of Pittsburgh, (bottom): Courtesy Paul Mellon; 54 (top): Courtesy Paul Mellon, (bottom): R. Carafelli; 57-58: Courtesy Paul Mellon; 59: AP/Wide World Photos; 61: AP/Wide World Photos; Photo courtesy D.C. Public Library

MR. MELLON GOES TO WASHINGTON

64 (bottom): Washington Cathedral Archives; 65 (top): Smithsonian Institution, (bottom): NGA Photo Archives, James M. Goode Collection; 67 (top): R. Carafelli; 68: José Naranjo; 69 (top): José Naranjo; 70: NGA Archives; 71: The Bettmann Archive; 73: NGA Archives

CAPITAL BUILDER

74: NGA Archives; 76-77: Washingtoniana Division, D.C. Public Library; 78: The Historical Society of Washington, D.C.; 79: Library of Congress; 80-81: The Historical Society of Washington, D.C.; 82: NGA Archives

MR. MELLON'S FOREIGN AFFAIRS

84: AP/Wide World Photos; 86: National Archives; 87: The Hulton Picture Company; 88: AP/Wide World Photos; Photo courtesy D.C. Public Library; 89: Courtesy Paul Mellon; 97: José Naranjo; 98 (top): Bettmann/Hulton, (bottom): NGA Photo Archives; 99: Mary Evans Picture Library

A TAXING CASE

102: AP/Wide World Photos; Photo courtesy D.C. Public Library; 104: AP/Wide World Photos; 105: AP/Wide World Photos; Photo courtesy D.C. Public Library; 106: AP/Wide World Photos; 107: AP/Wide World Photos; Photo courtesy D.C. Public Library; 111: AP/Wide World Photos

THE COMPACT

112: Courtesy Library of Congress, thanks to Marita Stamey; 114: Franklin D. Roosevelt Library, photo by Thomas D. McAvoy; 116: Franklin D. Roosevelt Library; 118-119: Library of Congress, thanks to Marita Stamey; 123: National Museum of American Art, Smithsonian Institution; 124-125: NGA Archives; 126-127: Courtesy Library of Congress, thanks to Marita Stamey

THE MASTER BUILDER AND HIS MASTERPIECES

128: Courtesy American Academy and Institute of Arts and Letters; 130: © Jonathan Wallen; 131: The Historical Society of Washington, D.C.; 132: © Jonathan Wallen; 133: Dennis Brack/Black Star; 134: NGA Archives; 135: Dennis Brack/Black Star; 136-139: Dennis Brack/Black Star; 140: NGA Archives; 141 (top): Dennis Brack/Black Star, (bottom): NGA Archives; 142: NGA Archives, photo by Samuel H. Gottscho; 143: NGA Archives

CONSTRUCTION AND DEDICATION

144: © *Washington Post*; Reprinted by permission of the D.C. Public Library; 146-153: NGA Archives; 154: Dennis Brack/Black Star; 158-159: NGA Archives

THE FIRST DIRECTOR

160: NGA Archives; 162-163: NGA Archives; 166: NGA Archives; 169: NGA Archives; 171: NGA Archives; 172: © *Washington Post*; Reprinted by permission of the D.C. Public Library; 173: NGA Archives

THE BROTHERS KRESS: FOLLOWING THE LEADER

174: NGA Archives; 177-179: NGA Photo Archives

THE WIDENERS' MOST MANIFOLD GIFT

190: R. Carafelli; 192 (top): R. Carafelli, (bottom): NGA Archives; 193: NGA Archives; 194 (left): NGA Archives, (right): AP/Wide World Photos; 196 (top, bottom left) Dennis Brack/Black Star; 200: Dennis Brack/Black Star; 203: José Naranjo

THE FOURTH PENNSYLVANIAN

204: NGA Archives; 207: NGA Archives; 213-215: NGA Archives

WAGES OF WAR

216: NGA Archives; 218: NGA Archives; 220-221: © *Washington Post;* Reprinted by permission of the D.C. Public Library; 222: Dennis Brack/Black Star; 223-224: NGA Archives; 227: Library of Congress, photo by Esther Bubley; 229: NGA Archives; 231-235: NGA Archives

THE MIDDLE YEARS: CHESTER DALE

236: NGA Archives; 245 (top): NGA Archives; 248 (bottom left): NGA Archives

A SUCCESSION AND ITS SUCCESSES

250: AP/Wide World Photos; 252-253: NGA Archives; 254: AP/Wide World Photos; 255-256: NGA Archives; 258 (right): José Naranjo; 259 (right): R. Carafelli

THE GALLERY'S LORENZO, THE PERICLES OF PLEASURE

267: Courtesy Paul Mellon; 269: © *Washington Post*; Reprinted by permission of the D.C. Public Library; 270: The Bettmann Archive; 271: © *Washington Post*; Reprinted by permission of the D.C. Public Library; 272: The Bettmann Archive; 273: © *Washington Post*; Reprinted by permission of the D.C. Public Library; 274: NGA Archives; 275: Magnum Photo Library, photo by Henri Cartier-Bresson; 276: © *Washington Post*; Reprinted by permission of the D.C. Public Library; 277: AP/Wide World Photos; 284: © *Washington Post*; Reprinted by permission of the D.C. Public Library

THIRD DIRECTOR, SECOND BUILDING, FIRST TRANSFIGURATION

286: James Pipkin; 288: Dennis Brack/Black Star; 289-290: NGA Archives; 298-299: Pei Cobb Freed & Partners; 300-305: NGA Archives; 306-309: James Pipkin; 310-311: NGA Archives; 312 (upper left): James Pipkin; (lower left): Dennis Brack/Black Star; 312-313: Dennis Brack/Black Star; 316 (top) NGA Archives; (lower left): NGA, Department of Design and Installation; 317-319: NGA, Department of Design and Installation, William Schaeffer, Kathleen Buckalew; 320-321: James Pipkin; 322-323: Dennis Brack/Black Star; 326-327: Dennis Brack/Black Star